The Patchwork
Cloak of Kamal Bey

ALSO BY JOHN ZADA

Veils of Distortion:
How the News Media Warps our Minds

In the Valleys of the Noble Beyond:
In Search of the Sasquatch

THE PATCHWORK CLOAK OF KAMAL BEY

AN EAST-WEST MEMOIR

JOHN ZADA

TERRA INCOGNITA

Copyright © 2025 by John Zada

All rights reserved. No part of this book may be reproduced or used, stored in a retrieval system or transmitted, in any form or by any means, without the prior written consent of the copyright owner or a license from Access Copyright, The Canadian Copyright Licensing Agency.

For a copyright license, visit www.accesscopyright.ca or call toll free at 1-800-893-5777.

Cataloguing data available from Library and Archives Canada

ISBN: 978-1-7773571-2-2 (paperback)

ISBN 978-1-7773571-3-9 (ebook)

Cover Design: Michel Vrana

Visit the author's website at:

johnzada.com

Pour Kamaleddine

I have become a queer mixture of the East and the West, out of place everywhere, at home nowhere.
  – Jawaharlal Nehru

If I ever found a place where I belonged, that in itself would be an identity crisis.
  – Mitski Miyawaki

Home's where you go when you run out of homes.
  – George Smiley, in John le Carré's
  The Honourable Schoolboy

AUTHOR'S NOTE

This is a work of narrative nonfiction. Most conversations and dialogue come from my recollections. The rest are drawn from travel notes, journal entries, articles I've written, and other forms of documentation gathered over the years.

Time is also used here as a literary device. The chapters inside of the original frame story of the bus journey to Mardin, although generally progressing chronologically, do at times move back and forth.

Finally, the names of certain characters in the story have been changed to ensure privacy and anonymity where circumstances warrant it.

Contents

Prologue: The Road to Mardin — 1

Part I: The Lure of the Exotic
Run-ins with the Riffians — 9
West of East — 22

Part II: Cairo
The Suffering Bastards Club — 37
The Incident at the Moulid — 51
Lost and Found on the Sea of Reproach — 67
The Cairo Beard — 83
Goma'a — 97

Part III: Spies, Informers and Agents Provocateurs
The Curious Case of Rabia Abbas — 109
The Patchwork Cloak of Kamal Bey — 125
"There is No Mossad" — 141
The Hezbollah Encounter — 156

Part IV: Borderlands and Liminal Zones
Escape from Lebanon — 169
The Forever Kingdom — 182
The Cyclone — 206
The Colonel's Caravan — 221
Interview with a Partisan — 248
The Road to Mardin — 269

Part IV: Beyond East and West
Anatolian Dreams — 275

Afterword	291
Appendix: Some Historical Background on the Mardin Family Connection	295
Acknowledgments	301
About the Author	303
Request	305

Prologue: The Road to Mardin

The overnight bus lurched to a sudden stop somewhere in the lonely scrub-brush mountains south of the city of Erzincan. The abruptness shook me out of my slumber: a drowsy stop-and-go time warp between anonymous Anatolian way stations. When I opened my eyes and gazed out the window, there was no bus terminal as expected; no glowing depot in the dead of night with its steaming round-the-clock cafeteria offerings, its local insomniacs, and its uprooted souls carrying their lives on their backs in the endless drift towards better opportunities. Looking out, I saw nothing but complete darkness.

Inside the dimly lit coach, most of the passengers, largely men travelling solo across Asia Minor, also stirred awake. Only the man sitting beside me in the aisle seat, a bearded religious Kurd, remained still with his head slumped over his chest. The young man had earlier told me with great pride and in the few words of English he could muster that the three people he loved the most in the world—even more than his parents—were Jesus Christ, Sayyid Qutb and Sheikh Said. All his role models, I noted, were political troublemakers who were executed by the authorities they challenged.*

The bus remained immobile. I thought maybe there was an accident on the road, or perhaps a local traveller had flagged the vehicle down to hop on between stops. Only when the front door of the bus hissed open and two tense-looking soldiers brandishing serious weapons climbed into view, did I realize we had hit a Turkish military checkpoint. We were in the remote eastern half of the country in 2012, where a guerrilla insurgency had been flaring on and off for decades.

Terse banter erupted at the front of the bus. The driver shut off the engine and resentfully dismounted the vehicle. Then one of the soldiers slowly walked through the aisle, scrutinizing individual passengers with his flashlight and waving a few of them off the coach, telling them to take their belongings with them. When he reached me and my fellow passenger who had since awoken, he pointed to both of us and said something in Turkish, waving us forward.

"What's happening?" I asked the soldier in English. The idea was to make clear I was a foreigner and that I had no part in their conflict.

The soldier snapped back in his own tongue. The Kurd translated to me: "He say for you to go out."

I stepped off the bus, leaving the scent of unwashed upholstery, mutton and dirty socks for the refreshingly cool and effervescent mountain air. Pinpricks of light in the distance confirmed we were in a rolling landscape. Somewhere, perhaps on a nearby ridge, what sounded liked a very large dog barked. Around me, more soldiers wearing helmets, flak jackets and balaclavas, some brandishing flashlights, milled about. The reflection from their torches revealed the dim outlines of an armour-plated jeep with a

---

* Sayyid Qutb was a 20th century Egyptian Islamist revolutionary and author who espoused political violence. Sheikh Said fomented a failed Kurdish rebellion more than half a century earlier in the area we were in.

gun atop it, and a pair of larger armoured personnel carriers with turrets, parked haphazardly in the middle of the road. The passengers who had stepped off the bus before me, including the bearded man sitting next to me, were retrieving their bags from the luggage hold lit by a soldier's flashlight.

One of the soldiers closest to me mumbled something curt, prodding me in an unfriendly manner towards the hold.

I had been pulled into a dragnet. My heart began to race.

I took some deep breaths and uttered to myself some half-convincing mantras about how this was all a security routine. I pulled out my large backpack from deep inside the hold. Then, following the example of the others, I took my place in a lineup beside the bus, on the shoulder of the road near the edge of what seemed like a steep drop off. Each of our bags was placed in front of us and we were told to open them. Soldiers started rifling through the bags in succession, emptying our clothes and contents onto the asphalt, turning them upside down, inside out, and feeling around into any pockets they could find. Meanwhile, a pair of soldiers began frisking the passenger standing at one end of the line and checking his documents, asking rapid-fire questions. When the passenger remained silent after repeated queries, he took a cuff across his head from the questioning soldier.

Nothing I'd witnessed so far confirmed my self-assurances that these were casual checkpoint procedures. As a journalist, long-time traveller, and erstwhile resident of the Middle East, I was familiar with the conflict between Kurds and Turks in this far-flung corner of the country. Here young and old, male and female, guilty and innocent—all and everyone—found themselves caught up in the decades-long Kurdish insurgency demanding autonomy from the Turkish state. As in all guerrilla conflicts there was no firm delineation between fighters and non-combatants. People were killed, or were disappeared, regularly. This included the Turkish gendarmes who were ambushed with disturbing frequency. For all I knew, we were about to be attacked by rebels crouched-down invisibly in the shadows around us.

Though I was innocent of any wrongdoing, I worried that my angst and paranoia would show, causing suspicion. I told myself over and over again that this was only procedural. I'd been questioned by security people a few times and in different countries before, and all had been fine in the end. Yet I couldn't convince myself now. Dealing with war-weary soldiers under these circumstances bore little resemblance to fielding questions at an airport. Danger weighed heavily around us.

The interrogating soldier stepped up to me. What I could see of his eyes—under his balaclava and illuminated by the lights of his torch—appeared heavy with the gravitas of frontline duty. He asked me, I think, for papers.

I handed him my Canadian passport. He looked at it and asked another question.

I shrugged my shoulders and lifted my hands. "I don't speak Turkish."

He called another soldier over and handed him my passport.

The second pair of blinking eyes peering out of cloth looked me over. "Where you go?" he snapped accusingly.

I was en route to Urfa that night, via Elâzığ. But it was the next destination, beyond that, which was on my mind—and which I blurted out.

"Mardin," I said, indicating the hybrid Arab-Kurdish city near Turkey's border with Syria, to the southeast. It was also an area of political troubles—as were most places in the general direction I was heading. There were no right answers in that regard.

"Why go Mardin?"

"*Tourizm*," I said. The more precise answer involved other motives and was too long-winded to be intelligible. But given the power dynamic, and the country's politics, I wasn't planning on telling the soldier that I was visiting the city of my ancestors, who were non-Turks.

"No Mardin," he said firmly, before adding some words in his language.

"Why no Mardin?" I asked, assuming he'd understand.

He raised his hand that held my passport. *"No Mar-din!"* he repeated, annoyed.

My heart sank when he slipped the passport into his uniform pocket and without further explanation walked away. As his flashlight beam receded, all went dark. The other nearby soldiers also had their torches off now. When I turned to look at the other men beside me, hoping to meet someone's gaze who could commiserate, all I could see were their tired, humiliated and dejected silhouettes.

Suddenly another light went on and a pair of pant-camouflaged legs shuffled over to me. A hand gripped my left arm tightly, pulling at it. The man uttered some words in Turkish. I froze. The soldier raised his voice, yanked at my arm, while another gendarme holding a flashlight and shouldering a semi-automatic weapon approached.

Like a bad jump-cut in a film, the three of us were suddenly walking down the road, past the back of the bus, past another armoured jeep, further and further away from the vehicles. Fear threw my imagination into overdrive: these men were going to throw me off the cliff somewhere out of sight, maybe after putting a bullet or two in me. I was reduced to short breaths, a fast-pumping heart, a cold sweat and tingling arms. My legs stiffened again, refusing to go further, and I nearly dislocated my arm as I got yanked even harder. I thought I felt the second man stick the gun muzzle in my back.

We stumbled for another few minutes, rounding a gradual turn in the road. I could see more lights, flashlights, far ahead at what appeared to be an initial roadblock that our bus must have passed. It looked like cars were being turned back.

Then, we suddenly stopped. The soldiers let go of my arms, uttering something to me in Turkish. They both stepped away and just stood there. One of them lit a cigarette.

As the wind picked up, buffeting my ears and adding white noise to near-total darkness, I thought about what led me here to begin with; and how I was now fatefully ensnared at the forsaken intersection of soldiers and insurgents—and the forlorn land broken by their incoherent melee.

I slipped into a terror dissociation response, following paths of causation backwards in time to my original motives and obsessions that had driven me like the devil to this exact spot: the seductions of the East, the lure of the exotic, and the desire for a deeper sense of home. And like so many people thinking that they are facing their final moments, I experienced a sudden series of flashbacks. The key scenes of that lifelong trajectory came rushing from my memory: a great journey across epochs, which, at that moment, unfurled and vividly reconstituted itself on that windswept mountainside beside the checkpoint...

Part 1: The Lure of the Exotic

Run-ins with the Riffians

Our traipse through the narrow streets of the *medina*, the old quarter on the hill, felt interminable—like a long, endless march to nowhere. What was presented as a short hop to a nearby café became a furtive and convoluted journey into a featureless maze of empty passageways devoid of activity. Left turn followed right, up flights of stairs, and down long laneways past great ornate doors, many half open, percolating cooking smells and snippets of conversation in an Arabic dialect radically different from my own.

Setting the pace was Chaouki, a tall and lanky Moroccan tout with a halo-like profusion of thick curls, ripped jeans and scars on his face and arms. Curtis (Curt), my friend and fellow-Canadian travel companion, had summoned him from the ether by way of his blunt questions to several storekeepers about acquiring *kif*— the local word for cannabis.* With arms swinging buoyantly, the light-on-his-feet Chaouki took us ever deeper into passageways that became narrower as we pushed on. More than once we

---

* Etymologically, *kif* derives from the Arabic *kayf* whose various meanings and implications include: 'condition', 'state of mind', 'high spirits', and 'pleasure' (as in the Arabic expression, 'as you like it').

seemed to pass the same ornate red door set behind a tile-decorated horseshoe arch, suggesting to me that we had retraced our route. I realized later that we were likely being disoriented—in much the same way that kidnappers deliberately drive blindfolded abductees in zig-zags to keep them from accurately recounting where they were being taken.

We finally arrived at the café, an unmarked and cavernous space with crumbling walls of peeling blue paint, and rickety chairs. Two men in hooded *djellabas,* each sat alone at the far corners of the large room staring into space, seemingly content in their own company. The three of us sat at a table and Curt, who had become impatient and nervous, asked Chaouki in English when he would see the *kif.*

"Tell your friend he has to wait," Chaouki said to me bluntly in Arabic.

The Moroccan could speak broken English. But he disliked Curt, and preferred not to engage with him. Because I could converse in rudimentary French and a somewhat more functional Egyptian Arabic, I became the point man.

When I translated, Curt made a dour face.

"*Attends,*" Chaouki said delicately, but coldly, to him in French, bringing his fingertips together in the Eastern hand-gesture for patience. "Wait."

A server emerged from the kitchen carrying a large embossed silver teapot and three small glasses. The man poured a round of sweet mint tea. Chaouki spoke a few rapid-fire words to the server that were incomprehensible to me. The waiter nodded and returned to the back before he re-emerged carrying a long, thin object wrapped in a brown cloth sack, which he placed on the table beside Chaouki. Our host opened the sack and removed an absurdly long wooden pipe that measured the length of an orchestra conductor's baton. Chaouki dug into his pocket and removed a small ball of foil which contained hashish resin. He pinched off a piece of the brown cake and thumbed it into the bowl and raised the pipe to his mouth. He extended his arm and lit the small bowl at the end. Voluptuous plumes of thick sweet smoke curled upwards and danced in pirouettes around us. Chaouki handed the pipe and the lighter to Curt, who had been utterly spellbound from the moment the implement was unsheathed.

As my friend underwent the same ritual, Chaouki watched intently with a glazed and drowsy—but pleased—glance that spoke to things going his way. When the pipe and lighter were handed to me I took them, hesitatingly. A pang of anxiety shot through me. We had just arrived in Tangier on the boat from Spain—my first trip to Morocco, and 'the East'—and had barely dropped off our packs before Curt sought out his heart's desire in the most public and exposed fashion. I neither wanted to smoke or be anywhere near these port town underworld types. But I was 24 years old and amenable. And the siren call to misadventure, to anything exciting, found its receptivity in the rationalizations thrown up by a mind unwilling to muster any resistance.

EARLIER THAT DAY, we had stood on deck as our ferry seesawed on wind-whipped breakers through the Strait of Gibraltar. We gazed in breathless awe at the rugged sun-burnt shores of Africa looming beckoningly before us. Curt, standing beside me, revelled in the blissful knowledge he'd be high within hours.

"Tangier!" he shouted, bouncing on his tiptoes and gazing into the distance with the euphoric look of a pilgrim nearing the gates of his personal utopia. He went on to intone the names of the Beat Writers and other patron saints of post-war literary counter-culture who had graced the ancient byways of the approaching city and whom he idolized: William Burroughs. Allen Ginsberg. Jack Kerouac...

It was our first time on the road together, an event for which we established sobriquets. I called him "Colonel"—a play on

Colonel Kurtz from the film *Apocalypse Now*. He called me "Admiral," an attempt on his part at a corresponding military title that appealed to me if only for the little-known fact that the word derived from the Arabic term *Amir al-Bahr*, which literally translates to "Prince of the Sea." Our pseudonyms signified a puerile band of brothers pact devoted to adventure glory that only seemed to work against us.

We had been travelling for less than a week and had already found ourselves at the centre of an international commotion. Days earlier, Curt had been arrested and temporarily detained in Alicante, Spain, for not having a tourist visa. Canada and Spain were embroiled in a nasty Atlantic fishing dispute in the Grand Banks off Newfoundland at the time, in which their usual diplomatic niceties, including visa-free travel for each other's citizens, had been suddenly and resentfully revoked. In the end, Curt wasn't imprisoned by the interrogating Spanish plainclothes police bureaucrat in suspenders that he was taken to see. Acting on Curt's tearful pleas for clemency, and perhaps on a phone call from a higher authority, the policeman settled on him, and us, voluntarily leaving Spain within 72 hours. We were free to go.

The incident was enough to impress upon me an important observation early on: travel with Curt was a high-risk venture. He could draw trouble to himself even as he sat still. My rebellious friend with a Jesus complex, the son of kind but stern Baptist Christian parents, had a burning desire to live without boundaries and to seek suffering at any cost. Curt had spent the previous summer vagabonding with another friend through France and the Benelux countries on bikes, sleeping by the sides of roads, and getting drunk on cooking sherry. In Paris, the two hit their faux Beatnik strides when they jumped into the Seine from a bridge in the 7th arrondissement and were barely rescued in time from the fast-flowing torrent by a tourist boat filled with scandalized, camera-toting seniors. For these reasons I got him to agree with me early on in our travels that we could part ways if either of us felt compelled to continue on alone.

Though I was not impelled by such fiascos, I lived under a different yet similarly problematic spell—one that I shared with Curt and which made us otherwise simpatico travel companions: my enslavement to the exotic.

We had both grown up languishing in the ennui of North American suburbia, victims of its logical orderings, clinical subdivisions and manifold sensory deprivations. The suburban commuter existence marries the least desirable aspects of both rural and urban living, creating a bland insularity of existence. Morocco was a raw octane stimulant and antidote to the banality of our lives back home. For Curt, embracing its seedy underbelly was also a 'fuck-you!' to the world of convention, under whose thumb he had lived as the son of strict fundamentalist parents. For me, 'the mysterious East' was becoming an object of personal obsession. So much so that this ridiculous situation with Chaouki that Curt had cultivated in pursuit of life's exhilarating friction, was justified by me as a fleeting detour that had to be experienced.

JUST AS THE *kif* took its mind-warping effects, a friend of Chaouki, another scuffed-up ruffian in unwashed jeans, sailed into the café. Without a word he took a seat at our table, reached into his pant pocket and removed a brown rectangular object wrapped in several layers of cellophane. It was about as large as a man's thick wallet. Chaouki placed it on the table between him and Curt, with the deftness of a casino poker dealer

"*Voila*," Chaouki said, with self-satisfied finality. "*Le chocolat.*"

Curt gazed at the hashish, transfixed in wide-eyed incredulity. "Wow," he muttered to himself.

No one said a word for several seconds.

"But," Curt said, breaking the silence, after looking at me, "I don't think we need that much."

"*Mais*. This is what we have," Chaouki said.

Another long and uncomfortable pause ensued. Chaouki then broke the impasse with an uncaring exaggerated shrug.

"*Pas de probleme*," he said, taking the brick in his hand and pushing his chair back. "We go."

"No, no!" Curt implored. "What do you want for it?"

Chaouki froze and then slowly leaned back again into his chair. His expression lightened before bringing his hand to his chin. "One hundred dollar," he said.

Curt concealed his delight beneath a muddled smirk. He dug into his fanny-pack and extracted a crisp Benjamin Franklin and pushed the bill across the table. Chaouki examined the bill front to back like a money exchange clerk looking for signs of counterfeiting, before looking again to Curt.

"*Alors*. The rest, then?" Chaouki said, with a touch of sarcastic insult.

"The rest of what?"

He shook the bill like a flag flapping in the wind, "This one hundred. Price, *two hundred*."

It took our slavish minds, diverted by tangential thoughts that ended in cannabinoid cul-de-sacs of forgetfulness, more than a couple of beats to conclude what was going on.

Curt's face became contorted in outrage. "Heyyyyy," he scowled. "What kinda bullshit is this? You just said one hundred!"

"*Non. Deux cents*," Chaouki held his fingers in a peace sign and waved them back and forth deftly. "Two."

Curt turned to me: "He said a hundred. That's what you heard, too, right?"

"Clearly," I confirmed.

I turned to Chaouki. "You told him one hundred dollars," I said in Arabic. "Give him what he bought." I half-expected my cultural and linguistic bona fides, which meant nothing to Chaouki, would magically negate the scam and resolve all.

Chaouki leaned forward in his chair and grinned. His friend looked on with the quiet intensity of a chess match observer.

"*Mes amis,*" he began imploringly. "We have some smoke. We drink mint tea. This big piece *kif* is best Moroccan quality. For this: two hundred."

"You lied!" Curt said.

Chaouki shrugged. "*C'est pas cher pour vous.*"

Curt sighed. He looked at me and for a long time made a show of sitting on his haunches and deliberating. "Okay," he said, reaching into his pack. "But you're not getting any more."

Chaouki eyes fell again on the money.

"Did you hear me? I said I'm not giving you anymore."

Chaouki looked up at him and barely nodded.

"Give me the hash first," Curt said. "Put it near me."

As Chaouki did so, keeping his hand near, Curt slid him another bill and simultaneously took the block of cannabis resin. He held it in his hands in wonderment, and then smelled it, as if it were a long sought-after treasure with which the Fates had finally united him.

SILENCE HUNG over us as we sauntered slowly, lost in convoluted thoughts, through the empty byways of the *medina*. Curt and I neither knew where in the old town we were, nor in which direction we were heading. To say that all of the previous zig-zagging to reach the café had deliberately disoriented us would be technically inaccurate since we hadn't been in town long enough to become oriented in the first place. The mind-tricks wrought by the *kif* wrecked our navigational senses. The whole situation: the unfamiliar surroundings, the tawdry deal, Curt's self-immolation, and the kaleidoscopic and paranoid distortions of smoke put us in a tenuous place.

"Curt," I said, breaking the silence, "that thing you're carrying in your pocket... It's a problem."

Curt turned to me with a blank stare that transformed into a knowing, horrified look.

"Let's go back to the room," I said.

We were staying somewhere on the opposite end of the *medina*, but had no idea how to get back there. We decided to find the gate we had entered from by leaving the old town altogether and trying to locate it again from the outside. The *medina* was built on a hill and to leave it meant going down. We found the first of several staircases that led to the streets below. As we descended, I looked back over my shoulder and unexpectedly caught a glimpse of Chaouki and his band of hustlers poking their heads around a corner at us. I turned several times to confirm I wasn't imagining it. His orange "Good Vibrations" Sunkist t-shirt made him easy to spot. By the time we reached the bottom I knew we were being followed. The men shadowed us, making no effort to conceal their presence. They were aloof, keeping their distance, yet remained mostly in the open.

When we reached the road, I broke the bad news to Curt. He spun around and looked up at them on the staircase.

"What do they want now?" he cried.

Chaouki broke ranks with his myrmidons, and trotted down a ramp that led from the lowest level of the *medina* to the main avenue where we were standing. When he reached us, he was panting and appeared frightened.

"*Mes amis! Danger!* The police, they come. Quickly, go! *Vit vit!* " With that he glanced fearfully over both shoulders and dashed off.

Curt and I looked at each other, folded our map, and resumed our walking into the new town, but now more quickly.

Every few hundred metres another member of Chaouki's team reached us and conveyed the exact same message. With each subsequent rendering of that warning, the urgency was greater, the police closer, our implied detainment nearer at hand. The Moroccan law enforcers, the last of the grifters told us, could only be stopped if we coughed up payment—in US dollars.

Even as we put distance between ourselves and the *medina*, the surveillance against us did not abate. The opposite seemed to be the case: because of the effects of the smoke there appeared to be more of them, an ever-multiplying army of extortionists, new faces, who stared at us, from both near and far. When we found ourselves passing Tangier's busy train station, we felt ourselves sandwiched between our pursuers and the handful of police, soldiers and bystanders standing outside the terminal—some of whom eyed us with interest. The *kif* we'd smoked, which had been meant to confuse and frighten us, reached its pinnacle impact. Panic was cresting.

"That's it, I'm throwing it away," Curt said, shoving his hand into his pocket.

"*Don't*," I said tersely, grabbing his arm. "Not yet. Everyone's watching."

Curt seemed on the cusp of tears. I realized we needed to get back to our room as soon as possible and away from the eyes of the crowd.

"Let's split up," I said. "That will confuse them. They won't be expecting it."

"And then what?"

"I'll meet you back at the room."

"Alright," he said, before giving me a grave look and heading off in a different direction.

It took no more than a minute to realize that by leaving Curt, I had merely abandoned him to the sharks. Several glances over my shoulder confirmed that no one, not one hustler, was following me. Chaouki and his team, hawked-eyed and shrewd as they were, must have known Curt was still the keeper of the *kif*, and thus they stuck to him. A part of me simply wanted to distance myself from Curt's contraband—and I regretted my impulsivity. But it was too late. My friend had melted into the surroundings, nowhere to be seen amid the thick pedestrian street traffic moving to the pulse of a magical rhythm I'd left home to seek.

I EVENTUALLY FOUND my way back to the room, located in a small guest house with a *riad* and a few other units, beside a butcher's shop, which I recognized. I realized that Curt, who had not arrived yet, had the room key. I approached the manager to let me into the room. I spent the remainder of the afternoon waiting for my friend to materialize, while unknown people knocked and banged on a second door to our room that led directly in and out of the *medina*. Each time I opened it I found no one there. But I began to suspect Chaouki and company were the perpetrators. This was confirmed several knocks later, when I opened the door to find yet another of Chaouki's alley cats standing before me uttering the words "police" and "money" with his hand outstretched. I shut the door in his face.

Over an hour later Curt came shuffling through the other door leading into the *riad*. He looked upset and exhausted.

"You made it," I said, with huge relief. "All fine? Did you ditch the stash?"

"They took it from me," he said resentfully. "They pulled it out of my pocket when I was talking to them."

"Good riddance, let them have it," I said. "We should probably leave this place."

"Not before I get the stash back. Or my money."

"*What?*" I said with alarm. "What do you mean?!"

"I've changed my mind. I paid two hundred dollars. They can't just steal it from me. We made a deal."

"Dude, they're thieves, criminals. You won't win with these people."

"No, I've made my decision: I'm going out again to look for them," Curt said stubbornly. "I'll be back before it gets dark."

"Don't do it," I implored him, as he ignored me and stumbled wearily out the door.

Moments later, I went to my bag and pulled out my journal. I tore out a blank page from the back of it. After looking through my travel guidebook I scribbled a message to Curt instructing him to meet me at a certain spot in the central square of Marrakesh in five days' time. He and I had agreed after the Spanish debacle that we could part ways and meet up again later during our trip, if need be. I now unilaterally decided to enact this plan. A sense of foreboding hung over me. I envisioned no respite from this army of petty criminals who specialized in playing cat and mouse with travellers. Curt might yet tussle with Chaouki and his underlings in the backstreets for days to come. In any case Tangier had become another fiasco. I felt I had to exit and reset our situation to avoid entanglement in deeper trouble—possibly with the police.

I gathered my things and moved my note visibly into place on the table. I remember thinking, as I took my first steps towards the door, that I might not see Curt again on that trip.

I LEFT Tangier alone that evening on an overnight bus to the city of Fes. The decades-old vehicle whose gaunt innards resembled the metal interior of a cargo plane, hurtled through the Rif Mountains, between isolated villages, rattling and bouncing like an aircraft thrown around in a storm. It was a monotonous journey through almost total darkness broken only by a series of robed and hooded buskers, singing and playing an ancient-looking string instrument called a *kamenjah*. The musicians got on and off the bus at whimsical stops in the middle of nowhere, beneath the star-spangled sky.

Though I had abandoned Curt, Tangier, and my previous worries in a cloud of dust, giving the last of Chaouki's thugs the slip en route to the bus depot, I was walking into the embrace of a less heinous, yet still potent force which was to affect my life trajectory for years to come: the stimulations of the East.

The days that followed, first in Fes, then in Marrakesh, became a euphoric dreamlike procession through the exciting and emotive sensory impacts of a novel reality: rooftop sunsets amid calls-to-prayer while flocks of pigeons did cartwheels in the honey-tinted sky; supernovae bursts of carved Arabesques and geometrical textile displays in all colours intimating infinity; beguiling medieval labyrinths and their warren of alleyways bustling with hooded men and their beasts of burden; the sizzle and scent of foods cooking in a panoply of pans and cauldrons crowded by hungry, boisterous masses; a gregarious humanity alertly and creatively navigating life with a graceful, fatalistic dignity; and the ever-beckoning High Atlas with its conspicuous white snowpack resonating otherworldly loftiness.

The exoticism resonated and found fertile acceptance in a mind that was culturally familiar with, though barely exposed to, such close-quarter impacts. And like any pleasure or stimulus, the piquancy of 'the East', I would soon learn, could also become an addiction.

CURT SHOWED up on the fifth day. A lifetime seemed to have passed in the interim. He looked different: gaunt, sleep deprived, but also somehow calmer.

"I'm glad to see you," he said, embracing me, and looking momentarily free of his demons.

I felt the same. There were no recriminations—our paths had simply parted and rejoined. We went to a walled-in, open-air garden, where, in cushioned wicker chairs and under the soothing effects of mint tea, Curt wove a tale even more bizarre, fantastic and convoluted than our brief and sordid experience in the Tangier *medina*. In the time we were apart, Chaouki and his men hunted and assailed Curt until my friend paid Chaouki off as demanded. In return, the chief of Tangier's petty criminals offered

Curt a job in the Rif Mountains—from where Chaouki and his henchman hailed—at a plantation that processed *kif*. But all of this was for a price, which, of course, Curt paid. But when he arrived there, the drug mafia farmers relieved him of more greenbacks in every which way possible, passing him along like a football between themselves, while keeping him arm's length from their operations. Unsurprisingly, the "job" never materialized.

Hearing all of this, I felt vindicated in my decision to leave Tangier on my own. I asked Curt what he took away from all of it.

"I'm done with smoking hash. I'm a new man. And anyway, who needs drugs in a place like this?"

He then went on: "I've been thinking about it: that school in Cairo that accepted you for a master's degree—I hope you're going to go."

"I'm going to decide after the Egypt trip."

"You can't not do it. All of *this*," he said, raising his arms to encompass the scene, "this could be your life. Every day. For years. Maybe for your whole life, if you never leave. You could be another Paul Bowles!"

I smiled, and as I poured us another round of the sweet syrupy tea, a feeling of excitement at this prospect welled in me.

West of East

Read *Sinbad the Sailor's Voyages* and you will be sick of Aeneas's.
– Horace Walpole in a letter to Miss Berry, 1789

He took his pulpit once the dinner party was in full swing. The living room was crammed with adults, some sitting on tall-backed chairs pulled from the dining room table and all of them wearing their shoes indoors as if they were back in the homeland, and not in Toronto. A concoction of elegant perfumes, cigarette smoke, and the aroma of *kibbeh* and *warak einab* filled the air, creating the scent of occasion. It didn't matter in whose home we were gathered, when the social mood reached that crescendo of receptivity marked by the relaxed tinkling of glasses filled with Johnnie Walker Black in their second and third pours, it was his time. All he needed was his segue. Given that every social gathering of Arabs bristled with talk of politics, he didn't have to wait long.

"No, forget Carlos," Kamal Bey said firmly, waving his finger like a metronome in rapid swing. "And he is no cunning 'Jackal' by the way. The real player in the guerrilla world is a man named Sabri al-Banna."

"You mean Abu Nidal," someone said, trying to correct him, referring to the shadowy and faceless Palestinian militant whose name was all over the headlines.

"If you'll forgive me, I regard *noms de guerre* to be fantasies. I refer to people by their real names. It reminds us—including the name holder—of their humble origins. Speaking of which: Carlos, whose real name, if you'd like to know, is Ilich Ramírez Sánchez, is both a Venezuelan and a gun-for-hire. He isn't even an Arab. By contrast, al-Banna is his own man and makes Carlos look like a schoolboy."

The six-foot tall presence in the tweed blazer, bristling pyramidal moustache, and a steeply sloping bald head that screamed for a *tarboosh*, or fez hat, sat on the edge of his seat and began painting tales with lyrical brushstrokes, hypnotizing all who listened. Once Kamal Bey began there was little but the host's call-to-dinner to stop him.

"Obedience to al-Banna *is absolute*," he added, raising his index finger up to his nose, focusing our gazes and attention to him. "Each of his recruits, without exception, *even if they are his relatives*, has to sign a paper promising total and unquestioning loyalty to him. The least amount of faltering is punishable by death."

Complete silence fell over the room as the Egyptian singer Abdel-Halim Hafez crooned from the stereo speakers to his melancholy orchestra in the background, hitting nostalgic high notes to the rhapsodic cries of his recorded live audience. All of us waited with baited breath to hear more.

"If al-Banna orders you as part of your cover and operation to 'Drink alcohol,' then you will drink—even if as a good Muslim you have never touched a drop of booze in your life. If he tells you, 'Get married and have a child,' you have no choice but to take a wife quickly—the first suitable woman you can find—and start a family right away. If he says, 'Hijack this plane,' then you will do so without question—and forfeit your life in the process, as these jobs are little more than suicide missions. He sends his most expendable agents into those situations while telling them he is doing so because they are his finest."

Kamal Bey's first yarn was merely the launching point. His stories were streams of consciousness affairs, with one tale transitioning almost seamlessly into the next. An anecdote about Abu Nidal strangling a Palestinian rival in cold blood in Baghdad would imperceptibly segue into a story about the fierce battle prowess of Margaret George, the first female Christian guerrilla of the Middle East who fought alongside Kurdish *peshmerga* rebels in the mountains against their Iraqi oppressors in the 1960s. Listeners would then find themselves hearing about Haroun al-Rashid, an 8th century Islamic Caliph of the Abbasid Dynasty and character of *The Arabian Nights*, roaming around Baghdad in disguise at night in order to escape the insularity of palace life. If you stepped out of the living room to snatch a few seconds of conversation with the hostess cooking in the kitchen (and perhaps sample a stuffed vine leaf finger or two from the simmering pot), you would return to find Kamal relating the details of former Egyptian president Anwar Sadat's hashish fetish and his relationship to Nazi German agents during World War Two. Those anecdotal epics were rendered in the colourful tongue of colloquial Egyptian Arabic, interspersed with footnotes in English (sprinkled with vulgarity), and punctuated by French turns-of-phrase and proverbs that both created a sugar coating of cultured charm and drove his points home with utter elegance.

After listening to a particularly heated discussion about the gruesome massacre and deportation of Armenians and Assyrians by their Ottoman rulers during World War One, Kamal Bey interjected with an equanimity that few were able to match.

"The French have an expression: *À quelque chose malheur est bon*," he said to the group, who suddenly fell silent in order to digest the comment. "In each bad thing there is the good," he translated literally. It was the idea that negative, even terrible, events can often have some positive unintended consequences, especially when viewed from the distance of time. The proverbial, 'There is a silver lining in every cloud' conveys a similar notion. In this case, Kamal said, it was that many of the surviving Armenians, and their descendants, went on to forge highly successful diaspora lives in the West in the aftermath of their tragedy. It was something that few in his audience ever considered, although they may not have all agreed about his conclusion.

An Armenian at that gathering snickered cynically at his comment, to which Kamal Bey responded:

"Vartan, you enjoy driving a Cadillac and eating *filet mignon* in what is the safest, most affluent society in human history. This is in part owing to these long-ago events. See the bigger picture and give thanks."

Those present seldom asked Kamal how he knew what he knew—it was just assumed that he did. They were aware that my father's close friend from Egypt was a lawyer by education, a specialist in Islamic *sharia* law.* Kamal had great respect for Islam and was an almost unheard-of example of a Christian Arab who could not only point to deep wisdom in the Koran, but could even recite passages from it flawlessly at will. He was not just book-smart and learned, especially on anything to do with the Middle East, but he also lived a storied life in the region before emigrating to Toronto. Once in Canada, he found a secretive job with the government that he never discussed—but which also made him somehow 'in-the-know.'

My own drift towards the Middle East was catalyzed by the many warps and wefts woven by Kamal the storyteller. His compendium of random but interlocking tales did not just trace out the Arab World writ large but also breathed life into it and lent it a depth usually not discernible short of being there in person. All of it ignited a wanderlust that would drive my jour-

---

* A body of Koran-based principles that point Muslims toward living a proper Islamic life.

neys into unexpected corners of that region in search of what I deemed to be my cultural bequest—and which, I felt, my family's transplanting to the West prevented.

THIS AFFINITY and attraction to a culture I considered my endowment was bolstered by a taste for exoticism. I recall intense flickers of interest, when, as a child, I looked at my parents' travel photos from around the world. Nothing focused my gaze in those pictures more than the images of foreigners from other lands: I think of the Mexican cliff-diver in Acapulco posing in a photo beside my parents, or the pretty blonde Danish woman sitting on a park bench in Tivoli Gardens whom my dad befriended while on a university work exchange in Denmark.

The same tendrils of seduction, the same lure of the exotic, grazed me when I was exposed to anything to do with the Middle East in the media. Whether it was TV footage of crowds of commuters hanging off the exterior of buses or riding on the roofs of trains in Cairo; merchants plying their wares in the dimly-lit byways of the Damascus *souq*; or ragtag militiamen clad in undershirts and wrapped in coils of ammunition firing their guns helter-skelter along Beirut's 'Green Line' during Lebanon's civil war in the 1970s and 80s—all of it seemed intensely thrilling, foreign, and on the cutting edge of life.

The English word "exotic" comes from the French *exotique*, which in turn had its roots in the ancient Greek *exotikos* and the Latin *exoticus*—both literally meaning 'from the outside.' When the term first came into usage in Europe in the 1600s it meant 'unusual' or 'strange' in the sense of something being alien or outlandish. There's a tendency nowadays to condemn the exoticization of other cultures as a direct link or throwback to the attitudes and legacies of Western colonialism. It is therefore sometimes seen as an absolute moralistic vice. The late Palestinian-American academic Edward Said's landmark work, *Orientalism*, similarly described the history of Western perceptions and portrayals of the East as being servile to power. His magnum opus didn't just make exoticization a bone of cultural contention, but seeded the idea, adopted later, that its perpetration necessarily had political underpinnings. Certainly, objectification of 'the other' can grease the wheels of racism and exploitation—something which numerous cultures, not just the West, have been guilty of.* Contemporary Western civilization, as Said pointed out, has consistently misunderstood the East and cast it in a simplistic and monolithic light.

But, the propensity to exoticize can also be an entirely innocent and apolitical reflex that is simply core to being human: a basic psychological impulse more ubiquitous than the symptoms of political oppression, or aberrant cultural trivializing, that are often attributed to it.† At the most fundamental level, to be stimulated by something 'exotic' is merely to experience novelty, stimulation, and excitement born of our exposure to something unfamiliar. All of us are highly sensitized to the new. Our brains evolved to prioritize changes in our environment from an evolved imperative to survive. Anything unusual and different that enters our field of perception is prioritized in our consciousness. We experience a mental jolt from the unfamiliar: a stimulus that makes us acutely aware of it in the moment. It is the reason circus clowns and eccentrics wear bold, garish clothing to gain and hold our attention; and why travel to new and especially foreign places is so stimulating.

The Middle East—its colours, noises, smells, freewheeling

---

* The closest rendering of the word 'exotic' in Arabic is *ghareeb*, which can mean 'unusual', 'interesting' or 'foreign'. Ironically, it shares the same root consonants as *gharb*, meaning 'West.'
† There may be another reason why Westerners have shown a propensity to exoticize the unfamiliar. The West's capitalist-materialist culture and its constant access to a mind-boggling variety of new goods conditions its people to excitement and pleasure tied to novelty.

chaos, and expressions of high emotion—represented a kaleidoscopic carnival of stimulus to me. This 'exoticism' was made all the more acute by what I took to be the comparative dullness of my Canadian existence. The country's politeness, sterility, sedateness, culture of risk-aversion, vast spaces, sense of social alienation, and somber blue-grey natural light translated into a vacuity of experience and detachment from the grit of real life. For me, the remedy to that ennui was to throw myself headlong into the only opposite I could conceive: the stimulus-rich and frenetic human ferment that was the Arab World, which Kamal Bey described so vividly and with a very Eastern panache.

It was Kamal Bey who also first articulated and mirrored what would later be my own dissatisfaction with aspects of Canadian life. He would much later speak of it repeatedly.

I was in the back seat of his big white sedan, riding with him and his wife Lilly, down a four-lane highway, following my parents in the car ahead. We were on a daylong outing to Niagara Falls. I was probably ten years old and a fan of Kamal's yarns. Thus, a kinship of sorts with him had already been forged. He suggested I ride with them.

"Look at all of this space," he said to me, extending his hand outwards to encapsulate the residential suburbs on the outskirts of Toronto, including a vast wooded escarpment. "Everything: the size of the properties, the houses, how far people live apart, the empty spaces... we never had this in Egypt, this kind of space. It is nice to live in your own castle, to have a big backyard and drive everywhere by car. But this emptiness and physical distance separates people. The ease of life here creates boredom."

"Kamal..." Lilly said, tonally scolding her husband and suggesting he dial back his complaints. She needn't have. I didn't fully comprehend what Kamal was implying at the time. The magical spell of childhood had not yet evaporated.

"I have a feeling you're going to be a man of the world," Kamal said to me, putting on a smile. "When you're older and start a job, have a career, you'll move far away from these places."

"What is *your* job?" I asked him.

His wife turned to him in almost amused anticipation.

"I work for The Government," he said.

"Where?" I asked.

"At an office in Toronto."

"No, I mean for which part of the government?"

"I work for The Solicitor General of Canada. It is the office responsible for public safety."

"What do you do there?"

Kamal Bey paused before answering. "To tell you the truth: mostly paperwork. Lots and lots of paperwork."

WE SPENT the day at the falls, where one inland sea disgorges into another. It is a natural wonder without equal for Middle Easterners coming from the nearly parched wastes of one of the world's most water-deprived regions. My parents went to Niagara frequently in the early years to ogle at the incomprehensible torrent. But my eyes and ears that day were on Kamal Bey, who was in top raconteur form telling us how Niagara Falls was the site of peace talks between the United States and Mexico, who both nearly went to war in 1910. The two parties, he said, worked out their differences while overlooking the falls, "which humbled them and put them in a mood to agree."

At one point as I leaned over the thick cast-iron railing atop the old stone wall beside the Horseshoe Falls, and stared down into the beckoning, terrifying abyss, Kamal Bey came over and watched the spectacle with me. When we had drunk it in, he told me that he had once spent a whole day sitting on the edge of Victoria Falls in Africa, beside the Zambezi River, watching the incessant flow. Those falls were double the size of Niagara he said, surrounded by thick jungle and draped in towering clouds of mist and epic rainbows.

"There were no tourists, no crowds smoking cigarettes, no pickpockets, no cheap souvenir stores, wax museums, hot-dog stands, or honeymoon hotels. Just nature as God created it."

Kamal Bey was not intentionally sabotaging the moment. He was widening my horizons in any way he could when the opportunity presented itself. As a citizen of the world caught between East and West, he was given to transporting himself, and others with him, anywhere on the globe in an instant—with a flick of his magic storytelling switch.

LIKE KAMAL BEY, I also had an East-West problem. But it was more than a feeling of being caught between cultures. Simply put: my Middle Eastern side felt insufficiently Eastern.

Though I didn't understand this properly until I was older, my parents, despite being born and raised in Cairo, were not exactly Egyptian. They were a mix of Egyptianized Levantines (Eastern Mediterranean peoples) and Mesopotamians whose families had emigrated from other parts of the Middle East at a time when Cairo was a more liberal cosmopolitan crossroads home to many Europeans. Being middle class and Christian, they idealized and related to the West nearly as much as to their own local cultures—paying lip service to Arabism, while embracing the values, manners and pretensions of Europeans. London, Paris, Athens, Rome and Los Angeles were their beacons of cultural guidance.

The names of family members, close and extended, were testament to this unusual dichotomy of 'here' and 'there': names like *Albert, Edouard, Yvonne, Antoine and Angèle,* all pronounced in a French lilt, far outnumbered occasional Arabic names like *Fuad,*

Samir, Adel, Fatouh, and *Nahed.* They studied under priests and nuns at French mission schools and lived in a Cairo suburb called Shubra, which in bygone days was a more pleasant, merchant-class neighbourhood teaming with foreigners that has since morphed into a crowded lower-class district of densely stacked tenements.* My family was just as much at home preparing meals of *escalope* and *pastitsio* as it was the more local delicacies of *megadarra* and *molokhia.* They left their neighbourhood only to travel to the beach in Alexandria, or to their various social clubs around Cairo where they whiled away their time gossiping, playing cards and drinking whiskey.

In some ways it was the perfect mélange and meeting of cultures. Yet there was also something fragile and tenuous about the whole arrangement. The world they inhabited was an insular, westernized bubble with little durability in a tumultuously restless landscape that was growing weary of Occidental influence. People of their demographic were considered outsiders, second-class citizens, a Christian minority living in a Muslim majority country—and non-Egyptian Arabs at that. For my family, feelings of superiority *and* inferiority intermingled in this fusion of civilizations, making for an uneasy existence. My parents and grandparents were referred to in Egypt as *khawaga.* It is a word derived from the Persian *khwaja,* roughly meaning "Lord" or "Master," but which in colloquial Egyptian became both an honorific and a subtle disparagement meaning 'a person of foreign ancestry.' For their part, my family viewed the underclasses and more conservative Muslims as somewhat backwards and culturally anathema to all they stood for.

Indeed, by the late 1960s when Arab nationalism, an Islamist revivalism, and the wars with Israel became too great to bear, and

---

* Not just people of Syrian-Lebanese ancestry, like my family, lived in Shubra, but it was also where most Italians, Greeks, Maltese, Yugoslavs, Cypriots, French and Middle Eastern Jews resided. Today, an underclass neighbourhood, Shubra is considered one of the most densely crowded in the world.

having sent most Europeans living in Cairo packing years earlier, they too responded in the only way they knew how, given there was no going back to their ancestral cities of Beirut, Aleppo and Mardin: they emigrated west.

THERE IS A VERY old Eastern saying: *All that goes into a salt mine become salt*. The proverb captures both what happened to my family in Canada, and what I hoped to achieve by travelling East and immersing myself in the Arab World.

Where my parents were concerned, as time went on, certain of their cultural habits slowly evaporated in Canada. The large and frequent weekend family gatherings with extended relatives became fewer and more far between. Arabic music, which used to blare loudly and frequently, causing hands to clap and fingers to snap, went silent. Even some of the more conditioned, out-of-awareness 'back home' behaviours, like drinking tea from glasses, and shouting during long-distance phone calls (the landlines in Cairo, especially for international calls, were notoriously poor) came to an end.

As I became older and grew aware of the wider cultural heritage of the Middle East, I saw my family's connection to it as a watered-down version lacking the requisite colour, zest and spice. Even their version of Arabic was an archaic and simplified mid-century patois—an antiquated rendition of a colloquial dialect that had long since evolved, and only survived in the black-and-white films of Omar Sharif. I felt shortchanged, lacking sufficient Arab *bona fides*. What I wanted instead was the bolder, more evocative Middle East characterized by its most potent imagery: the shape-shifting whaleback dunes of the deep Sahara, the circle dances of the Lebanese and Kurds, the majesty of domed Islamic architecture and the Arabesques of the *souq*. All of these, though resonant of the exotic and romantic, felt nonetheless real and hinted at something bordering on the ineffable. They were things the rational, linear and imperturbable West could not deliver. Kamal Bey, it seemed to me, in spite of his own ambivalence and criticisms of North America, embodied all of it in equal measure —he was a more rounded version of both East and West, which I was still not.

This was driven home during another social gathering, this time at my family home when I was in my late teens. Another visitor who had met Kamal for the first time asked him why he had come to Canada.

Kamal's face became broody and perturbed—as if he was still struggling with the decision. His moustache and tufts of ear hair bristled, and his great bald head, flanked by wings of greying hair, broke into wrinkles.

"For *all* reasons," he said.

He was asked to elaborate.

"Egypt gave us a million reasons to leave. Count them," he said, raising his hands to tally one on each finger. "The bribery, the corruption, the *wasta*,* the societal rot, the religious conservatism, Abdel-Nasser's thieving and destructive socialism. Then there were our two daughters: we wanted them to live somewhere that would have the same rights for women as for men."

"Is that all?" one visitor joked sarcastically. Everyone broke into a chuckle.

"No," Kamal Bey declared, dead seriously. "I also came because I knew, in addition to being Eastern, I was also Western— I am of both worlds. My wife is also an Englishwoman born in Cairo. I needed to feed both parts of myself. I could only do that here, where I was more free to be both."

Kamal Bey's words stayed with me. I realized years later that his situation, in a sense, mirrored mine—but in reverse. My journeys eastward in search of completion paralleled his relocation West. And whatever stories I accrued in those travels and sojourns

---

* A word that roughly means 'nepotistic connections.'

along the way, my own patchwork of tales, would, on some larger plane, join up with his.

Part II: Cairo

The Suffering Bastards Club

When Mounir Barsoum said he was taking me to "the best bar in Egypt"—I thought for certain it would be one of those iconic Cairo watering holes that had seen better days. Perhaps the Café Riche, or the old colonial bar at the bygone Windsor Hotel. When he added that it was also Egypt's "most secret bar" my imagination shifted to those even more obscure booze joints barely clinging to life in the vicinity of Midan Talaat Harb. After all, Mounir was a bona fide man-about-town and a die-hard cosmopolitan: he, more than anyone I had met before or since, would frequent such places. But when his lime green Lada turned towards the Kasr el-Nil Bridge over the great river Nile, instead of striking deeper into the *belle époque* city, I knew that we were headed for an unpredictably off-piste evening.

Our destination, confounding all expectation, was a low-rise apartment building in the leafy middle-class suburb of Mohandiseen on the Nile's west bank. We followed a shrub-lined walkway around the side of the building and came to a large mahogany door with a small plaque inscribed with what I assumed to be the name of the establishment. The portal looked like any exterior entrance to a ground-floor apartment.

"You have to promise, for as long as I live, not to tell anyone about this place," he said with a gravity that bordered on the comedic, as his finger rested idly on the doorbell.

"Agreed," I said, wondering with even greater curiosity where we were headed.

Mounir rang the bell. The door opened a crack and then widened to reveal a concierge wearing a black tuxedo. He greeted Mounir politely by name and let us in. We walked into a dimly lit corridor lined with wall lamps and proceeded towards another door at the end of the passageway.

We finally stepped into an upscale tavern. It was still largely empty. There were a smattering of customers, mostly older men nursing drinks and a few couples who conversed quietly to the melancholic warbling of Mohammed Abdel-Wahab. A live band's musical instruments sat unattended upon a small stage. The bar looked like an imitation British pub you'd find in a hotel—not the underground Cairo speakeasy with its forbidden and scandalized clientele that I was envisioning.

"That's it?" I asked, feeling let down. "This is what the secrecy was about?" I wondered if my new friend was also a practical joker.

Mounir smiled coyly and led me straight to the bar where an elderly Nubian man, also in a tuxedo, but wearing a *tarboosh*, a fez hat, tended bar to a retinue of older male barflies—all of whom, though intensely morose, greeted Mounir with warm camaraderie. We took the two remaining stools at the end of the row.

"Your bottle, tonight, *oustaz* Mounir?" the bartender asked, in a shockingly hoarse voice.

"Thank you, Bashir." He then turned to me: "Do you take lots of ice in your whiskey, like your dad?"

I nodded decisively, without mentioning that I'd never before so much as tried the stuff.

Hours later, a rip-roaring scene of Dionysian excess wiped clean the staid beginnings of our night: the bottle of J&B with Mounir's name on it resting on the bar and reduced to a puddle beside a cascading pile of empty *mezze* plates; the *oud*, *doumbek* and electric keyboard players incanting modern Arabic love poetry and strumming their instruments with heartfelt bravado; every available space thronging with bodies with arms raised in suggestive gyrations of Eastern dance; women scrambling upon tabletops with their shoes off, some with their blouses off to reveal their bras, dancing above the crowd; Bashir the Nubian bartender calmly and methodically churning out new potables like the cocktail maestro from the 1940s that he once was; and Mounir clutching his rock glass in one hand, a cigarette in the other, and with one arm around a busty middle-aged woman wearing too much eye makeup, both of them laughing uncontrollably.

All of it seemed inconceivable—a few degrees shy of an illegal bacchanal. It was 1995. I had only been in Egypt for a week, but I already knew that the religious conservatism that suffused the culture, even in its more westernized and permissive quarters, made this beyond unusual. The fact that it was a middle-age crowd made it even more surreal.

Mounir caught my eye and came fumbling over, drowsily, in the stooped posture I would come to associate with his unusual profession. He plunged his face messily into my ear.

"What do you think about our party?" he yelled, before pulling back to reveal a mischievous smile grafted over years of fatigue.

"It doesn't feel like Egypt," were the words that automatically came out of my mouth.

He leaned in again. "You asked about the secrecy."

I looked at him and nodded.

"Do you see why now?

IT WAS my first trip to Egypt and the Middle East—as part of a backpacking trip with my friend Curtis—that kicked off in Spain and saw us traipse around the Mediterranean via Morocco, Tunisia and southern Europe. I continued on, solo, to Egypt, partly to scope out the country in preparation for possibly living there. I had been offered acceptance into a two-year graduate program in international relations at the American University in Cairo (AUC) and was leaning towards taking it.

"You have to see an old friend of mine when you're there," my dad said over dinner one night, before I left on my backpacking trip.

God, not another visitation, I thought.

Naturally, my parents were thrilled about my first trip to their home country, which they'd visited only once in more than two decades in Canada. Living vicariously through me, they made plans for me to see nearly *all* of their relatives. The prospect of meeting everyone was of course exciting. But now their long-lost friends and acquaintances were being furtively slipped onto the visitation roster. I was worried that I'd be spending all of my time in Egypt shuttling between invitations in which I'd be awkwardly gawked at and overfed.

"Mounir Barsoum is his name."

"What does he do?" I asked, trying to gage his worth as a contact.

My mother fielded the question: "He's a nail technician," she said. "He works at a manicure-pedicure salon."

I nearly spat out my beer.

My dad looked offended. "Why are you laughing?"

"It's a funny image."

"How?"

"Well, isn't that a *woman's* job?"

"Clearly not," he said, firmly, trying to head off my juvenile suggestions questioning his friend's manhood. "And Mounir is the best at what he does. He knows and admires women. He's a kind of Casanova."

"So, he got into pedicure work because he couldn't become a gynaecologist?"

My mom slapped my arm. "Stop it. Mounir is a decent guy. He's just independent and isn't interested in marriage."

"You're both just playing him up as a cool guy because you want me to meet him."

My dad made an annoyed face. He then turned to my mom: "Show him the pictures."

My mother ran upstairs and came back with an old 1960s string-bound photo album with Egyptian hieroglyphs embroidered on the cover. Among all the black-and-white images of Alexandrian bikini beach scenes and group portraits photobombed by the Sphinx, were a handful of party shots. A few of them featured a suave, moustachioed, and somewhat cocky-looking young man surrounded by attractive and well-heeled Arab women who were laughing, brandishing their breast cleavages and swooning all around him.

"*That's* Mounir?" I said pointing to a man tweaking his thin 'stache and ogling the ladies in another photo.

"Yes," my dad said, jabbing his fork into the salad bowl.

My mom stood up and took my dad's empty dinner plate. "Egypt's most famous belly dancers and actresses call on him at the salon," she said, almost braggingly. "They all love him."

"*Belly dancers?*"

"Mounir goes to nightclubs," my dad added, sweetening the deal. "He knows everyone in the city. He'll show you a good time."

I suddenly felt affronted. "Why didn't you tell me about this guy before?"

"We're telling you now," my mom said, placing a second serving of *bamya* and rice before my father.

My dad picked up his fork, "So, what do you think?"

"Give me his number," I said. "I'll call him as soon as I get there."

I'D NEVER MET a mani-pedi Don Juan before, but I was intrigued. What was it like to be entrusted with the beautification of a woman's hands and feet—a job whose demands of particularism and perfection could no doubt have been anything short of toilsome? What did Mounir talk about with them? Did these ladies, especially the repeat clients, take Mounir into their confidence? And if so, how deeply? And as an Egyptian Casanova, how did he maintain complete professionalism in the face of his libertine impulses? In his moments of weakness, did he employ foot reflexology as a flirtation device? Did the act of prostrating at a woman's feet in a more or less misogynistic society cause the ladies to look upon him with secret scorn? The embryonic journalist in me was on fire with all possible lines of inquiry.

But as with most romanticized depictions of life, the reality turned out to be otherwise. It wasn't until my next meeting with Mounir at his clandestine speakeasy on a quiet weeknight among his sullen bar-fly confrères, that he let me in on some of the details.

"I'm tired," he complained, while rubbing his eyes and forehead. "What used to be a paradise is now a prison."

The old salon life described by my parents, he told me, was gone. His glamorous and high society clientele had been watered down by an influx of commoners—brash and "vulgar" customers who had emigrated to the capital from the provinces. The work was laborious; his patrons ever-more demanding and finicky. The physical aspects of the work, he lamented, had also aged him. He had developed a slightly hunched back after decades of stooping at his customers' feet. And Cairo, imbibing an austere religious conservatism that had swept the region, had lost its cosmopolitan playfulness. His late fifties were thus no longer the years of freewheeling folly he once lived.

"This is our last refuge of the old life," he added. He turned to look at the bartender: "Right, Bashir?"

The Nubian server, who stood opposite us making a drink,

smiled and uttered a deep-throated chuckle. "May God preserve it, *effendi*."

Eager to know, I asked Mounir how he became a nail technician in the first place.

He poured more whiskey atop the mountain of popping ice in his rock glass.

"Everyone asks me this question," he said. He then paused and became more circumspect. "I hated my father," he began. "He used to beat us. That was the foundation."

Mounir explained that his mother, whom he was close with, died when he was a teenager. When his father remarried a woman he disliked, Mounir made the decision to leave high school and get a job so he could afford to move out and live on his own. None of the odd jobs he took paid well enough, or worked out for him.

"Then one night at a bar," he continued, "a friend-of-a-friend noticed that I was easy-going and popular around women. He told me that I could probably make a lot of money by learning how to do manicures and pedicures. He said I'd get rich on the tips alone if I could also entertain these women—and who would love getting their hands and feet done by a man. What he said made sense. Back then only upper-class ladies with lots of money got their nails done at salons: wives of big businessmen, actresses and famous dancers. I knew how to make women laugh. So, it was the perfect job for me."

Mounir beat a path to the best nail salon in Cairo: Maison Lucie, an Armenian-owned parlour located in an alleyway off Kasr el-Nil Street. He was hired on the spot by the salon's namesake owner who had an eye for spotting talent. As one of the only male technicians in the city who also had a gift for the Egyptian gab—a form of playful and poetic Arabic banter replete with punning turns of phrase and clever idioms—Mounir eventually became a sensation. A flirtatious edge that didn't cross red lines also added to his appeal. Some of the most well-known belly dancers and actresses in Egypt at the time became Mounir's clients.

"What did your friends and family say?"

"My father disowned me after having disowned me several times before," he said, taking a sip from his glass. "Most people, men especially, didn't understand—even when I tried to reason with them about the benefits. Even now most of Egyptian society still sees this as a woman's job. It's considered lower-class work by some because you're touching people's feet, which is just an old Bedouin hang up. But that didn't bother me. The money was good and I was meeting women—some of my clients set me up with their friends."

Then Mounir's face became slightly cold. "That's why I never emigrated like your parents."

"You never considered leaving?" I asked.

"Some people are not meant to be parted from their homelands. Besides, I thought it would be crazy to leave."

Bashir the bartender placed a small bowl of nuts before us. I could tell by the look on his face that he'd heard these stories a million times before.

"I was optimistic," Mounir went on. "I thought the situation in the country would improve. But it only got worse."

MOUNIR DEMONSTRATED ambivalence where my family was concerned—especially when he became sodden with firewater, which was nearly every time I saw him. On the one hand he waxed lyrical about his friendship with my parents during the days of the *ancien régime*. On other occasions resentment towards them, and anyone else who left Egypt, tied to feelings of abandonment, came to the surface like a geyser stream.

One night I decided to repay Mounir's generous patronage by inviting him to an unobtrusive downtown Cairo watering hole that I discovered and proudly claimed as my own, called Cafeteria Port Tawfeeq. From the moment we stepped into the bygone-era and slightly seedy saloon, tucked within Midan Orabi's crumbling architecture of faded grandeur, Mounir recoiled in loathing. I could tell that the bar's aura of licentiousness and its fall into decrepitude marked by its cheap local beer, imitation contraband liquor and blue plastic tubs filled with fava and lupin beans from which the bartender filled our bowls for snacking, hit a nerve. The bar symbolized the decline of the old Egypt in microcosm.

When Mounir, who had already started drinking before arriving, asked for a double of Johnnie Walker and was offered instead "Johnnie Talker," a knockoff moonshine likely distilled in someone's bathtub in Bulaq, he rolled his eyes.

"What is this?" he said, lifting the top of the bottle with his fingertips as if it were a dirty rag.

The bartender wore a joking smirk. "What's the matter uncle?" he said. "Are you looking to impress a woman? Whiskey is whiskey."

Mounir lost his temper and turned to me: "Look at this place! *This* is what happened to the country after all the good people left."

I had no idea what to say.

"Calm down, Captain," the bartender said, patting Mounir on the shoulder before reaching below the counter. He pulled up another bottle, this one labelled "Gordoon's Special Dry Cairo Gin," and placed it on the bar. "How about this? As God is my witness, you won't taste the difference."

MOST OF MY relatives in Egypt, family who had stayed in the country long after everyone else fled to greener pastures, sometimes felt similarly. For them, religious conservatism and economic mismanagement had since ruined the place. Those who had emigrated, like my parents, were partly seen as facilitators of the societal decay, which they had sped up through a kind of cultural and political version of brain drain. Feeling as if they'd been left behind in a place turned utterly unsuitable, all of these people—my wider Cairo family, Mounir, and his forlorn drinking buddies—were shellacked with self-pity and cynicism. They were the forlorn and growingly impoverished victims of the great slow motion financial collapse that was decimating Egypt's middle class at the time. Chronic nostalgia, a permutation of denial, was their main, but ineffectual, coping mechanism. Mounir's clandestine speakeasy was an alternate reality, a mirage, a form of life support, that he and the barflies used in order to convincingly roll back the clock to that easier period of East-West equilibrium and material plenty. Even Bashir, the ultimate prop to that unrecoverable age with his great red *tarboosh* and deferential white-gloved manner, seemed duped enough by his own getup.

"I'm the oldest bartender in Egypt," he said to me proudly, tapping his chest slowly, on our next visit to the tavern. "I made drinks for British Army officers. I even learned bartending from Joe Scialom."

"Joe *Shalom*?" Mounir said, enunciating the man's name while pulling a cigarette from his pack of Cleopatras. "Was he Jewish?"

"He was the Jewish bartender at the Shepherd's Hotel. His nickname was: 'International Bar Man of Mystery.' Joe could speak seven languages. His Arabic was just like yours or mine."

Mounir put down his lighter and exhaled smoke. "He must have been a spy."

"That I don't know. But he created a world-famous drink. He called it in English, 'The Suffering Bastard.'" *

"Suffering *what*?" Mounir asked.

"*Bastard*."

"What does that mean?"

---

* Cocktail ingredients for The Suffering Bastard: equal parts gin, bourbon and lime juice; a dash of angostura; topped with ginger beer.

Bashir pondered for a moment. "It is a person who has no parents. I don't think there's a word in Arabic for it."

A portly barfly sitting beside Mounir turned to us in his stool: "A bastard is a child of *uncertain* lineage."

Mounir's brows furled. "Oh. You mean someone who doesn't know who their father is."

Bashir snapped his fingers: "That's it."

The barfly nodded: "When I was growing up in Alexandria, the Italian kids used to call me that—for no good reason. They would chase me through the street and yell: '*Fottuto bastardo! Fottuto bastardo!!*'"

Mounir pulled on his cigarette. "Bashir, you should have told us about this drink before."

"No one orders it anymore," he said, with a defeated tone. "It's gone, with the old days."

"I would have served it to my fiancé and her family," Mounir said. "They were very much of uncertain lineage."

"You were married?" I said, surprised.

"Engaged," he said with a distant look in his eyes before drifting back. Then he slapped his hand on the bar. "*Yalla*, Bashir! You have the ingredients: make us two suffering bastards."

"I'll have one too!" the barfly said, raising his hand.

"Three!" Mounir added. "The third for our *fottuto bastardo* friend, here."

The bartender pointed to each of his lower eyelids—an Arabic gesture indicating humble compliance and servitude—and set to work.

Mounir turned to me. "What do you think of my family here: King Farouk's barman, the society of whiskey-drinking men, and now, you, the son of an old friend?"

"I think I see myself moving here," I said, smiling.

On my last full day in Cairo I visited Mounir's nail salon, where he gave me a complimentary pedicure in which he revealed his legendary prowess in revitalising the outer aspect of the human foot.* We drank that night at the speakeasy with his usual band of cohorts. I shared with Mounir my official decision to do my schooling in Egypt and we made plans to become fast and furious wingmen of the Cairo night when I got back. Part of that included getting my dad to come to Egypt and initiating him into 'The Suffering Bastards Club,' as we called it. On the drive home that night with Mounir, he momentarily lost control of his car during a left turn taken too fast and too hard. The vehicle went up on the curb and grazed a pole, knocking off the side mirror on the passenger side. Though a reckless moment, that incident somehow cemented our newly minted brotherhood.

Four months later I returned to start my graduate program at the American University in Cairo. After finding an apartment and roommates and settling in, I decided to pay a surprise visit to my newest friend at the salon.

"I'm here to see Mounir," I told the receptionist.

The woman blinked a few times and stared at me as if she didn't understand what I was saying.

"Oh, you're his friend who came here a few months ago," she said, finally recognizing me.

"Yes. Is he working today?"

Her eyes darted sidewards in lightning quick calculation. "Just have a seat. Can I get you something to drink? A Fanta?"

"Sure," I said.

I took a seat on the couch, wondering what was up. Around me, nail technicians worked studiously on the hands and feet of female patrons who were sprawled out every which way, some

---

* I also went to the salon hoping to meet Egyptian Nobel laureate, Neguib Mahfouz. But the legendary literary fiction author, a client at Lucie's, cancelled his afternoon appointment that day. Mounir told me that Mahfouz, who was stabbed in the neck by a religious fanatic the year before, missed his bookings when his injuries flared-up.

engaged in conversation, others with their faces plunged deep into Egyptian gossip magazines.

A few minutes later the salon owner who I hadn't yet met, the famous and inimitable Lucie, came over with my drink and sat beside me. She could barely look me in the eye and after handing me the pop can, she began wringing her hands anxiously.

"I'm sorry."

"What is it?" I asked.

"May Allah have mercy on his soul—Mounir is dead."

I tried to speak, but no words came out.

"I guess you didn't hear. It happened over the summer."

"No," I said, grimly. It felt like only days had passed since I'd last seen him.

"We didn't know what happened to him at first. He didn't come in to work, and wasn't answering his phone. His sister finally found him and told us that he died in his sleep."

All I could think of was how upset my parents were going to be when they found out—and that I'd have to be the one to tell them.

"Mounir was a lonely man," Lucie said. Her chin wrinkled and quivered slightly. "His sister said he died from a broken heart. He died from loneliness. He told me not that long ago that he was waiting for his friend's son to come back from abroad. That he hadn't enjoyed himself, as he had with you, for a very long time."

With swollen eyes and constricted throats, we both stared at the salon's black-and-white checkerboard floor for a long time in silence.

Sayida Aisha (Cairo), Egypt, 1996

A crowded commuter bus fights its way through traffic in roaring fits and spurts on a swelteringly hot day. Two young boys holding colourful backpacks and no older than the age of six or seven, deftly hop onto the vehicle through the rear doors, unattended. They squirm through the legs of the towering, perspiring adults to a spot near to where I am sitting. There the boys stand silent, grasping a pole and looking as bored as any commuter on any transit system the world over.

It is mid-afternoon and I conclude the boys are returning home from school. I am shocked by their independence and freedom of movement without adult supervision. The other people on the bus don't even notice them.

I turn to an Egyptian woman sitting beside me and say to her, pointing at the boys, "This is something you never see in my country."

"What is?" she asks.

"Children at that age travelling alone across the city."

She chuckles. "Really? Why?"

"In the West parents don't trust that kids can take care of themselves or do anything alone, until they're teenagers. They'd never allow their kids to go out alone at that age—not even down their own street—in fear they would be kidnapped."

The woman stares at me in disbelief before suddenly keeling over in laughter. The other passengers, including the boys, turn to watch the laughing woman as they hold onto dear life amid the erratic race car-style bus driving.

"Kidnapped!" she says, letting out another cackle.

"Is there no child kidnapping in Egypt?" I ask.

"Mister, we have so many children here in Egypt that people are willing to give them away for free. Nobody wants more of them."

The Incident at the Moulid

A sign is enough for the alert, but a thousand counsels are not enough for the negligent.
 – Arabic proverb

There is no worse deaf person than the one who does not want to hear.
 – French saying

The warnings came in triplicate. Two mild cautions, and one stern. They arrived as we walked along a forlorn street in the Sayeda Zeinab district of Cairo at night. All of them delivered within minutes of each other. All of them destined to go unheeded.

The first injunction came from a group of young Egyptian women passing alongside us.

"Are you going to the *moulid*?" one of them asked in Arabic, clutching a pile of books under one arm.

"Yes," I said, as we headed towards the muffled ruckus in the distance. She pointed to my four American friends, three of whom were women. "It won't be good for them." She spoke curtly for effect and left it at that.

The next warning, also from a female, was exactly the same in message and tone—and just as fleeting and ambiguous. Neither had bothered to elaborate. In their minds, the message was sufficiently implicit.

Moments later a young couple, also pedestrians, beckoned me with a wave. When I reached them, they looked at me incomprehensibly at first, trying to size me up. I was wearing the traditional clothing of a rural Egyptian *fellah* or farmer: a black *gellabiyah* winter robe, white headscarf, and a gargantuan embroidered scarf slung around my neck and over my shoulder. I held a heavy, wooden walking stick.

"Are you taking those foreigners to the *moulid*?" the man asked.

When I answered in the affirmative, both clicked their tongues in disapproval and stared at me with wide-eyed astonishment.

"No, no, no. May Allah preserve you: take your friends and go back," implored the man.

"There is danger there," the woman added. "This event should *not* be attended by women."

I knew that the working-class neighbourhood we were in held something of a reputation for roughness, even sordidness. But a certain stubbornness and hubris gripped me. The three women accompanying my roommate Soren and I—Betsy, Claire and Virginia—were year abroad students attending the American University, where I was also doing graduate work in my second year. They had recently moved into the apartment above ours. I had told them proudly, having already lived in Cairo for a year already, that I would personally take them, as a sort of welcome gesture, to the annual *moulid* of Sayeda Zeinab: a raucous religious festival held not far from Garden City, where we lived.

I had a desire to impress the others and to use this occasion to put my Egyptian bona fides, my local cultural prowess, to a sort of test.

When the warnings were delivered, I threw up the best rationalizations I could muster, rather than embarrassingly turn tail. *These are worst-case prognostications. The detractors are mistaken. I've done this before. All will be fine*, I thought.

"What did those two people want?" Betsy, who was from Maryland, asked as I fell back with the group.

"Just to be more careful than usual because of the crowds," I said.

IN THE MIDDLE EAST and Islamic world a *mawlid* is a public celebration of the birthday of a Muslim saint that is held in the vicinity of his or her tomb, or shrine. The most famous and widely observed *mawlid* is that which marks the birthday of the Prophet Muhammed. But there are scores of other such holy days held across the region that celebrate more locally-known saints, and which culminate in mass observances, and sometimes riotous merry-making by the thousands in the street.

In Egypt, such an occasion is known as a *moulid* and is celebrated among some of the country's Coptic Christians, who have their own saint-days, as well. The Egyptian *moulid* has a twofold face. At one level it is a pious religious observance in which the pilgrim seeks to make personal contact with the saint's divine essence, their *baraka,* that emanates from the spirit of the deceased and their place of burial. Worshippers brave the unspeakably large and crushing crowds—some second only in size to those they might experience in Mecca—to touch, kiss or circumambulate the shrine of the holy person. Among them are great numbers of the sick coming to be cured of their ailments, and the childless who seek a miraculous cosmic intercession to correct their infertility. But the *moulid* also has a secular side. At the same time it is a carnivalesque whirligig of bacchanalian excess, in which the general populace, especially the impoverished and downtrodden, come to blow off steam and have an all-round good time.*

Some *moulid*s last for a few days, others as long as a week. In nearly all cases, the public squares adjacent to the saints' tombs become transformed into a makeshift fairground draped in a garish latticework of blinking lights and lanterns—and replete with cotton-candy sellers, boat-shaped swings, fortune tellers, conjurors, acrobats, and snake charmers. Some of those rites and customs date from as far back as the Pharaonic period. Large groups, in some cases whole extended families, sprawl upon the ground, picnicking and congregating around gas stoves to brew endless rounds of tea for any and all comers. Enormous canvas tents, decorated in colourful Islamic motifs, host the ecstatic gatherings of the various lodges and orders of the Sufi brotherhoods. At night, the tents fill with groups of men swaying shoulder-to-shoulder in the trance-inducing ritual of *zhikr*† to long musical repertoires and chanting, whose tempos become increasingly frenetic. Every *moulid* culminates in a climactic evening of celebration and observance called *Al-leila al-kebira*, or 'The Great Night': one last hurrah of devotional and secular activity for which Egyptian *moulid*s are known, and in decades past also involved much more of the profane.

"Several years ago... I witnessed a queer sight at the dawn of the last day from my window in the square, a sort of burlesque, but harmless at the time, called locally 'zeffet el-Sharamit,'" writes Joseph McPherson in his 1941 book, *The Moulids of Egypt*. "It was a procession of gaily decorated carts bearing the prostitutes of the town with their admirers, with much music and song. At that date the secular side of the moulids had become rather too like

---

* One of the reasons the blinkered and orthodox-conservative Salafists and Muslim Brotherhood types disapprove of these celebrations.
† Arabic for "remembrance" or 'reminder' of the spiritual unity between the soul and the Godhead state preceding Earthly life.

ancient Greek and Roman feasts, with Lesbian and mixed dances of a pronounced character, and other unseemly things."*

Just the year prior, I, along with several others braved the treacherous, accident-prone Alexandria Road to attend the Great Night at Egypt's largest *moulid*, which up to two million flock to from around the country: the Moulid of Sayed Ahmed al-Badawi in the city of Tanta, in the Nile Delta. The feast commemorates the birth of a 13th-century Arab Muslim mystic and miracle worker born in Morocco but who relocated to Egypt, and who hailed from a Syrian Bedouin tribe. † In spite of its size and crowds, the Tanta moulid was mostly a family affair that had a patina of benevolence to it. There was only one hair-raising moment in which we were nearly crushed to death in the throng of worshippers in the Al-Badawi Mosque. We had lined up to kiss a stone slab in which the suspiciously rectangular imprints of the Prophet Muhammed's feet were allegedly cast (a custodian with a stick beat worshippers away if their smooching went on for too long). Beyond that we witnessed no other negative incidents at that *moulid*.

I had successfully braved the Tanta throng, and those of two

---

* McPherson, an eccentric Englishman who lived in Egypt for 45 years during the first half of the 20th century wrote the one and only book on Egyptian *moulid*s. In it he lists 126 different village celebrations—many of them now gone. Given to travelling around Egypt in disguises, '*Bimbashi*' (Major) McPherson worked in various military, intelligence and police capacities. He rose to the rank of Chief Inquisitor and Director of Egypt's secret police, investigating organized crime groups, corrupt officials and secret societies. British author Lawrence Durrell, in his *The Alexandria Quartet*, based his fictional character Lieutenant Commander Scobie at least partly on the real-life McPherson and his interests in *moulid*s. Durrell's Scobie was a cross-dressing Englishman and *bimbashi* of the secretive Q Branch of the Cairo Police. While prowling the docks one night in drag he is beaten to death by scandalized British sailors. Yet Scobie is mysteriously canonized by Alexandrians and reincarnated into the holy man known as "El Scob," replete with his own shrine and an annual festival held in his honour: "The Mulid of El Scob."

† Al-Badawi and his troupe of forty disciples are said to have dwelt on the city's rooftop terraces, earning his spiritual order the informal name of "The Roof Men."

other festivals that year, all without fracas or fisticuffs. Because of that, I assumed the *moulid* of Sayeda Zeinab would also offer no drama or difficulty—even on its Great Night. Part of the reason for this assumption was that Sayeda Zeinab festival was much smaller than Tanta's. This was despite the fact that it was also somewhat more important: one of three big Cairo *moulid*s involving the Prophet Muhammed's family. Sayeda Zeinab was the Prophet's granddaughter. Zeinab was the child of his daughter Fatima and her husband Ali—the fourth Caliph of Islam, the Prophet's cousin *and* the revered founder of the *Shia* faith. Vectors of celebrity, sainthood and exponential holiness criss-crossed this woman and her feast every which way. Because of all this, Sayeda Zeinab's mosque and mausoleum is one of the largest and holiest religious venues in Egypt and Islam.

Neither had I considered, which is perhaps more to the point of the story at hand, that Zeinab's namesake neighbourhood is known as one of the more crowded and rundown places in Cairo. Its residents have a reputation among Cairenes for a certain brashness and rudeness stemming from an indescribable neighbourhood frustration said to inflict them. I was later told by locals that the *moulid* there was known for its rowdiness, drunkenness and *bango* (marijuana) smoking. Even had I known this in advance, the fact that every *moulid* drew its handful of troublemakers meant I still wouldn't have paid the warnings I received much heed.

My laissez-faire attitude explained why I had even dressed the part: donning the garb and staff of an agrarian *Sa'idi* from Upper Egypt. Those southern farmers partake in an ancient ritual stick-fight at *moulid*s, which is also part-dance and part-martial art. It was the reason the three heralds bearing warnings on the street approached me—and not my friends—as we neared the festival grounds: I was clearly the group leader. If I was as Egyptian as my appearance suggested, I would have known better than to take women into the *moulid*'s feverish—and maniacally male—inner vortex.

The Incident at the Moulid

WE REACHED the edge of the party zone with its ambient ruckus of *mizmar* trumpeting, frenzied tambourine drumming, and the amplified reverb effects of the chanting of *sheikhs*. As we wove through the hoopla of magicians, carnival rides, book vendors, frankincense dispensers, and popcorn sellers, nothing appeared or felt disconcerting. On the contrary, I found myself in my element: amid the sensual, emotive and pleasure-inducing stimuli I'd felt lacking back home and which I'd sought by coming to Egypt. But what I didn't notice quickly enough, as we left the periphery and pushed deeper towards the square and mosque, into the thick of the party zone, was that the presence of women and children evaporated. By the time we entered the square, the crowd that gathered were all men. Nearly all of them were staring at the odd spectacle that outdid every other *moulid* extravaganza before them: a young Egyptian dressed in the robes of an elder *fellah* leading four young westerners—three of them attractive Western women.

Several old men brandishing ear-to-ear grins threw me thumbs-up signs; a kind of congratulatory pat on the back, I assumed, for the ladies who had literally taken my arm out of nervousness. The point at which we began to palpably sense menace came swiftly thereafter. It was also the point of no return: when a crowd-within-a-crowd formed around, and began to shadow us, growing larger as it did. Events at that point unfolded at breakneck speed.

"Let's leave the square," I said alarmed, raising my voice above the deafening din.

But when we moved in the opposite direction, so did the mob. The circle of men who fixated on us then began to tighten and close ranks. We were just as much a pageantry to these people as they and their *moulid* were to us. Some of them, I am certain, seldom left their neighbourhood and had only seen foreigners from a distance, and rarely at that. In the permissive and jubilant environment of the festival, and emboldened by their numbers, they naturally came in for a closer look. The overly-enthusiastic greetings in broken English co-mingled with lurid jokes and mocking laughter, and then all too soon, groping hands. They were like the first intermittent raindrops of an approaching torrent.

"Don't fucking touch me!" Betsy screamed, kicking and hitting one of the men in the arm as hard as she could.

Soon after, with rage-fuelled strength, Claire, a fellow Canadian, pushed one of the scruffy-looking hooligans in the chest. "Stop it! Get away from me!"

An indescribable deep-seated terror gripped me as I realized that not only were we completely surrounded and cut off from any exit and assistance, but that the scene was spiralling into a form of mob violence. In surreal slow motion I watched as the crowd, seemingly hundreds of anonymous men, their honour besmirched by the stinging retribution of the Western women, came alive, and set themselves upon us—pushing and pulling us apart from one another like separate cross-currents and eddies of explosive energy. I thought of the experiences of surviving avalanche victims, in which they describe the helplessness of being subsumed into an unstoppable force that exponentially dwarfs them.

I tried hard to fight back, even thrusting at the attackers and bopping at their heads with my *Sa'idi* fighting stick, but there was no repelling them. My friends grappled and punched and pushed as countless hands reached at their private parts. I knew that there had been rare incidents at other smaller festivals in more remote communities, where family vendettas existed— vicious fights and brawls—that ended in people being killed. I surrendered to the idea that some, or all of us, might possibly die, and that I bore responsibility for leading us into it. A defeated acceptance turned me limp, like driftwood, as I was pushed and pulled by the tsunami of bodies crashing and colliding into us in successive waves that could scarcely be resisted.

Then came a strange moment, a beat, in which the irresistible momentum of the mob felt uncertain, tentative. From within the very crowd that assailed us came a counter-movement. The horde began to churn inside-out, turning in on itself. Many clean-cut men, most in black leather jackets, appeared by our sides, as if surfacing from the depths of some tumultuous sea. They began resisting and even pummelling our attackers. One of them grabbed my arm and pulled me towards the edge of the square. I saw that my friends too were being yanked and physically cajoled by what I could only conclude were people intent on rescuing us. Some of these men, moving ahead of us, blazed a corridor through the human masses, yelling, screaming and threatening, telling everyone to move back.

With growing ease and speed, these undercover officers whisked us through the crowd to a makeshift police post at the edge of the square, located on the grounds of a gated cinema building. As soon as we arrived, three officers slammed the heavy cast-iron gates shut. No sooner had the doors closed than the wake of the crowd, following on our heels, collided head-on against the bars, rocking the gate nearly out of its foundations. Screaming faces pressed against the bars, their hands and arms clawing at us through them.

We sat exhausted on the ground, or paced in adrenaline-fuelled circles, trying to process what had just happened. Beside us, a group of policemen, some uniformed, others undercover, formed a circle around an impoverished-looking older man who was intoxicated and had slipped through the gates with us. The officers yelled at and shook him at first. Soon each officer took turns punching the man in the shoulders and chest.

Betsy, who was already short-circuiting from the incident, fell into hysterics at the sight of the old man being brutalized.

"Stop it! Stop it! That man tried to help us! Don't hurt him!"

The officers ignored her. After delivering several more blows which knocked the old man down, the police took him to the gate, opened it a crack, and threw him into the crowd. He was engulfed into the mass of humanity which fell upon him like a large boiling school of piranhas.

Virginia, my Spanish friend, sitting on the ground near me, looked up and stared in wide-eyed horror and disbelief at the scene.

"Did you see that?" she said.

"I did."

"Those people just ate him. They devoured that man whole. I've never seen anything like that in my entire life."

A TALL OFFICER dressed in black with a commando-like physique, and who had been part of the circle of police who beat up the old man, approached us calmly. He looked at all of us for a while, without saying anything, and then approached me.

"What prettiness is this?" he said straight-faced in Arabic, gesturing at my clothing. He had used an Egyptian expression of astonishment about one's appearance that could be spoken in one of two ways: either as a literal compliment, or, as in this case, its opposite: sarcasm.

He narrowed his eyelids and made a skeptical face. "You're not Egyptian," he declared, shaking his head slightly.

It was a stinging rebuke. I must have been deeply absorbed in deciding which of many insufficient comebacks to employ, because I didn't respond.

"Where are you from?" he continued.

"Canada," I finally said.

"Ah, yes. Of course. I should have known from your clothes," he said with a wry smirk.

"My parents were born here," I added.

He ignored my comment before adding. "And your friends?"

I pivoted to face them as they looked on, calmer, but still shaken. "Two Americans. A Spaniard. A Canadian. We go to the American University."

I saw the officer's studied demeanour become marred by a touch of annoyance. "I'm the commander," he said. "We're not allowed to keep you here the whole night. You're going to have to leave."

"We're not walking back out there," I replied.

"I wasn't suggesting that. I'll get a car and drive you myself."

"Drive? But the square and streets here are full of people."

He shrugged. "They'll have to move out of the way."

As the Great Night of the *moulid* reached its crescendo, we were spirited into the Peugeot station wagon like rock stars fleeing ravenous fans and paparazzi.

"Tell your friends to lock their doors," the officer said once we got inside, as he began to slowly drive into the crowd.

It was like moving through a car wash. The square, and the streets feeding into it, were still thronged with people. We could barely see where we were going. A panorama of faces peered through the windows to catch glimpses of us inside. The officer kept his own window half-open and constantly barked orders for people to get out of the way while honking his horn. The car picked up pace, bumping into people and at times virtually running them over. My friends, crammed in the backseat, gasped and at times covered their eyes. Occasionally groups of people swarmed the driver's window to beg for a ride. One of them was a very old man who clutched at his chest and claimed he was having a heart attack. He held onto the car and tried to climb onto the hood.

"Get away, you filthy dog!" the officer yelled, picking up a handgun lying below his seat and flashing it menacingly at the man, who in his terror, fell away as we passed.

Once we were out of the carnival zone and back on the less crowded road, the tense mood lifted somewhat. The officer began to make light-hearted small talk with the girls in his very broken English. Claire and Virginia politely engaged him. Betsy, stern-faced with her arms crossed, said nothing. She was furious about what had happened—chiefly at me, but also at the policeman. At one point she opened up, interrupting the banter.

"Ask him why he beat up that innocent man!" she barked at me.

I translated, reluctantly.

The policeman paused before responding calmly, looking at Betsy in the rear-view mirror.

"Tell your friend," he said "that my country is different than hers. Here, people misbehave at every opportunity. The only thing that stops them, the only thing they respect, is strength."

Everyone became awkwardly silent.

The vehicle soon pulled up beside our building. All of us were exhausted and grateful to be back home. We politely thanked our rescuer and bid him farewell.

MANY YEARS LATER, after picking up a copy of Joseph McPherson's 1941 book, *The Moulids of Egypt*, I came across this somehow apt excerpt about the Sayeda Zeinab festival with which the retelling of this episode may well be brought to a close:

> Some ten years or more ago there was a serious *bagarre** at which a number of people were killed, mostly 'Sa'idis', a most

---

* French for a 'brawl.'

rare occurrence, as a moulid crowd is full of piety, and fun, and good temper. And ladies whom I have taken into the thick of the Sayyida Zeinab crowd would add 'good manners', for a way is always made for them politely and pleasantly, and every consideration shown. On one occasion my lady companions were invited into the mosque to visit the tomb, a favour which delighted them and left them most appreciative and grateful. 'Sayyida Zeinab was a lady,' one of them remarked, 'and her votaries here are gentlemen.'

Cairo, Egypt, 1962

Egyptian President Gamal Abdel Nasser and his gaggle of advisors saunter slyly into the exhibition pavilion, a band of brothers in sharp suits. Egypt's baby-faced leader and his retinue are touring a commercial fair and have stopped to visit the country's Chamber of Tobacco with its display of cigarettes and cigars. Kamal Bey, along with his boss, both of whom work at the Chamber, greet the president and his henchman with the deferential niceties befitting men of high authority.

Kamal shows the big shots around the displays before handing out sample smokes to everyone—including a Belmont cigarette, Egypt's top selling brand, to Abdel-Nasser himself.

Nasser, though a chain-smoker, politely declines. "I have my own," he says, reaching into his pocket and pulling out a pack of illegal contraband Kent cigarettes made in the United States.

Without missing a beat Kamal Bey lights Nasser's cigarette, as all of the president's deputies look on awkwardly and with a touch of embarrassment. By smoking the banned American cigarettes, not only is the nationalist-socialist leader breaking the law, but he is also favouring a capitalist Western product over Egypt's locally-manufactured brand—a deep faux pas, especially in front of the tobacco-men.

Nasser notices the change of mood and uncomfortable glances. He chuckles self-consciously.

"Sorry, guys," he says to his hosts. "I'm used to smoking Kents. Any change of brand would irritate my lungs."

Kamal Bey and the tobacco-men vehemently dismiss the great leader's concerns in polite unison. But awkwardness and embarrassment still hangs over the meeting.

"I'll tell you what," Nasser says to the executives. "If you make me a cigarette similar to this Kent, I promise to stop smoking the American brand and be your first and best client."

Kamal Bey's boss, Joseph Matossian, the chairman of Egypt's tobacco chamber, straightens his back and clears his throat before nervously stepping forward. It is his come-to-Jesus moment.

"Mr. President," he says proudly, "your wishes are our orders."

DAYS LATER, Matossian summons Kamal Bey into his office.

"Kamal, we promised the President that we would make him a new American-style cigarette. I want you to go to the black market and buy three cartons of Kent. We'll have them analyzed to see what the exact blend is. Then we'll simply recreate it. The President won't know the difference."

In the weeks that follow, Matossian instructs his designers to create a box that is similar to the Kent's packaging to deepen the illusion of likeness: white with gold inlay.

The only thing left to decide is the new cigarette's name.

Matossian holds a big meeting with his most trusted colleagues, including Kamal Bey, to decide the matter. At the time, the Hollywood film Cleopatra, starring Elizabeth Taylor and Richard Burton, was in production and was making headlines around the world—in part owing to the adulterous affair the two stars were having on set.

"I think 'Cleopatra' would be a perfect name," Kamal Bey declares during the meeting.

The tobacco-men stroke their chins and grumble, unsure.

"Yes, she was a Ptolemy of Macedonian origin—and a Westerner," Kamal continues. "But she was also the Queen of Egypt and remains a historical icon. The name is instantly recognizable to anyone, anywhere. Plus, if we call the cigarettes 'Cleopatra,' we can time our launch with the film. The movie will do much of our early promotion work on our behalf."

Matossian claps enthusiastically like an excited child, "This is brilliant, Kamal! Egypt's best-selling cigarette will be called 'Cleopatra.' Cleopatra!! It is decided, then."

WEEKS PASS, Kamal Bey and Matossian are in a car driving to the Koubbeh Palace, which was then the site of Egypt's presidential offices. The men are carrying with them four cartons of Cleopatra cigarettes wrapped with golden paper and silver ribbons. Because the cigarettes were created at Nasser's behest, Kamal and Matossian reasoned the first person to try them had to be the president himself.

There, they are received by the Nasser's chief of staff, Abdel Magid Farid, who thanks them profusely on behalf of the President himself, and promises to deliver the gift to him.

Weeks elapse. And then months.

No word ever comes from the president, or his office, about the new Egyptian cigarette produced specifically at his request and to his taste—and named after an Eastern *femme fatale* with a penchant for sleeping with Roman warlords.

MONTHS GO BY. Kamal Bey and his wife are attending the wedding of a family friend who was marrying the daughter of President Nasser's aide-de-camp. The reception is held at the once swank Heliopolis Palace Hotel, which will much later become the presidential palace of both Presidents Hosni Mubarak and General Abdel

Fattah el-Sisi. Kamal and his wife know both families and are seated close to the main wedding table. There is a long delay in serving dinner as rumours are rife that President Nasser is expected to attend.

Nasser, the de facto guest of honour, and his entourage of bodyguards arrive 90 minutes later. The President is given a seat wedged between the married couple at the main dinner table—just several meters away from Kamal and his wife.

Nasser is a chain smoker and Kamal Bey knows that the first thing he will do is light a cigarette.

After hugging the newlyweds and sitting down, Nasser reaches into his pocket and pulls out his pack of smokes and puts them on the table in front of him. The President, Kamal notices, isn't smoking his usual Kents, or the Cleopatras designed to replace them, but L&M—another contraband American product...

Lost and Found on the Sea of Reproach

> When Jesus was young, someone said to him, "Where did you gain your education?" He said, "From nobody. I looked at the ignorance of fools and avoided it."
> – Abu Hamid Al Ghazali's sayings attributed to Jesus

Kamal Bey had once said, "When a person has a genuine need or yearning, life will often provide opportunities to fulfill it—and sometimes in a way that is no less miraculous for its subtlety." One such moment unfolded on an April day in Cairo, under a dust-filled sepia sky in which the sun's usual magnificence was reduced to a tepid moon-like pallor. It came in the form of an old and water-damaged copy of *Egypt Today* magazine that a recent visitor to our apartment had left behind. The English-language monthly, lying unobtrusively at the edge of our cluttered dining-room table, might have easily been ignored, or sooner thrown out.

It was spring of 1996—several months before the incident at the *moulid*. I had been living in Egypt as a student. My three North American roommates and I had largely acclimatized to the city and its chaotic rhythms. But Cairo's hydra of encumbrances seemed to reach new levels of maddening that spring, testing the limits of our human adaptability. It wasn't just the non-stop bleating and psychic emanations of the city's colossal population. The air pollution, political tension and the incessant waves of *khamaseen* dust-storms all simultaneously crescendoed, triggering red-line stress that plunged us into catalepsy. We suffered from what I called "Cairo Fatigue Syndrome." Like most people living in what is known endearingly to its natives as 'The Mother of the World' (*Umm al-Dunya*), we craved the healing purity and stillness of anywhere *not* Cairo. The usual touristy getaway spots in Sinai and the Nile Valley wouldn't cut it. We needed a deeper reality shift to a place that was more ethereal and refined.

But where?

The solution, materializing with the implausible magic of an answered prayer, appeared as a travel feature in that abandoned *Egypt Today* magazine. The article was entitled "Hiking in Devil's Country." It was a first-person account, by a Western writer, of a trek along a remote mountain footpath that wound its way between two Coptic Orthodox monasteries deep in Egypt's Eastern Desert. The trail, a part of history in its own right, formed the one and only physical link between the earliest beacons of Christian mysticism: the Red Sea monasteries of Saint Anthony and Saint Paul.

The monks at the monasteries allege it is the path blazed by Anthony when, in answer to a vision, he sought out and encountered fellow hermit Paul in the fourth century AD. Invitingly obscure, the trail had no name and appeared on no maps of the region. Offering neither shade nor water, and subject to alternating fits of heat by day, and cold by night, for much of the year, it runs through a desert whose monastic denizens refer to ominously as the "Sea of Reproach."

When I brought the magazine article, and trail, to the attention of my roommates, they were all in favour of making the trip. The fact that none of us had any backcountry experience and that the writer of the article himself got lost, ran out of water, and only found his way back with the help of some passing Bedouin, made little difference in our calculus. Cairo had broken us to the point where our only salvation lay in something akin to spiritual redemption, and which only the desert could provide. Dangers be damned. It was for this reason that when we decided to throw ourselves upon that Boschian wasteland far beyond the Nile's periphery, we didn't so much as ask ourselves what we were doing.

WE THREW off the last residues of Cairo after watching a nerve-fraying kung-fu flick with Arabic voice over, and stepped off the bus into the stillness and pitch black of the desert night. The preliminary leg of the trip involved taking the overnight coach to Hurghada along the Red Sea Highway and telling the driver to let us off at a nondescript, almost invisible turn off past Ras Zafarana. Ahead of us, a paved 10-kilometre road led inland to our embarkation point for the hike: the Monastery of Saint Paul.

Known locally as *Deir Anba Bula*, the Monastery of Saint Paul is situated roughly 300 kilometres southeast of Cairo on the edge of the Red Sea Mountains near the Gulf of Suez. It was founded above the cave where the anchorite Paul of Thebes lived alone for more than eighty years and where his remains are to this day kept. Legend has it that Paul, the first Christian hermit, fled the persecution of Roman officials in the Nile Valley and lived a life of solitude in the desert until the age of 113 in 341 AD. He purportedly subsisted with the help of a raven who brought him a loaf of bread to eat every day.

The monastery's larger and more illustrious twin, *Deir Anba Antunius*, the Monastery of Saint Anthony, rests beneath the northern edge of the same range in a valley known as *Wadi Arabah*, 30 kilometres to the northwest. Its namesake, Saint Anthony the Great, considered the forefather of early Christian monasticism, spent the last 45 years of his life in a similarly austere seclusion. Like Paul, he too resided in a cave, where he is said to have sheltered from a host of demons who frequently swarmed and beat him with truncheons, cudgels and maces. He died in situ, also a centenarian, in 351 AD.

A barren and windswept desert plateau rising 1,000 metres divides the two monasteries. Over the plateau and between the monasteries twists the inconspicuous path on which we had set our sights. In commemoration of Anthony's journey to find Paul, monks at both monasteries once a year traverse the path to meet at the mid-way point on the plateau—keeping the trail physically visible.

As the bus growled away and resumed its laboured itinerary, becoming a speck of red light in the distance, the four of us were swallowed by an all-consuming solitude. A blustery gale, blowing off the Gulf of Suez, underscored what all of us were thinking: that by seeking reprieve from one set of adverse conditions, we'd done little more than place ourselves in the hands of another.

We lifted our packs and headed west in the direction of the monastery. Deciding soon after to call it a night, and careful not to stray far off the road and into the landmines said to be waiting in ambush there, we found a stretch of soft sand and curled into our sleeping bags to ride out the remainder of the night in what small bliss we could garner.

Day 1

"A terrible wilderness of mountainous country constitutes the immediate environment of St. Paul's," writes 19th century German traveler, Georg August Schweinfurth. "It is a precipitous cliff into the abyss, a gate of hell, more horrible than the fantasy of Dante could express it."

When daylight made its return, it became clear that the spectacle described by Schweinfurth, albeit hyperbolic, was not that far off the mark. Before us was a bleak and shattered terrain of rock, sand and scree. Not even an anaemic shred of dry desert flora was evident.

We again took to the road and eventually rounded the final stretch of pavement leading to the monastery. St. Paul's twin-towered gateway came into view and stood out like a portent. At the compound we found a scene more reminiscent of Cairo than of a secluded monastery in the desert. A large throng of Coptic Christian pilgrims from all over Egypt—men, women and children—filled the site. Moving through the crowds were St. Paul's beacons of piety: Egyptian monks in black robes exuding a smiling benevolence from beneath their trademark cross-embroidered hoods. They were everywhere: from young novices running errands, to older patriarchs with grey or salt-and-pepper beards of huge length engaged in small talk with visiting housewives. What we failed to realize until we arrived was that it was Good Friday in the Orthodox calendar: by coincidence our hike was taking place over Egypt's Easter weekend.

Our first order of business was to find the trailhead and get any navigational advice we could from the monks. But between all of their busyness and religious emoting and celebrating with pilgrims, we weren't getting much help. At first the monks who stopped to listen to our entreaties for direction said they didn't know where the trailhead was—and that they would ask someone else, though never to return. Others among them warned us in the most stringent terms against making the journey. Their responses varied, but all were decidedly ominous:

"This is definitely not good."

"They will have to call in the army to rescue you."

"You must be fond of dangerous Bedouin."

This went on for hours.

Just as we began to think that our journey had reached a dead end, our momentary salvation appeared: a down-to-earth looking monk who was a misfit in manner and seemed to be on our frequency. He was devoid of the outward show of either pomp or deep piety so prevalent among his brothers. The man approached us in light, tempered steps, and wore an inquisitive smirk.

"You look lost," he said in English.

We explained to him our harebrained plans.

"I see," he said pensively, stroking his feeble wisp of beard. "Do you have a compass? A map?"

We had a photocopy of the writer's magazine article which described the landmarks and terrain along the way, we told him.

"I see. And have you been informed of the dangers?"

If you mean the hodgepodge of demons, devils, djinn and unpredictable Bedouin,* we replied—then yes, we have.

"Then there is nothing more to say. Follow me."

With a wide grin, the monk escorted us to the trailhead at the rear of the compound and volunteered to accompany us part way along the path. As we hiked into the foothills the monk quipped that he wanted an excuse to escape the chaos of the pilgrim infestation at the monastery. When we asked him how long he'd been a monk there, he told us that he couldn't remember.

The path was a faint foot-and-a-half wide trail that snaked its way into the distance through the litter of rock surrounding it. Every so often the monk would stop to point out the trail that stretched away like a faint scar upon the horizon that was the top of the plateau.

"Do you see how much more clear the trail is further away, compared to up close?" he asked. "If you want to avoid getting lost, keep your sights on the path *in the distance*. If you only fixate

---

* Not all of the monks frowned upon the Bedouin living outside the monastery walls. One father told us many of them were friendly and helpful—and that they even prayed to Saints Paul and Anthony in times of need. "Though the Bedouin are Muslims, they recognize these men to be saints," he said. "But they prefer praying to Paul over Anthony. Paul, they tell us, responds more quickly to their prayers."

on the path directly at your feet, you will mistakenly be led into a fork and go the wrong way—and you'll become lost."

He told us this no fewer than three times.

An hour into the climb, our guide stopped and informed us that he would go no further. With hands raised and speaking in the ancient and incomprehensible Coptic tongue, he invoked the protection of the supreme deity for our ad hoc enterprise. Once done he turned heel and ran down the mountain back towards the monastery far below. We watched as he receded into the distance, his figure swallowed up by immensity of the rugged mountains we'd thrown ourselves upon.

WE CONTINUED our ascent into the late afternoon that same day, plodding against an austere and scree-cluttered landscape that littered our path like broken glass. The difficulty of the climb and the periodic scrambles up steep rock faces were indescribable given the heavy packs we were shouldering.

Trekking in the desert requires carrying ample water—a life and death consideration with no equivalent save the necessity of not getting lost. Our packs, worrisomely bursting to excess with payload, consisted of 10 litres of bottled water each. They bore into our constitutions with each strained step. What little room we had left in our bags was crammed to capacity with sleeping bags, sweaters and the bread, dates, boiled eggs, and canned tuna we brought to eat.

We reached the true plateau just before dusk, after passing many a false summit, with barely enough time to witness the transformation for which the entire desert now seemed braced. The retreat of the sun beneath the western horizon, marking the desert's changing-of-the-guard into night, was an event which had no equal in spectacle, or importance. The evening quickly descended in waves: plummeting temperatures, and the arrival of a more obstinate and mischievous wind. One could feel the entire desert shifting and changing, like a curtained theatrical stage between scenes.

We moved quickly. Selecting a small rock formation as a barrier against the wind, we cleared the area in front of it of as much sharp rock debris as we could, and laid our sleeping bags side-by-side there using our packs as headrests. In the final moments of dusk, we had our dinner and slipped into the protection of our bags, closing them firmly around us.

As darkness fell, the mind-boggling cluster of stars and galaxies forming above was complemented below by another breathtaking display of lights from the countless cargo ships parked outside the Suez Canal.

How sleep could have come so quickly to the others in view of the night's dramatic events is something I still marvel at. As exhausted as I was, there was to be little slumber during the operatic performance of the elements that evening which I viewed with terrified palpitations of the heart: billowing clouds with morphing faces; gales that grew colder with each passing hour; whispers echoing back-and-forth across the plateau. These were St. Anthony's devils come to wreak havoc upon fresh souls cast adrift on the Sea of Reproach.

Seen another way, it was the desert's response to Cairo's cacophonous symphony of street activity, which, from my standpoint at the time, had never seemed more benevolent or welcome.

Day 2

Our hike across the largely featureless plateau was a silent and monotonous drudgery.

The monk at St. Paul's was right to have taken pains to drill into us the need to remain attentive to the trail. The path was at times barely visible, at other times it vanished briefly into heart-stopping obscurity—expunged by a gully, or some other disturbance that rendered it invisible. It was at these frightening junctures in the hike where one had to rely on instinct and keep plowing ahead, maintaining directional momentum, while constantly looking out for the path on the horizon.

When the trail didn't veer wildly or meander nonsensically, it would fork annoyingly into branches of twos or threes and run parallel for kilometres at a time, before sometimes fusing back into one stream. It constituted the veritable story of its progenitors, chronicling every whim, turn, calculation, and error of their original journey. It was our only marker, and we followed it unquestioningly.

Marching together in single file, the hiker who steered the group at the head of the pack would over time relinquish his command and retire to the back of the line, allowing the person behind him to take the lead. This was our mantra as we moved step after step, mile after mile, through the day's sensory deprivation.

There was little occasion for talk. Words were an abomination, a vulgarity upon the sacrosanct stillness. We spoke only when necessary: during navigational decisions and to consult the magazine article which mentioned landmarks along the route. We spoke softly and in hushed tones stripped of their urban volume and abruptness.

But from this silence there also followed the perverse treachery for which all deserts, everywhere are renowned. The immense void, in collusion with our minds, played havoc with us during that march—sowing visual distortions and illusions across the way. The absence of scale left us at a loss about how distant—and large—landforms were, and how much progress we were making. After seeing what appeared to be a Bedouin sleeping at a cave entrance on the slope of a distant hill, our thoughts were commandeered by the ghosts of those two vanguards of Christian asceticism whose exploits seemed to us increasingly inane. Visions assailed us of Anthony tramping barefoot in animal skins—followed by a company of lions—as he waged his protracted war against Satan and his club-wielding marshals of temptation. And also of Paul, draped in palm leaves, staggering about the parched wilderness, living from handouts of bread delivered to him by crows and foxes.

Their memories pursued us relentlessly across the plateau that day, only to disappear as suddenly in a spiralling dust devil two hours from dusk.

ASCETICISM AND MONKERY are rituals as old as the religious traditions in which they manifest. The idea underscoring them all is that denial of the world and the mortification of the self—the inculcation of personal suffering and deprivation—brings one closer to the spiritual realm, and God. That nearness to the divine is considered proportional to the extremity and duration of denial suffered. The more and longer the monkishness, the better.

Other more level-headed mystics, especially the Sufis in Islam, claim that asceticism as understood by conventional religionists of various faiths, is a misinterpretation of an old exercise, now taken to absurd lengths. The version practised by religious monks, they allege, was originally meant as an activity of *limited duration* and a means to an end: to transcend worldly things *just enough*. Ascetic practices marked a temporary stage to help get functionally beyond attachments, in a much longer process of inner development, which required detachment as a prerequisite.

Ideally, the aspirant should become nimble enough to be able to use, *or forego*, things of the world at will. That flexibility helps prevent one becoming a slave to worldly things, and its seemingly opposite behaviour: self-enforced asceticism. The goal of humanity and its development, Muslim mystics allege, should not be to retreat from and deny the world *in extremis*, but instead, as one aphorism has it, "To be *in* the world, but not *of* it." Asceticism as an absolute, lifelong goal, pursued on autopilot, they add, encourages the mental conditions which the aspirant is trying to escape: self-indulgence, pride, fixation, excessive attachment to a process, and too much desire (in this case for salvation).*

It is partly for this reason that Rabia al-Adawiyya, a 9th century Sufi of Basra, when asked why she was walking with a torch in one hand and a bucket of water in another, said, "I am going to quench the fires of Hell and burn Heaven, so that both these barriers to understanding will vanish from the eyes of pilgrims, so that they may seek Truth without hope or fear."

Day 3

Disorientation.

As we neared the edge of the plateau, and the segment of the trip where we had to find our way back down, we came to the sinking realization that the path we thought we were following was really nothing of the sort. It was an imposter, a diversionary laceration that petered out in a deceptively subtle swoosh upon the horizon. Looking back across the plateau, we saw nothing that resembled the real trail.

Gone was our path, as the nameless monk had warned.

We were lost.

In a desperate attempt to reorient ourselves, we rifled through the magazine article whose observations and descriptions of the terrain we had used to chart our progress. In it we learned nothing beyond what we already knew: that we were seeking the exit off of the plateau to which our now missing path led; specifically, a *wadi* —a dry river bed or drainage system—of which there appeared to be several in our vicinity. Which of the numerous drainages was the one that safely led off the plateau was anyone's guess.

A moment of panic took hold of us.

---

* In his book, *Meditation and Modern Psychology*, Robert Ornstein writes, "In the Zen and Sufi traditions the emphasis is solely on the psychological state of non-attachment and not on prohibitions in actual practice. Both Zen and Sufism emphasize, as they do in the exercise of self-awareness, that one can do whatever one wants as long as one is not attached to it."

With our provisions running low, we had few options. We could do either of two things: attempt to relocate the path and the right *wadi* leading off the plateau but risk searching for days with limited supplies; or attempt a retreat, a three-day forced march back in the direction of St. Paul's. After much silent but strained deliberation, we bravely and unanimously opted for the first plan, and vowed not to look back.

As the day wore dangerously thin, and after spending hours feverishly zigzagging quadrants of plateau, following false *wadi*s to their disappointing cliff drops, we chanced upon the semblance of a path and ran with it. Within minutes, the trail split into yet another of its sadistic forks: the left leading in what appeared to be the direction of Sudan, and the right towards an entirely new *wadi*. With no time to waste we took the right fork and descended the steep gully.

The desolate drainage bottomed out in a run-up to a dry waterfall at the edge of the plateau and a 1,000-metre drop to the valley below. Our trail ran to the waterfall, but then veered right at 90 degrees, taking the form of a brittle, meter-wide footpath that skirted a cliff wall and empty space.

We stopped dead in our tracks. This precisely matched the description in the article. It was our path off the plateau, but was also the most exposed cliff face I would ever see—or hike.

With paralyzing reluctance, and after sacrificing much of our remaining water to ensure physical balance, we slowly, gruellingly, began stepping along the most hazardous segment of the trail. Each of us faced our vertigo demons in turn as the thud of explosions from a distant granite mine reverberated from the valley below.

Day 4

Our first glimpse of civilization was a corner of concrete that jutted out from around a hill in the distance. As more of what we saw came into view, our wounded march was transformed into a vigorous trot. It was now clear that the Sea of Reproach would not consume us, not co-opt our bones into its mythological landscape. We would again see, hear and taste the bittersweet imprecations of the city we had so hastily fled. We were now cleansed by our experiences, founded in a new appreciation of the world.

Our arrival at the entrance to St. Anthony's monastery from the rear elicited stunned perplexity from the monastery's superintendent. Shooting incredulous looks from us to the horizon and back, the *bowab* pointed in the direction of the path and spoke to us with brow-bending incredulity.

"You came from... *there*?"

Yes, we said, on the path leading from *Deir Amba Boula*.

"*Mish Maaoul!*" he proclaimed in Arabic, expressing his disbelief. "Wait here."

With that he turned, and in a shuffle of plastic flip-flops went back into the monastery. Moments later he emerged behind a robed monk whose decisive hurried steps exuded a strange importance.

Father Deoskoros, St. Anthony's *hougemenos* or head monk, a congenial but domineering figure, ushered us on a guided tour of the monastery.

"You know, you were very lucky," he said. "Just last year the army was called to search for a German tourist who had decided to try the route alone. They never found her."

It was Easter Monday. Only a trickle of worshippers from a much larger throng over the weekend remained. The patriarch was not only in a buoyant mood and but had time on his hands. He proudly showed us the shrouded remains of Abuna Yostos: a long-deceased, yet famous monk whose body was cured-in-piety behind glass. As we continued our walk, we passed the cell of another soon-to-be monastic legend who was in his seventh year of isolation. We continued on to see the impressive vegetable garden sprouting abnormally large wares (Deoskoros: "Have you ever seen such large cucumbers?"). The tour ended at the monastery's cistern for a refreshing, if slightly phosphorous-tasting, drink.

I would often think of that moment, just prior to leaving the monastery, where, had I been more inclined to abandon the world for good, I would have made the decision there and then to don the anchorite robes and make a go of the ascetic life.

Having heard that the monastery's spring water had travelled hundreds of kilometres underground to the compound from its source in Upper Egypt, I asked the good *hougemenous*, "From where exactly does the spring flow?"

Father Deoskoros sported a momentous, cherub grin.

"Why, from God."

Heliopolis (Cairo), Egypt, 1980

Kamal Bey, during a visit to Cairo, came across a tense and emotional gathering of residents at the entranceway to his sister's apartment building, where he was staying. The people were having an impromptu discussion and were at their wits' end. The imam of the mosque next door, who was also its muezzin (leading the call to prayer), was abusing his position, they complained. He was using the mosque's loudspeaker to broadcast non-religious business, creating all sorts of noise pollution for them. The single megaphone, which faced the building, roared whenever the imam *needed a plumber, an electrician or a fruit seller. The* imam *castigated the Americans, the Israelis and sometimes even his wife and children when he was upset by them. His calls to prayer, moreover, were rent with coughing, drawing phlegm, and bad vocal notes, as singing was not his strength. The mosque keeper had refused to hire a proper* muezzin *after his last colleague died. And there was nothing the neighbourhood could do to change his ways.*

"The man has connections at Al-Azhar and at the Ministry of Religious Endowments," *one resident exclaimed in desperation.*

After listening to their complaints, Kamal Bey introduced himself, and told the group he would speak to the imam *on their behalf to try and alleviate the situation.*

The next day Kamal paid a visit to the mosque.

"Peace be upon you, oh great shaikh!"

"And unto you be peace," *the* imam *responded tentatively, not knowing who Kamal was.*

"I am here representing the people of those far-away buildings across the main road there in the distance," *he said, pointing in the* opposite *direction to where the upset residents lived.* "You are renowned for your beautiful voice and sagacious language. I am honoured to make your acquaintance."

At those flattering words, the imam *went from a glum look bordering on suspicion to a face beaming with pride.*

"The honour is mine. And you are not the first to tell me that, by the way," *he said.*

Kamal continued. "The Creator has bestowed you with a voice as clean and pure as jasmine. Your singing is like the harmonies of paradise that will resound following the Day of Judgement, inshallah. There is no equal to you in this regard."

"Thank you, Effendi. Tell me, what can I do for you?"

"Your Presence: because there are so many of us living over there as compared to this one building next door that your megaphone is pointing to, we would be forever indebted to you if you could turn your loudspeaker to face us so we could hear you better."

"You mean, point the loudspeaker in the direction of those distant apartments?"

"Yes, Your Presence."

The imam *hesitated for a moment.* "But what of the good people in this building right here? I am told they are happy with my services?"

"My dear imam, as you can see, there are many more of us living over there than there are people here. There are hadiths quoting the Messenger of Allah, peace be upon him, as saying, 'If you see differences, you must follow the great majority.' I'm sure these people next door, living so close to your great wisdom, know this already—and will not object to you siding with us."

The flattered imam *smiled.* "Who am I to contradict The Messenger? It would be unjust for me to deprive the majority of their desire. Alright, I'll have the loudspeaker turned in your direction."

"May God's list of blessings for you be as long as your illustrious beard! A thousand thanks indeed! When do you think the operation may be completed? In a day or two?"

"I'll use the megaphone to call for a handyman. Inshallah, *if I call every day, someone usually turns up within two months."*

The Cairo Beard

"All true devotees wear a beard," said the Imam to all his audience. "Show me a thick and lustrous beard and I'll show you a true believer!"

"My goat has a beard far bushier and longer than yours," replied Nasrudin. "Does that mean he is a better Muslim than you?"

– Idries Shah, *The World of Nasrudin*

A hallmark behaviour of certain Westerners living in the Arab World is their desire to maintain a tight delineation between themselves and the visiting tourist—both in their own minds, and in those of their friends, family and colleagues back home. Although most foreigners in the region seldom, if ever, attain the coveted designation of 'honorary local' in the minds of their hosts, some Westerners will do all they can to assimilate and gain the insider knowledge and access which make them *seem* like they do—a crucial cornerstone on which the 'expat' status game rests. I call the mindset behind this posturing the 'Our Man in Cairo complex' epitomized by the Egyptian character Sallah, played by Welsh actor John Rhys-Davies, in the Indiana Jones movies. Sallah, whose full name is Sallah Mohammed Faisel el-Kahir, is an archeological excavator friend of Jones in Cairo. He is a baritone-voiced and British-accented global man of intrigue, an exotic figure who sports safari suits, turbans and fes hats; a fixer-type who locally knows everyone and everything, and operates with almost espionage-like implications.

Many Westerners living in Cairo that I met aspired to that unspoken archetype, even if they weren't aware of it. If you lived there long enough as a foreigner, you picked up a few words of Arabic, learned more or less how to beat the cab drivers at their own games to pay local fares, and cultivated your own in-the-know network of obscure restaurants, *qahwas* and stalls at Khan al-Khalili *souq*, where if you were likeable enough, the merchants would consider you a pal and refer to you by your first name. All these things not only sufficed to put you on a higher pecking order over the tourists to impress visitors from back home, but it was an indication that you had sufficiently 'made it' in the local milieu.

I was more vulnerable than most people to the Our Man in Cairo complex not just because I aspired to it as someone looking to shore up my Arab bona fides, but because I was born with a foot in two worlds: East and West. Playing that character came naturally because I bridged both cultures. My family network, which spread over parts of the city few foreigners visited, combined with my functional colloquial Egyptian Arabic, gave me a leg up in terms of the people, places and things I knew about and could access. Many Egyptians trusted me and took me into their confidence as an Egyptian, while also conferring upon me the graciousness and hospitality granted to the foreigner—part of the ancient Arab honour code. I enjoyed the best of both worlds. My assimilation was so fast and deep in comparison to my foreigner friends in Egypt, that I became *their* man in Cairo when they themselves needed help. I embraced the role with relish.

One of my more impressive Our Man in Cairo connections I

cultivated was access to the Giza Plateau late at night after the site had closed to the general public. A local friend knew an Egyptian stable-keeper named Mumtaz (the name meaning 'excellent' in Arabic), who managed one of several horse-riding outfits that offered trips during the day for tourists visiting the Great Pyramids. My friend tipped me off that Mumtaz was also hireable to take people out for rides at all hours of the night. For some *baksheesh* (tip money) and some apples and carrots for his horses, he would take you out for as long as you liked. All I had to do was drop my friend's name and I was in business.

"*Mumtaz!*" I said, thanking my friend for the hot tip.

For the remainder of my time in Egypt, I visited Mumtaz around once a month, usually during the dark of the moon, and with a few friends in tow, to ride his horses near the pyramids in the middle of the night—after the Giza Plateau had closed to the public. The connection was also a boon beyond its use for my global man of intrigue pretence. Every visit to the site was a magical interlude. The silence of the desert, absence of tourism, and the late-night view of the pyramids as dark silhouettes ever so slightly backlit by the megacity, made it a sublime experience.

Mumtaz himself was barely less interesting—and certainly not your usual stable-keeper. The short, middle-aged man, who lived on site and wore a dark brown *gellabiya* over flip-flops, proclaimed himself a "close friend of the Pharaohs." Like most Egyptians who worked near, or at, antiquity sites, he was smitten by the ancients to the point of nearly having Western New Age pretensions that verged on religious heterodoxy.

"The Pharaohs were the Muslims before Islam," he said matter of factly, as we had stopped to gaze in awe at the ghostly pinnacles during one visit. "The pyramids were made to elevate the minds of the people. They contain the spirit of Allah. His *baraka*. Their tops are like heaven, and below them are all the layers of creation."

Mumtaz pushed the boundaries of eccentricity in my mind when, on another occasion, he told us that one of his horses, named Khamees ('Thursday' in Arabic), the very animal I was riding that night, could speak to him. I had gotten to know Mumtaz after several outings with him, and I knew that this was more than just a put-on for the tourists and foreigners. He was completely and utterly serious.

"Khamees wants to tell me something," Mumtaz said that night, approaching my horse.

"I hope I haven't ridden him too hard," I replied, playing along.

Mumtaz, who always accompanied our rides on foot, put his ear to Khamees's mouth. He nodded a few times as if listening to the horse and stepped back to look up at me.

"He wants to know why you have let your beard grow so long."

IT WAS a question many people were asking me—either explicitly, as in the case of my perplexed Egyptian relatives, or implicitly, in the baffled looks from strangers. The Cairo beard was less an aesthetic statement and more a spontaneous stunt. Just prior to travelling to Egypt, a close friend and I, under the influence of some intoxicant or another, made a pact to grow our beards indefinitely. It wasn't just a fun experiment, but also a competition to see who could grow theirs the longest and resist the societal pressures to shave. This long predated the hipster facial hair revival and lumberjack beard of the early 2000s—a cultural development that marked the reintroduction of facial hair across much of the Western World (and the more clean-shaven parts of the East that tended to imitate it). My pal and I were both admirers of the ancient philosophers, men like Plato, Marcus Aurelius, and Epictetus. Insofar as we embraced any dogma tied to the beard, it was that a monumental tuft of facial hair was a powerful symbol both of social non-conformity, and the unencumbered life: think Diogenes the Cynic meets The Big Lebowski.

However, the Cairo beard came with lots of unintended baggage. Facial hair can be a much more loaded symbol in the Arab and Islamic worlds—even in today's more beard-friendly era that has normalized manicured whiskers in secular quarters of the East. A large beard in the Middle East is predominantly considered a hallmark of devoutly religious men, especially Muslim men. Jewish rabbis and Christian priests in the region also sometimes brandish bristles of Biblical length. But its more potent symbolism resides more within the realm of Islam. Though there is nothing explicitly stated in the Koran about the requirement to wear a beard, the Prophet Muhammed is generally believed to have had one. Some pious Muslims wear one, too, to emulate him. There is even a *hadith*, an anecdotal saying of the Prophet, collected by Imam al-Bukhari in the 9th century, in which Muhammed advises his male followers to let the beard grow while clipping the moustache. Wearing a big beard, along with having what is called a *zabiba* in Egypt, the prayer callus on the forehead,* can by today's terms sometimes be considered a kind of virtue signalling.

The hot button nature of the Middle Eastern beard lies less in that, and more in that blinkered *political* religionists also tend to favour beards—giving facial hair a bad rap. Members of revolutionary Islamist movements such as Hezbollah, Hamas, Iran's Revolutionary Guard, the Taliban, Al-Qaeda, Islamic State (or ISIS), and run-of-the-mill Wahhabi *imam*s, have often sported some manner of scruff. In Egypt, members of the opposition Muslim Brotherhood party, as well as its erstwhile militant confreres in the late 20th century *Al-Jihad* and *Gama'a al-Islamiya*,

---

* Literally meaning "raisin" because of its appearance, a *zabiba* is found on the forehead of some deeply religious Muslims. It is created in the act of prostration by pressing one's forehead to the ground during prayer. It is thus considered an ornamental symbol and proof of a person's devoutness.

did, or do so too. The religiopolitical beard is a declaration of noncompliance (yet compliance from within), and also serves as a banner of moral superiority.

But the dogmatist's beard has another practical function. Beards mean business. They represent toughness and can thus be tools of psychological warfare. They warn opponents to think twice before tussling with their wearers. They enlarge the face and amplify the eyes, which, when empty of humour or good-naturedness, as is often the case with ideologues, combines to create a mask of bone-chilling dread. The beard is such a potent and ubiquitous symbol of the political and religious firebrand, its associations with sternness and inflexibility so strong, that it is no surprise they inspire fear and paranoia from the Middle East's more moderate clean-shaven.

This is why investigations, police roundups and persecutions of bearded upstarts has been a *de rigueur* reflex in many countries, even outside the Middle East. In Tajikistan in 2016, a country with its own stream of religious fanaticism, authorities shaved off the beards of nearly 13,000 detainees who they deemed radicalized. That same year, Sweden, some of whose nationalistic citizens fear foreigners, investigated a local chapter of a brotherhood of global hipsters who called themselves 'The Bearded Villains' (a member of the public informed on them to the police, thinking their black and white flag was an emblem of ISIS). China's brutal crackdown on its Muslim Uyghur citizens began with a law banning "abnormal" beards. Beijing's re-education program of the Uyghurs includes daily shaving. All of this stands in ironic contrast to the Afghan Taliban policy of harassing and persecuting people *who don't have beards*. An act of brazen noncompliance in one nation can be an enforced orthodoxy in another.

I had more than an inkling of these dynamics, and their potential problems for me, before moving to Egypt—a country facing, at the time, a militant insurgency, involving *real* bearded villains who were shooting and bombing innocent people in an attempt to overthrow the Mubarak government and impose their vision of a utopian society. But the pressure to agree to, and uphold, my end of the frivolous 'Beard Pact', as my friend back home and I called it, won out. To help ease the dissonance I rationalized that the facial hair would simply be an accoutrement that would take my Our Man in Cairo act to an unbeatable level. It was also a method of total immersion, of quantum assimilation. I'd be going all-in, all-East—becoming local in a way that not even my parents were able to when they lived in Egypt.

The most immediate palpable consequence of this subjective social experiment was the reaction from Cairo family members. "When will you shave this beard?!" they all asked upon every visit in a half-joking, but actually dead serious, tone. Societally upstanding cousins I had never met, or known, shunned me from the get-go, refusing to be seen in public with such taboo-violating riffraff. Mediterranean-style kisses on the cheeks exchanged upon arrival and departure at gatherings were met with displays of face-scratching heebie-jeebie revulsion designed to send a message. "Okh! Remove this dirt from your face!" they would implore me, barely smiling nervously. "You look like a terrorist."

Instead of perhaps adopting a more prudent approach, I dug in my heels and made it all about them: their vehemence was a reflection of their own lack of tolerance and small-mindedness. Not to mention their Western pretensions. Did it not occur to them that one could have a beard and *not* be a terrorist? What about Marcus Aurelius? What about Kenny Rogers? What about Jesus? And what about Baba Shenouda, the Egyptian Coptic Christian patriarch, and his cloistered minions with beards every bit as pubic and bee-hivey as mine—each sculpted with the beard oil of religious piety to which my relatives claimed fealty? It was such a double standard. My family would never understand the beard, I told myself. Their disapproval was simply one of many Cairo inconveniences—like broken 19th century elevators and dust storms—that I had no choice but to put up with.

Yet, just as my family and I had reached a sort of workable

détente, things began to get stranger—and more serious—in other quarters.

One day while walking in downtown Cairo, my beard at that point having attained prophet-like dimensions, I noticed another bearded Egyptian man walking in my direction who eyed me critically and then gave me a solemn nod as he passed. I asked myself: *Did that just happen?* I quickly dismissed it as a hallucination. But it was no desert vision. In the weeks and months that followed, scores of other bearded menfolk all over the city either winked or nodded at me as if they knew me personally and I was in on some secret or conspiracy. It didn't take me long to realize they were the furtive greetings—the secret signs—of the Muslim Brotherhood, and/or their splinter-group cronies. I had penetrated their ranks without so much as filling out an application form. You couldn't fault them for assuming I was one of them. For who else in their right mind would sport such a cascading Cairo beard, when the authorities viewed such people with suspicion, and sometimes used their beards as a pretext for arrest? And if they were noticing me, their opponents on their tails at every step—Egypt's G-men—had surely caught whiff of this bearded stranger too. During this period I got more hassles than other foreigners from security checkpoints and metal detectors at hotels and other buildings. Police and security forces in the street made snickering remarks as I passed calling me, *"shaikh," "mufti,"* and the best nickname: *"Shishani"* ('Chechen', owing to my relatively pale skin and red streaks in my beard). One cab driver, who I suspected was an informant, asked me where I could get a banned copy of the book *Signposts on the Path*, by Sayid Qutb, without arousing the suspicion of authorities. Qutb, an Islamist revolutionary writer and Muslim Brother godfather, was executed by the regime in the 1960s for allegedly plotting to assassinate Egyptian president Abdel-Nasser at the time.

After that particular incident it hit me that I had taken the 'Our Man In Cairo' scheme way too far. I had gotten *too* inside for my own good. Khamees, the horse I rode at the Giza plateau, or rather, his keeper Mumtaz, astutely called me out on it with the question about the beard.

It also struck me how just changing one detail, one factor, one ingredient, in a larger picture can lead to such an unintended and radical transformation in a situation.

THE CAIRO BEARD finally met its demise as many ill-conceived projects do: on the heels of incidents in which one's follies are too plainly exposed to further deny.

The first incident occurred on the Giza Plateau during yet another late-night ride by the pyramids with Mumtaz the stable-keeper and a small group of friends. As our horses sprang into a gallop, my animal Khamees, who happened to be weak and underfed, tripped and fell forward to the ground, throwing me over him. I was badly shaken but luckily not injured. As I dusted myself off amid a minor rush of adrenaline, Mumtaz approached in his characteristic half-run of flip-flops scraping the sandy plateau. When he arrived, he completely ignored me and attended to Khamees. He then took the horse's reigns and stood still with his ear to the animal's snout, as if he were again listening to it speak. He nodded a few times and then stood up, appearing visibly upset. Mumtaz turned to me.

"Khamees fell because your beard is too long," he said, accusingly. "You are too heavy. He will not carry you anymore. I will walk him back."

"What? That's ridiculous."

Mumtaz said, "No!" and raised his finger in the air with a finality that could not be appealed. "What is this nonsense clinging to your chin? Give up this foolishness and show people your real, handsome face."

. . .

THE SECOND INCIDENT occurred a week later.

My father, back in Canada, had asked one of his Cairo friends, who had connections in the local textiles industry, to buy him several pairs of a certain brand of Egyptian cotton briefs. He had long pined for them, owing to their unequalled comfort. I was set to go home to Canada for the summer break and he wanted me to bring the underwear with me. My dad hatched a plan for me to get the briefs from his friend's daughter who also attended The American University where I was studying—and who I'd never met. The girl, according to my dad, was attractive and unmarried and suddenly the proposed rendezvous with her took on a whole different meaning. Although it wasn't deliberate (my parents were too modern to play the arranged marriage game), the meeting also smacked of a romantic set-up. Whatever the case, I naturally became intrigued. In my own mind she was interested, too. We set up a time and place to meet on campus. And so this unlikely 'cotton briefs handoff', as odd a blind and romantic encounter as could be conceived, was set in stone. I envisioned us sitting down for some hibiscus tea and playful conversation on wicker chairs beneath the towering garden palms of the verdant campus. With any luck we would meet again on my suggestion to drink ice cold Stella beers at the vintage Al-Hourreya café down the road after class one day: an in-the-know Cairo institution which would cement my Cairo bona fides.

I first saw her, as I approached from a distance, standing outside the library entrance, holding a large plastic bag containing what turned out to be my dad's two dozen briefs. Like most girls attending AUC, she was Westernized, done-up and attractive, and seemed to be anticipating me with a nervous air as she bounced on her tiptoes and swayed from foot to foot. She didn't notice me, even as I arrived by her side.

"Hi," I said, catching her unawares, and sporting a gentle smile.

She glanced at me, grinned back politely, but then looked

away and proceeded to ignore me as if I were not the person she was expecting. I introduced myself again, this time by name.

A sudden dramatic transformation in her manner ensued. It was a sort of implosion fusing astonishment and deep disappointment—the type which occurs with unexpected news of a loved-one's death. Dumbstruck and stricken with fear, her mouth fell open and the bag containing the underwear slipped from her grasp. In that disturbing moment I could tell she had seen me before: I was that strange foreign student with the unruly, monstrous beard, with whom everyone on campus was familiar and wary of: the wannabe Eastern imposter who had defiled their Westernized university campus sanctuary.

All my attempts at small talk and appearing normal, even busting out my most Western slang, failed to undo the damage. All she could see was the bearded face that hovered over our meeting like a stern and rebuking Wizard of Oz. The only coherent words that came out of her mouth, when she pulled herself together, were: "Nice to meet you. I have to go to class now."

She picked up the bag with the underwear, handed it to me, and hurriedly rushed off.

Sayeda Zeinab (Cairo), Egypt, 1997

"I'm here to pick up a package," I say to the postal clerk, handing him a yellow slip with my name on it.

The employee, a tall and lanky young man, looks at the paper before glancing at his preoccupied colleagues. He silently motions me with his hand to an office down the hall.

Once inside, we sit across from each other at an old scuffed up wooden desk from the 1950s. We're in an otherwise bland and empty green-coloured room containing numerous small parcels stacked on top of each other.

"You usually deliver packages to my door," I say to the clerk. "Why do I have to pick this one up today?"

The man does not answer, but instead reaches below his desk and pulls up a small padded brown envelope, which he flashes before me. I see from the handwriting that it is from a close friend in Canada with whom I exchange mail frequently.

Since moving to Cairo, my friend and I have played a sort of mutual game in each of our letters. We give the other a random or nonsensical nickname placed in quotes between the first and last name on the envelopes. Some recent honorifics addressed to me include "Nakamichi", "Sly Man" and "Vilcabamba". The pointless and silly joke adds an element of surprise and comedy to our correspondence.

Just as I reach to take the envelope from the clerk, he pulls it away and places it on the desk closer to him. The man makes small talk about my time in Egypt, asking what I am doing here, and whether I like Cairo. I have no idea what he is up to and I become worried that he is toying with me as a policeman or security official would before announcing some accusation. Am I in trouble because of *something* inside of the package, I wonder?

"Your Egyptian is very good. But you can speak your normal

Arabic now. Don't worry, I'll understand you," he says, followed by a grotesquely absurd wink

"What other Arabic?" I ask confounded.

"Kuwaiti, Saudi, Qatari—whichever dialect you speak." He makes that ridiculous wink again as if a midge flew into his eye.

"What?"

"Or maybe you're from Bahrain. Zada *is Iranian, or* Shia, *isn't it?"*

"I told you already—I'm from Canada."

"I understand. But where are you from originally?"

"My parents were born here!"

"No," he says, shaking his head sourly, almost insulted. "I don't think this is accurate."

"I have to go. Please give me my package."

The clerk leans back slowly and grins. *"With the will and permission of Allah. But first: how about giving me a little something, if you will, for services rendered,* Oh Emir."

That explains it: he wants baksheesh, *a bribe. I lose patience and put down a five-pound note on the table—the equivalent of a couple of Canadian dollars at the time, more than enough for handing over what was mine.*

The man looks at the money and winces painfully. "But you are an emir. This is like one millime *for you."* *

At first, I think the references to being an emir, *meaning "prince" in Arabic, is simply the usual Egyptian flattery and wordplay—like when someone calls you a "Pasha" or a "Bey," old Ottoman titles, as an honorific. But when he says it again and again, I see the clerk has the look of a man smitten with gold fever. He actually thinks I am a wealthy royal of some variety. Because of that he is holding out for a sizeable handout.*

"Listen, I'm not a prince. There must be a mistake."

"Oh, *but you* are *a prince."*

---

* A *millime* is a unit of value used in Egypt to denote a thousandth of an Egyptian pound, and is thus practically worthless in the sense of a 'penny'.

"Look at me! I'm obviously not!"

"Then what is this?" he asks in the tone of a man about to play his trump card. He shows me the parcel as if he were slamming down the winning domino. I see that the package, sent by my friend, is addressed to me with the nickname:

John "Prince of Thieves" Zada

It takes me a moment to realize what has happened. I burst out laughing at his mistake.

"Ha! I caught you! Do you think I'm stupid and can't read?" he says with a self-satisfied grin. "What do you say now, Oh Emir?"

Goma'a

Three things cannot be retrieved:
The arrow once sped from the bow
The word spoken in haste
The missed opportunity.
  – Hazrat Ali, son-in-law of Mohammed the Prophet

The first time I heard the doorbell ring at my new apartment in the Hassan Mourad Building in Garden City—not a single press of the bell, but a wild fury of frenetic rings that mimicked the masturbatory cadence of Spanish guitar strumming—I was waiting for my landlady, Madame Narouz, to come for her first instalment of the rent. It was 1998, and I was spending several more months in Egypt working after finishing my schooling at the American University.

As I swung the door open I was surprised to find a traditional Egyptian woman in a colourful headscarf and her young pre-teen daughter standing before me. At the end of a rope that the young girl held was a lamb that brayed and tried to scurry away at my appearance. A saccharine smile beamed from the hefty mother, who carried plastic bags teeming with vegetable produce.

"*Asalama aleikom, ya oustaz,*" she said raising her hand, and addressing me figuratively with the Arabic title for teacher—a term of respect.

After I returned the greeting in the traditional manner, the two stood smiling at me in awkward silence.

"Yes?" I asked.

"Can we go up, please?" the mother asked, pointing at the ceiling.

"Go up where?"

"Upstairs."

"There is no upstairs," I informed her. "This is the top floor. And this is my apartment."

"Yes, we know."

"I don't understand," I said.

"We live on the roof."

"So, what do you need from me exactly?"

"We need to go upstairs."

I took a deep breath in frustration and looked back into my flat, wondering if I had missed something.

The daughter chimed in: "We want to use the outside stairwell that's behind your kitchen. Instead of climbing all ten floors, we sometimes take the elevator here and then go up just one flight of stairs through this apartment to the roof."

"Look at how much we are carrying," the mother added.

"The people living here before you always let us come through," the daughter added, not missing a beat, as she took the skittish lamb in her arms.

"Please, if you will," the mother implored, breaking into a more confident and genuine smile, which this time anticipated success.

I wasn't so thrilled about setting a precedent by letting them in, but I also wasn't so heartless as to turn them away in the moment. I pulled open the door and stepped back.

The two beamed with happiness.

"May God lengthen your life and give you good health, *ya oustaz!*" the mother exclaimed, as she clutched her bags and stepped inside with her daughter.

I followed them as they walked straight to my kitchen and accessed the open-air stairwell through a back door there. Without looking back the two deftly ascended to the rooftop landing above and vanished from view.

When my landlady, Madame Narouz, a diminutive Coptic grandmother with a Napoleon complex arrived an hour later, I related to her what happened.

"You did *what*?!"

"But they said it was okay."

She smacked the envelope she was holding, swollen with rent money, against the table with each word spoken as if she were delivering punitive blows of the lash.

"These peasants are liars!" she exclaimed.

Although Madame Narouz knew I was of Egyptian ancestry and could speak Arabic, she made a point of mostly addressing me in English.

"Do not listen to them! And do not let them up under any circumstances! Do you hear me? These are illegal people. Squatters! No one in the building lets them up."

"How was I supposed to know?"

"They ask you because you are a foreigner and they know that you do not understand. They are laughing at you!* They do this with the other foreigner living down the hall. The rest of us in the building won't stand for it. There are several families living on the roof. We're waiting for the day when the roof crashes down on top of us because of the weight of all of these people, their animals, and the many children that they can't stop having."

---

* 'They are laughing at you' is a literal translation into English of the colloquial Egyptian Arabic phrase meaning 'They are tricking you'—in the sense that a person is being made a fool, and is being laughed at by the perpetrators.

I was a bit amused by the prospect of a rural-style village scene with all of its soap operatic dramas existing right above my apartment. I must have smiled to myself because Madame Narouz glared at me as if I had blasphemed in the worst possible way.

"You find this funny? Tell me something: do you think the French allow such things to happen in Paris?"

Madame Narouz's outrage may have seemed excessive, but the issue of informal housing in Egypt was a serious one. No one really knows how many of Cairo's 20 million-plus inhabitants live in makeshift, illegal, or unregulated dwellings, but it is thought to be a huge number: up to ten percent of residents. Egypt's continued population growth, its unceasing human migration to Cairo from the provinces, and a lack of affordable housing, makes it impossible for some people to *not* improvise when it comes to setting down roots in the city. Micro-shanties, like the one above my apartment, are found on rooftops all over the city. No inhabitable space, regardless of its lack of amenities, goes unoccupied. Scores of such squatters live in the so-called 'City of the Dead': a sprawling expanse of cemetery known for its old medieval Mameluke and Fatimid-era tombs and mausoleums.* Those who have some money buy or rent units on additional floors built illegally onto pre-existing buildings and which lack proper quality controls. They are hard to see and spot from ground level. But if you scan the rooftops from any high vantage point you will easily spot the unwieldy Jenga-like extensions. Partly because of these additions, which can pile up precariously, but also because of age and maintenance issues, residential buildings in Egypt collapse without warning with disconcerting regularity. People die in such

---

* The area, referred to in Arabic as *Al-Torab*, means both "cemetery" and "dust" (as in the dust we return to after death).

events, seemingly every year. Madame Narouz's hyperbolic and seemingly sarcastic comment about the roof falling down was an allusion to that reality.

Her harsh warnings and uncompromising attitude, which she repeated, eventually rubbed off on me. But I could inspire no such compliance in my newest Cairo roommate. Julie, an Arabic-language student and salt of the earth American from Kentucky (she claimed to be a descendant of Daniel Boone), was unable to turn the rooftop short-cutters away. Her Appalachian conviviality and desire to practice Arabic at every possible opportunity made it hard for her to play the vigilant bouncer.

To fit in with more cosmopolitan Egyptian norms, and to counterbalance what I took to be Julie's naïveté, I became a more stringent gatekeeper. I allowed only the most desperate cases to pass. Madame Narouz's last departing caution, uttered with a wag of her finger, echoed in my head: "If you give these people one *kirat* of land and they will take a whole *feddan*."

But word got around the rooftop community of Julie's leniency, and in no time an almost daily stream of pedestrians—plus their visiting friends, family and various geese, chickens and goats—started traipsing through our apartment. The issue of the interlopers became a source of tension between Julie and I when on more than one occasion I came home to find these strangers using our apartment.

In one instance I discovered the woman who first came through with her daughter, rinsing enormous bushels of *molokhia*, a leafy vegetable delicacy, using our bathroom shower.

"What are you doing here?" I asked Fattouma, with a deliberate tone of annoyance.

"The madame let me in. We're having water problems upstairs again."

"Can't you do this in the kitchen? This is the bathroom."

"No, because my sister Zohra is in there now bathing her child."

Another time I returned to the flat to discover one of the

rooftop dwellers sitting cross-legged with another woman beneath our large dining room table. They were both staring into a small Arabic coffee cup. Julie approached me at the door and made a 'shushing' motion with her finger held to her lips before I could speak. I pulled her aside and asked what was going on.

"Fortune telling," she whispered. "Nahlah says she needs to sit under a table made of strong wood for it to work. It attracts the spirits, or something."

I glanced at the roof dwellers again in disbelief.

A molasses-slow smile then formed on Julie's face: "Oh, and she read my coffee cup too. She said that there is a man 'nearby' who is a foreigner but speaks Arabic and who secretly has the hots for me and—"

"This has to stop."

"What does?"

"All these people coming here. We can't let them in anymore."

"Why are you being so uptight? I thought you were Egyptian."

"I am!"

"So, be an Egyptian. This is Egypt. This is what people do here. We're being neighbourly."

"Even neighbours here are not *this* neighbourly."

Julie groaned and rolled her eyes in frustration. "Don't take this the wrong way: but I sometimes feel you really need to get more in touch with your Arab side."

Julie and I eventually came to a compromise. Only people carrying goods that were too difficult to transport up 10 flights of stairs, or the infirm, would have access to the rooftop bypass. One person whom we never turned away, and who came through most regularly, was an elderly man named Goma'a, whose name in Arabic means 'Friday.' We didn't know much about this frail man with the white embroidered skullcap and grey *gellabiya* who walked with a laboured shuffle while holding a cane. Goma'a was the complete opposite of a lot of Egyptians who tend to be social and verbose in the extreme. He was a man of very few words, and seemed at times to be even mute. He only spoke to say "thank you" and some inaudible blessings, praising us for letting him access the back stairwell. His comings grew into a ritual to which we became habituated. Goma'a must have accessed a neighbouring apartment to reach the elevator on his way down, as he only travelled through our flat to go up. When leaving the building, I sometimes found him sitting on a chair by the main entrance leisurely watching the world go by with childlike interest and wonder—as if the Cairo street dramas were his sole love and preoccupation. Neither Julie nor I had ever seen with him with another person. Apart from his membership of the pantheon of roof dwellers, Goma'a seemed to be Egypt's most solitary soul.

Months later, I was finally leaving Egypt after years spent living there, mostly as a student. I was booked on an early morning flight out of Cairo and had to catch a cab for the airport at 4am. When I left the building, dragging my oversize suitcase through the broken pavement onto Kasr Al-Aini Street, the main thoroughfare next to where I lived, I was unable to find a taxi. I walked ten minutes up the road to the nearest large intersection and was eventually picked up by a driver working the nightshift.

When we got to speaking, the middle aged man asked me what I was doing in Egypt and where I had lived. When I answered, the man's face lit up slightly with a look of recognition.

"So you must know Goma'a!" he said.

I stared at him, baffled. How was it possible he knew that I knew the man? In a paranoid reflex, I wondered whether I had been under surveillance and the cabbie might have been an agent.

All foreigners were watched to some degree by the authorities in Egypt. But the difficulty and randomness with which I found the driver seemed to belie that.

"Yes, I know Goma'a," I replied, trying to disguise my astonishment. How do you know him?"

"I've driven him places. I live near here and work in this area."

The cabbie went silent for a moment before speaking again. "It's also hard to forget a man like that," he said.

"Goma'a?"

"Yes. He has such strength and faith in God—to keep on living after what has happened to him."

"I don't know any of it," I said.

"His life has been one long streak of misfortune, one disaster following the next."

"What happened to him?"

The driver chuckled, almost sarcastically. "What *hasn't* happened to him? First, he was taken prisoner as a soldier by the Israelis in the Sinai War in 1956 and was physically abused by them. After his military service, he returned to his home in Fayoum and got married. But soon after, his wife was killed by a *gamoosa*."

I told him that I had never before heard that domesticated water buffalos killed people.

"What were the circumstances?" I asked.

"Allah knows. But it happens a lot," he said. "Some of those animals are possessed by *djinn*. Then Goma'a was in a bus crash a few years later in which his brother died. *Then—*"

"There's more?!"

"Yes! I told you, it's one long soap opera of misfortune. Years after that, he was badly injured on his first and only trip to Mecca."

"I didn't know Goma'a is a *hag*?" I said surprised, referring to the Egyptian honorific for someone who has been to Mecca.

"He's very modest. He doesn't flaunt it, like others."

"So, what happened to him there?"

"He was caught in a stampede at the Stoning of the Devil ritual."

"Is that why he walks with a cane?"

"Yes. He lost his job as a bricklayer after that. Now the poor man has absolutely nothing. He's living on that godforsaken roof, sleeping on a dirty mattress. Even his own people—his niece took him in—treat him badly. May God have mercy on him."

I was still reeling from this truly odd coincidence, when I was struck broadside with remorse for not getting to know Goma'a better and easing his burdens in whatever way I could by offering him food, conversation, or the kindness of prolonged company. Instead, I saw him mostly as a person to endure. I thought I was doing him a favour and was being charitable by letting him through the apartment. In actuality, the gesture was the bare minimum I could have done. It struck me that I had let an important opportunity slip by. I was already feeling sentimental about leaving Cairo and this news did not make things easier emotionally.

When we arrived outside the departures terminal of the airport, the cab driver helped me remove my bag from the trunk, after which I paid him.

"By the way," the driver said, "if you want to give me some money to help Goma'a, I could go to the building and deliver it to him."

I froze. My years of dealing with street swindlers in Egypt suddenly came to the fore. In an instant, I saw the possibility that all of this was some kind of a scam: albeit an excessively elaborate and somewhat implausible one. Or maybe the cabbie just saw an opportunity to make a few extra pounds? Whatever the case, my paralysis and inability to fully trust, an automatic impulse to being a foreigner in Egypt, was laid bare as a kind of disability.

"It's up to you," he said, with complete normality bordering on something that resembled indifference. "There's no obligation."

For a moment it felt like the driver was saying and doing all of this to reveal to me my own hesitancy: as if he could read my mind. It was possibly all above board, I reasoned. But again, the skeptical side of me took hold. Would my final transaction in Egypt after years of living and assimilating here, I wondered, be just another foreigner hustle? If so, it would be a dire mockery and invalidation of my efforts to fit in and move beyond such things.

With profound reluctance I pulled out a 20 pound note from my wallet (around 7 US dollars at the time) and handed it to him. I did not give enough credence to the possibility, or even likelihood, that he was telling the truth.

I don't know if it was because he was expecting more money, or because of my hesitancy which he undoubtedly picked up on, or perhaps both, but the driver seemed disappointed—more in me than in anything else.

It felt as if I had failed some kind of a test.

Nonetheless, he nodded humbly and acceptingly. The cabbie then thanked me, and wished me a safe trip before disappearing into the last tinges of the expiring dark from which he had emerged.

Part III: Spies, Informers and Agents Provocateurs

The Curious Case of Rabia Abbas

> Now, walking around the city, I began surveying the streets more closely. They all had eyes and ears. Here a building janitor, there a guard, over there a motionless figure in a beach chair, a bit farther on someone standing idly, just looking. Many of these people were not doing anything in particular, yet taken together their multiple lines of vision created a crisscrossing coherent, panoptic observation network covering the entire space of the street, on which nothing could occur without it being noticed. Noticed and reported.
>
> – Ryszard Kapuściński, *Travels With Herodotus*

The day I concluded Rabia Abbas was a spy, my flatmates and I had just returned from that gruelling four-day trek between two Coptic monasteries in the remote Eastern Desert of Egypt. Rabia, a brash, but innocent-looking 18-year-old who always wore an imitation New York Yankees baseball cap, dropped in, as usual, unannounced. The timing of his visit, the day after we came back, struck me as suspicious.

He planted himself in the living room and boldly requested a double serving of Jim Beam taken Egyptian-style in a glass overflowing with ice. That was one of the perks of his visits he enjoyed most: access to our liquor cabinet. Once properly lubed, Rabia promptly began to ask a battery of questions in his broken English with an authority that seemed oddly excessive:

Why did you go?
What did you see?
Did you talk to other people?
Did you take photos?

And then again: "Why did you go?"—as if our first answer didn't suffice, or was being scrutinized for inconsistencies.

It's true that Rabia might have just been genuinely curious—even to excess. Like many Cairenes, he had seen little of his country outside the capital, let alone such desolate, far-flung parts. Most Egyptians don't deliberately seek out the deep desert, which is considered by many to be an empty and unattractive void. Rabia was also weeks away from beginning his mandatory military service. It was likely he'd be posted somewhere in the desert, which is one of the most dreaded environments for a fresh recruit.*

But there was also an intentional probing quality, a tension and mental strain, to his questions that went above and beyond the manners of a casual query; even one driven by the concerns he held. He spoke with a tone of suspicion.

"But *why* go—where it is nothing?" he asked us a third time. Our repeated responses that ranged from "We wanted to escape Cairo" to "Because it is there" only increased his aggravation.

---

* Poor, working class Egyptians like Rabia who have no socio-economic status or political connections are often exiled to some of the most austere and isolated outposts in the country to serve out their military duties. The deserts of Egypt, where most of the country's military zones are located, are venues known for their hostile temperatures and overbearing silence and monotony.

He turned to me, as he often did, when he became frustrated at not being understood, or not getting the answer he desired.

"Ask them," he said in Arabic, referring to my roommates David and Tom, "who wanders around such an empty place with nothing to see?"

Maybe because I knew Arabic and was now acting as translator, he spoke as if I was no longer one of the suspicious foreigners who had been on the trip. He also wanted to hear the answers *directly from them*.

"There is a peacefulness and beauty in the desert," David answered through me. "That's why we went. It's quiet there. Cairo is loud. That's it."

Rabia smirked wryly, almost skeptically, as if he were being fed malarkey. The fact that he could barely hide his dissatisfaction on a topic that shouldn't have mattered so much, sealed the spy question for me.

Our visitor downed the rest of his bourbon, shaking the ice in his glass before draining the last of the diluted dregs, hinting it needed a refill. David stood up and poured him another.

As Rabia changed the subject, asking yet more questions, this time about a trip to Luxor David and I were planning to take, my eyes narrowed and I vowed that henceforth nothing he said, or did, no matter how small, would escape my scrutiny.

IF THIS 'EVIDENCE' that the Egyptian teen was a spy strikes as less than circumstantial, keep in mind there was more to the curious case of Rabia Abbas than what the details above suggested.

My flatmate David—a fellow Canadian who we called by the Arabic name 'Daoud'—was our connection to Rabia. He first met Rabia when the latter approached him in the street and struck up a conversation. But it took not one, not two, but *three* 'accidental' encounters in the street before they became chums. The 'fatedness' of that friendship greatly stretched credulity. It also went against an important maxim in the 'see dubiousness in everything' intelligence world, articulated by British spy-author Ian Fleming in his book *Goldfinger*: "Once is happenstance. Twice is coincidence. Three times is enemy action."

I was more attuned, perhaps, to these matters than most people. I became a spy buff in my late teens and early 20s and had devoured scores of fictional thrillers and intelligence memoirs, becoming somewhat versed in the shenanigans of that odd segment of humanity that enjoyed double lives and skulking in the shadows. The modus operandi of spooks existed at the forefront of my mind. I knew, or thought I knew, theoretically, what to look for. And so I sought matching suspicious circumstances in the external environment.

Rabia became more suspect in my mind when I later noticed that other foreigners we mixed with in Cairo had similar Egyptian sidekicks who fit Rabia's description, temperament and demographic: wily and unemployed young men from poorer neighbourhoods who brimmed with street smarts and had a sort of scrappy edge.

One time, Rabia, Daoud and I were walking home from a local coffee shop when we ran into an American couple we knew from Connecticut. They were accompanied by their local hanger-on, who was a Rabia dead-ringer in appearance and attitude. Moments later, a third student from France ran into us on the sidewalk with *his* crony, another young tough. As all of us Westerners broke into conversation, there was a moment in which I noticed Rabia and the two other Egyptians edge away in opposite directions from one another in small, incremental steps. They would neither acknowledge, nor speak with one another. What seemed certain is that they were cut from the same cloth. Might they even know each other, I wondered? Or had I begun to drift into paranoia?

That these young men were an archetype was something that

my Egyptian friend Ahmed confirmed in no uncertain terms, when I brought up the subject without mentioning my suspicions.

"We call them *khirtiyya* in Arabic," he said. "That's the plural word describing Egyptian hustlers who chase after foreigners." Ahmed explained that the singular form, *khirti* was a slang play on the Arabic word for parasite which is *khirtagi*.

"Right," I said, "but you're talking about those swindlers who go after tourists, trying to trick them into buying perfume and papyrus from their cousin's store in the *souq*? Rabia isn't one of those."

"A *khirti* is anyone who sticks to you for any sort of gain. The way to know that they're not natural occurring friendships is from the fact these people approach you directly on the street—they come out of nowhere. They see you from a distance and approach. That's what happened with Daoud, right? More than once, you told me?"

"Correct."

"Then this Rabia is a *khirti*, one hundred percent. You just haven't figured out what he wants yet."

It did occur to me that Ahmed's judgements might have been stereotypes born of Egyptian class prejudices. But when I thought about it, I was actually able to envision and cluster the various sub-categories of street hustler I'd encountered in Egypt: there were the tourism *khirtiyya* I spoke about with Ahmed, which also included people selling their services as illegal makeshift guides. There were the romancer *khirtiyya*: young men who preyed on lonely, middle-aged, female tourists smitten with Egypto-mania. These *khirtiyya* manage to seduce and eventually marry these women with astonishing frequency, turning it into a lifelong occupation. They cycle back and forth between Cairo and the Western cities of their wives after their inevitable divorces to seek out other women and begin the process anew. There were also "bango" *khirtiyya*, the easygoing, droopy-eyed Bohemian Egyptians with Rasta attitudes and silent cackles who befriended expats to sell them powerful Sinai-cultivated marijuana, known locally as *bango*. Other hustlers, who I would call '*khirtiyya* without portfolio', were those who, after knowing you a short time, could suddenly ask you for money, or a gift, or an invitation to your home country that might get them a visitor's visa.

Rabia, by contrast, didn't fall into any such category and revealed no obvious agenda apart from maintaining a casual friendship that involved spontaneous visits to our apartment for conversation, and to drink tea or alcohol.

In other words: perhaps he was a genuine friend—hardly a shocking possibility.

"You know," Ahmed added with a single raised brow, interrupting my thoughts, "he *may* be an informer *khirti*."

"Go on," I said, sitting up.

"All *khirtiyya*, because they work the streets and know a lot, can offer information to the police or security services for a little *baksheesh*. But the informer *khirti* specializes in this one job. Their talent is... what is the expression in English? *Infiltration*? They go around like freelancers seeking any information, which they can turn around and sell."

I watched as he thought the matter through.

"Or..." he said, not finishing his sentence and holding it in the air.

"Or...?"

"Or," he repeated, "and I don't want to alarm you: they're specifically recruited to spy for the state."

MY FLATMATES WERE oblivious and indifferent to this prickly issue of spies, even though we all found ourselves neck-deep in a police state that likely regarded us as suspect. The average citizen in the West doesn't think as much about political informers on a daily basis as in other parts of the world. Authoritarian regimes, which use such agents to intimidate and keep their populations in line are not yet a hallmark of the West. Nor is there yet any official ideology, or dogma, which requires a secret police body to enforce and uphold. Instead, Western domestic security and intelligence services focus primarily on thwarting malign foreign agents, hostile espionage and intelligence operations, transnational crime, and internal political agitators with violent intent. Government agents remain otherwise mostly out of sight, and therefore out of mind, for the regular Western citizen. Moreover, media scrutiny and various democratic and legal checks and balances on the power of the state force domestic Western intelligence people to be more constrained and discreet than their professional counterparts serving the autocrats. A growing reliance on technological collection methods also means fewer spooks are pounding the pavement. As a result most Westerners go their entire lives without real-life spies *explicitly* coming into their awareness, beyond perhaps a government official materializing suddenly to ask questions around a friend or relative's security clearance for a job.

It is a different story in the East, where intelligence services, often run by the trusted cronies of a strongman or dictator, also serve to keep a leader in power and quash public dissent or opposition. Often thug-like, they tend to throw their weight around more willy-nilly in public and make themselves felt more widely, and for infinitely smaller infractions (like making a derogatory comment about a leader). The Arabic word *mukhabarat* is the generic term for an intelligence service.* The word is also used more informally to refer to an entire national security apparatus, in aggregate, where more than one spy agency exists in a cluster in a country, and which sometimes includes the investigation divisions of the police services. It can *also* mean the enforcement arm

---

* The word *mukhabarat* shares the same consonantal roots with the Arabic words *akhbaar*, a noun meaning 'wide-ranging news', and *khabar*, also a noun for a single piece of news (as well as a verb meaning 'to report').

of the paternal authority figure—his innermost 'Praetorian Guard' as it were. As such *mukhabarat* is a profoundly loaded word brimming with unspeakable—and unspoken—terrors referring to the unyielding brutality that answers to no one, sometimes not even to the top leaders themselves.* In some countries you don't want to hear that word outside of a hushed conversation about politics, as it means you, or someone you know, is likely in trouble. The manifold security and intelligence services in the deeply tribal Iraq of its former leader, Saddam Hussein, for instance, whose minority Sunni faction held on to power only through maximum coercion and control, were famous for their sadistic forms of brutality. Comprising upwards of a dozen official and unofficial services before the regime fell, some of whose jobs included watching and countering *one another*, the Iraqi *mukhabarat* made themselves felt at the societal level as both an implicit and explicit threat. They were an omnipresent brandished stick. The same held true in Syria, where the erstwhile Assad regime, another minority tribe, interpenetrated the entire population with watchers, informers and random toughs. They exercised the same proactive and punitive brutality through their own *mukhabarat* made up of many composite parts.

What also sets the various Middle Eastern *mukhabarat* apart from their domestic Western counterparts is that they rely upon, and also employ, a huge body of informers within the local population who are constantly on the lookout for any malfeasance. The internally focussed American FBI, British MI5, or Canadian CSIS, for instance, will mostly employ specialized professional "watchers" or "surveillants," minor intelligence staff working at street level. They do recruit citizens to be informers—but those

---

* Cambridge University sociologist Hazem Kandil writes in his book, *Soldiers, Spies, and Statesmen: Egypt's Road to Revolt*, "The armed forces and security establishment are full partners in any country's ruling bloc. They work *with* rather than *for* the political apparatus—no matter what the constitution says. And while the interests of these three partners usually coincide (projecting an image of unity), they are never identical."

are usually with regards to specified targets, beats and operations. The strength of Egypt's domestic spy network, for instance, is that it can leverage, theoretically, legions of people from the whole of its dense population crammed cheek by jowl into the narrow strip of the Nile Valley. There is no anonymity in Egyptian cities, whose neighbourhoods function like villages: everyone knows everything going on and very little goes unnoticed.

The late foreign correspondent and author Ryszard Kapuściński, no stranger to secret police in his own communist Poland, saw all of this during a trip to Egypt in the 1960s. He not only astutely pointed out the utility of an omnipresent mass of watchers, but also the susceptibility of people, especially the unemployed, underemployed, and inactive, to render their services in support of a national omniscience operation.

"All dictatorships take advantage of this idle magma," he writes in his book *Travels with Herodotus*. "They don't even need to maintain an expensive army of full-time policemen. It suffices to reach out to these people searching for some significance in life. Give them the sense that they can be of use, that someone is counting on them for something, that they have been noticed, that they have a purpose."

Kamal Bey, who worked in an obscure security capacity in Canada and thus knew the professional ropes, so to speak, was also familiar with the Egyptian surveillance state from his life as a citizen in Cairo. He couldn't have agreed more with Kapuściński.

"Get used to the idea," he said to me matter-of-factly before I moved to Egypt, as if it were a coming-of-age talk between a parent and child, "that the government there will know everything about you: where you are going, who you are meeting, and even what you are saying. They'll get their information through everyone around you: your building's doorman, your maid, or your grocer."

"You're making it sound like I have to watch what I say or do," I said with a flicker of worry.

"No, no, no," he said, waving his hand dismissively. "Take my advice: don't let any of this bother you. Learn to put it out of your mind. It's *normal.* This is how life is there. We all had to endure it. Let them do their work, and go about your own business in peace."

KAMAL BEY'S QUIPS, combined with what I gleaned from books and films, made me aware, perhaps even a bit paranoid, of the shadow people upon my arrival in Cairo. And while there, things indeed came to pass as Kamal predicted. The landline phone in our flat was almost certainly, although quite primitively, bugged. The line was plagued by incessant clicking sounds and the occasional heavy breathing of an uninvited guest. When we threw parties at our apartment, crowded affairs of booze-infused revelry, we found suspicious solo Egyptians—complete strangers —standing alone against the wall watching the proceedings. Their *khirti*-like appearance, cut from a demographic that was clearly *not* the well-heeled and westernized Egyptian of the American University set, gave them away. Letters we received from abroad were steamed-open and Scotch-taped closed with bothersome frequency. In one instance a postcard a friend sent me from Canada was spliced open at the side, pulled apart at one corner, as if to see whether anything had been concealed *inside* of it. I wasn't sure what was more troubling: the fact that the card had been peeled open at all, or whether they had allowed it to be delivered to me left like that—in all likelihood a kind of message.

The fact that Egypt, like a lot of Arab countries, had a history of grappling with meddling foreign powers, including the Israelis, meant that all of us in the apartment, though welcome and treated with respect by most of society in general, were under suspicion of being foreign agents. The *mukhabarat* complex in the Middle East is so ubiquitous, so engrained in the culture and psyche of its people, that even as a foreigner, your Arab friends or family will sometimes half-jokingly quip to your face that you might be a spy.*

Kamal Bey was right: it was a state of affairs that simply had to be accepted. Yet I found it hard to take his advice to just 'let it be.' In fact, the contrary occurred: I became more and more paranoid with time.

WHEN RABIA CONTINUED to visit us in Cairo while on leave from his military posting, and usually in his army uniform, which he was required to wear while off-duty, I became particularly alarmed. Surely the Egyptian military didn't like their members, even the lowliest recruits, fraternizing with foreigners.† Perhaps this meant he had the official blessing to do so. Could he have been trying to entrap us by luring us with bits of information? On his first visit he told us he was posted near the militarily sensitive Suez Canal Zone, in Sinai, but said nothing more. This, I concluded, was just the beginning of what would turn out to be a wider entrapment operation. I told my roommates not to pry too deeply into what Rabia did, so as to not inadvertently trip any wires.

For months he continued to visit, sometimes alone, other times with Mustafa, another baby-faced recruit who liked to wear a military beret. Without us asking, Rabia began to volunteer stories, many of them strange and unexpected, about random aspects of his military service.

"While we're on duty we lose interest in women—and in sex,"

---

* An example, par excellence, of psychological projection on a collective level.
† When he was a young man and a reservist in the Egyptian Army, Kamal Bey was ordered to divorce his wife, a Brit, because a new law had just been passed forbidding soldiers and diplomats from having foreign spouses. He refused and resigned from the military, abandoning his much-loved early career.

he complained, placing his glass of whiskey on the coffee table loudly in protest. "We feel no desire."

"By God, it's true," Mustafa concurred. "The officers are putting a chemical in the lentil soup. This poison is stealing our manhood."

"How do you know?" I asked. "It could be that you're just feeling bored or depressed, because there's nothing to do in the desert."

"No," Rabia said vehemently. "We all feel it. It's a chemical. Once we're home it wears off and we have desire again!"

Mustafa laughed: "Maybe the army is scared us soldiers will have sex with each other and be too in-love to fight."

The information shared on Rabia's subsequent visits was the same marginalia: strange tidbits that included details of sightings by fellow soldiers of evil spirits—*djinn* and *afreet*—and the souls of the dead in the vast desert wastes. One long exposé by Rabia detailed how he had learned to fall asleep standing up, while on guard, which allowed him to pass the time more quickly.

The fact that none of the information was state secret quality, not even remotely close, caused my roommates to relax. But it didn't matter to me. To my mind Rabia was still monitoring us while at the same time dangling the prospect of information in his own mocking way.

One night, as we sat in the fading evening light of our Nile-view balcony overlooking Roda Island, with the river bats flying erratic pirouettes over our heads, I told Daoud that I'd had enough. Rabia was definitely a spy, and he had to stop coming to our apartment.

"Even if you're right, I don't really care that much," he responded, somewhat defiantly.

"How could it not matter to you?" I shot back.

"Because I know that he also regards us as real friends—even if he is also doing a job. And I also like him."

"But, that constant smirk and look in his eyes suggests he has an agenda," I said, in a failed effort to drive home Rabia's duplicity.

"Rabia is just a regular guy who likes having foreigner friends. He likes drinking our whisky and getting a glimpse of a world not afforded to most of his friends and family. And if it's more than that, then so be it. We're not doing anything wrong. I'd rather have Rabia reporting on us than someone we don't know well, or can't see."

I remained silent.

"If anyone's acting like a spy, it's you," Daoud said. "You're like a counter-spy obsessed with Rabia."

It was true. I had become fixated to the point of actually morphing into that which I opposed. The irony, I realized, didn't end there. Daoud was thinking more like a Middle Easterner, more laissez-faire, more naturally accepting of the ambiguity and uncertainty of the situation. He followed to perfection Kamal Bey's advice to just go with the flow—something which I wasn't able to do. Deep down he didn't care. Meanwhile, I had to know, define, and control the situation. I couldn't just let it be.

I realized later, too, that maybe I was just revelling in the intrigue, which was new and stimulating. The perceived (or real) cloak-and-dagger threat was exciting. It also made me feel somehow important.

WE NEVER DETERMINED, or found out for certain, whether Rabia was an informer. Certain mysteries remain forever concealed. Yet an exchange occurred that has since tilted the verdict slightly more in one direction over the other.

"Daoud, do you have something to eat?" Rabia asked during one of his later visits, and after having a whiskey poured for him.

"*Soudani?*" Daoud replied, offering him peanuts, in flawless Arabic—one of ten well-worn words in his repertoire.

"Okay," Rabia said, with a sweep of his hand, indicating anything would do.

Daoud went into the kitchen.

Following a long moment of uncomfortable silence, I asked Rabia how his military service was going. After telling me he had been reassigned to another location, he said out of the blue: "I recently learned that the head of Egyptian intelligence is a man named Amin Nummur.* Some officers at the base were talking about him over coffee."

It was the first time he had ever spoken about anything spy-related. By the time what he said had sunk in, I knew that I had taken too long to respond.

"I wouldn't know," I remarked.

Rabia studied my reaction for a moment more then took a long sip of his Chevas Regal before holding it aloft and looking into his glass.

"What is this? It's not what I usually drink when I'm here. Do you have any of the whiskey you used to give me before? I like it much better."

---

* I learned later, well into the internet age, that the said gentleman was in fact a former Egyptian spy chief, but who had served a decade before Rabia's mention of him.

Downtown Cairo, Egypt, 1995

Tahrir Square, the great commuter crossroads of Cairo. Here the 'Mother of the World' wheels on its axis to the sound of car horns and peddlers' calls. It is my first trip to Egypt. A young Egyptian man intercepts me as I cross the square and tries out greetings in different languages. He claims to be my friend. When I speak Arabic with him, he doesn't believe I am Arab, and says that I am Israeli. After the fourth time telling him I'm not interested in buying his perfume, or papyrus, or in hiring his services as a tourist guide, he drops his act, soberly disengages, and ducks away as quickly as he appeared.

Each time I walk through the square on that trip it is the same scene repeated, over and over: me running a veritable gauntlet of exuberant, street-smart Egyptian men who fling themselves at me from every hidden niche, brandishing well-worn, rapid-fire introductions and promises of products and services on the cheap.

But when I move to Cairo as a student later that year, I notice that the touts no longer approach me—not just in Tahrir, but all over the city. It's as if in the intervening period the hawkers had been driven away. Yet they are all still there. I see them as plain as day, haranguing others or lying in wait, ever watchful, scanning, calculating.

Yet none approach me.

I am burning with curiosity about this: why do they now leave me alone? When I finally meet a hustler sitting with two older British tourists at a coffee shop near the square, I tell him all of this and ask him point-blank in Arabic why he and his colleagues have stopped approaching me.

"Because," he says smiling, "we know the difference between tourists and the foreigners living here. We prefer the tourists who are more gullible."

"You can tell the difference by the clothing?"

"Not just the clothing. It's also the behaviour. The tourists walk slowly because they don't know where they're going. They look up, they look to the side, they turn behind them. They stop. They point. Their hands are close to their pockets guarding their money. Things are new to them. They are unsure. They are afraid. When people are afraid, it shows in their body."

"And the foreigners living here?" I ask.

"Like this," he says whistling and cutting his finger horizontally through the air in a quick straight line. "From here to here—direct. They are not afraid. We don't waste our time with these people."

"So you just stand around all day watching every person before deciding who to approach?"

He laughs. "Brother, we don't even have to watch. We can be minding our own business, doing something, talking to someone even. We just sense it—like suddenly something is wrong in the flow on the street. Tourists catch our attention."

"I see," I say.

"Here in Egypt we feel," he continued, resting his palm over his heart. "You foreigners, you live inside of your heads."

The British couple sitting next to him watch us amusedly, unaware that he is speaking mockingly. He smiles at them, and turns back to me and points again to his head.

"Like birds living inside of a cage."

The Patchwork Cloak of Kamal Bey

Kamal Bey, whom the Fates decreed should become a spy of sorts was inadvertently 'spotted' by the wife of a Royal Canadian Mounted Police (RCMP) Security Service officer in Brampton, Ontario, Canada in 1971. The woman was a repeat customer at the Italian suit store that Kamal Bey managed after emigrating to Canada. She went there on occasion to buy clothes for her husband. Kamal, being the inveterate Middle Eastern gentleman and charming character of cosmopolitan proportions, made her feel welcome in his shop. As she perused the shirts, ties and socks, Kamal regaled her with colourful anecdotes about the East, transporting her from her parochial suburban existence at the far-flung edges of greater Toronto to such places as the cat-infested and incense-anointed byways of the Khan al-Khalili *souq* in Cairo and the tribal marshlands of southern Iraq: venues she had barely heard of. Kamal fascinated her. Of course, her husband Jim, being a "Mountie," an RCMP intelligence officer, and a guarded spouse, heard about all of this and decided to see who this Kamal Bey character was for himself.

When Jim dropped into the shop, he found Kamal Bey sitting behind the counter reading a book called *The Problem of the*

Southern Sudan. He introduced himself as the husband of Kamal's female admirer, shaking his hand with a tight policeman's grip. Jim made no mention of his employer.

"What are you reading?" he asked, looking at the book Kamal had just put down.

"It is a history of Sudan. The chapter I'm reading now is about the Mehdi uprising and the assassination of the British Major-General Gordon Pasha," Kamal added, hoping to spark a conversation on the subject.

"Sudan," the man said, wonderingly. That's a country in Asia, right?"

After some slightly prying questions about Kamal Bey's past, in which he not only discovered that Kamal was a lawyer by education specializing in Islamic *sharia* law, but was also multilingual, a former reserve officer in the Egyptian Army, and was later head of Egypt's tobacco authority, travelling around the world to negotiate deals, Jim made his pitch.

"I don't understand," he said, "how a smart guy like you is working at a job like this. Have you ever considered a career with the Canadian government?"

"No, but if the work doesn't involve selling suits, I'd be happy to let you talk me into it."

Jim returned days later with a stack of forms for Kamal to fill out. Kamal didn't know what job he was applying for and asked his new friend what the position was. Lying, Jim told him the job was undetermined and might be in any department of the federal government.* In the enduring archaic tradition of British Commonwealth secrecy, Kamal was not even allowed to know that he was being vetted for a civilian domestic intelligence role within the RCMP. He submitted to a battery of cloak-and-dagger style interviews and tests, often held in nondescript Holiday Inn

---

* Jim had told Kamal that he himself worked as an administrator in the Ministry of the Solicitor General, the branch responsible for public security and law enforcement—a half-truth and obfuscation.

hotel rooms in and around Toronto. Interminable background checks, reaching all the way to Egypt, scrutinized every detail of his past. The whole time Kamal believed—as was his deep want—that he was being considered for a position in the Canadian diplomatic service. He had always considered diplomacy to be the most useful, refined and prestigious craft among all government work. He assumed his travels, language skills, and international business experience made him a shoo-in for a diplomatic role.

But Kamal Bey's G-man candidacy hit a fatal snag a year and a half into the process. The twin Canadian cultural pillars of risk aversion and a fanatical adherence to regulation compelled the very martial Mounties to reject his application. The news came by way of a terse and rude letter of a few paragraphs, surreal in its sternness, sent in an official Government of Canada grey envelope. Kamal Bey's application, they regretted to inform him, had been rejected. The reason cited, almost cryptically, was the debts Kamal had accrued since coming to Canada. Two of his businesses he had started after emigrating had gone belly-up—Kamal owed creditors money which he was in the process of paying back.* The letter, which Kamal read after returning home from a long day at the suit store, ended by warning him harshly, as if he were some criminal, not to re-apply for the job which, ironically, he had been recruited for, and which had no title or description. Who were these phlegmatic, uptight Canadians, he thought to himself, tossing the letter into the trash bin?

Yet unbeknownst to Kamal Bey, a fatalistic die had already been cast in the summer of 1972. That year, a Palestinian militant group, Black September, killed and kidnapped members of the Israeli Olympic team at the Munich Summer Games. Canada was set to host the next summer Olympics in Montreal in 1976, and officials in Ottawa would need to prevent a repeat of what

---

* It was later learned that the debts, which weren't monumental, made Kamal Bey, in the mind of his potential employers, susceptible to bribery by a hostile intelligence service.

happened in Munich. So, when a third Canadian cultural tendency, its government's short-sightedness, saw the RCMP severely understaffed and backlogged in its security checks for the upcoming Montreal Olympics, the Mounties changed their minds about Kamal. They needed Arabic speakers badly and they practically begged Kamal Bey to reconsider the nondescript government job he had applied for.

"Forget about the debt," they told him over the phone, calling him in a panic. "That's neither here nor there. Can you start on Monday?"

Kamal quit his job and the next week he was sworn in to the force—not as a roving international diplomat as he had very much hoped, but as a civilian member in the intelligence arm of a hierarchical and militaristic federal police force swearing allegiance to the Queen. Though appreciative of the new opportunity, he also found himself somewhat crestfallen.

Kamal Bey liked to tell this story, which he shared with me in adulthood on numerous occasions. But during his last telling of it, like a good storyteller, he tacked on an epilogue that I had not heard before.

"I have always regarded life as my greatest teacher, and this episode contained a big lesson about disappointment," he said. "My despondency at not becoming a diplomat helped prevent other painful disappointments in the future."

"How so?" I asked.

"I learned to harbour few, if any, expectations."

I KNEW and became close with Kamal Bey because he and my father were friends in Egypt—both emigrated to Canada at around the same time in the late 1960s. I owed much of my fascination with the Middle East, as well as my desire to travel and live there, to Kamal. He was a larger than life figure who straddled civilizations and could combine, or shift between cultural modes in an instant, as if executing eloquent dance moves. It was his storytelling ability in particular, a very Eastern quality, that captured me.

Kamal Bey was a force-of-nature raconteur who hypnotized listeners with his manifold yarns of intrigue. Donned in his patchwork cloak of stories, he delivered ever new matrices of tales that left you reeling from vivid imagination overload: the story of Kamal escaping an unwanted encounter with Ethiopian Emperor Haile Selassie's pet lion; his adventures translating the user manuals of French battle tanks for Egyptian Army mechanics while under fire in the 1956 Suez War; apocryphal tales about the extramarital affairs of Egypt's last monarch, the corrupt hedonist King Farouk.

The anecdotes of his interlocutors, culled from the staid and deflated chronicles of domestic life in Canada, were unable to compete in the storytelling colosseum. I recall the occasional male guest at gatherings—usually would-be blabbermouths—sailing in frustration out of the room with their drink and cigarette in hand as Kamal's next ribald comment threw the mesmerized congregation into uncontrollable fits of tear-streaking laughter.

But such displays of resentment were rare. The vast majority of people who met Kamal Bey fell under his spell. His character was underscored and bolstered by many of the noble qualities that the Arabs of yesteryear seemed to more frequently strive for and hold in the highest esteem: honour, humility, generosity and an uncompromising respect for truth. All of this imbued his storytelling with a strange, almost magical repertoire of subtle expressions and gestures, giving it a magnetic, almost hypnotic charge—as well as a flavour that smacked of something aristocratic, respectably imperial even. The fact that Kamal Bey came from a family of notables (including a 19th century Ottoman governor of northern Syria) showed itself in his manner. Yet he was quite humble and devoid of any social pretensions.

Kamal and I naturally took to each other. I was fascinated by his tales, and he, not having a son, grew to regard and treat me as a sort of surrogate heir. In adulthood, I began to visit him on my own, which kicked off a deeper and longstanding friendship that grew independent of my family's relationship with him—and which was predicated on the transference of not just his stories, but also his knowledge and something I'd describe as wisdom.

"There is an important Arabic expression," Kamal said to me one day, in the course of a discussion about the follies and failings of Middle Eastern despots. "*Sayyidu al-qoumi khadimuhum.*"

He said it with that penetrating and utterly serious gaze that on the surface resembled anger, but in actuality communicated gravitas.

"What does it mean?" I asked, not understanding the classical Arabic.

" 'The master of the people is the one who serves them.' "

My relationship with Kamal entered a new phase, and my fascination with him compounded, when I confirmed his intelligence connections at the impressionable and credulous age of 21. My family always knew he had some vague security role with the RCMP, which he sometimes mentioned obliquely in passing. What he did say made it sound administrative and boring, and so I'd never thought to question him about it prior to that.

He and his wife were visiting us for lunch one day and he was wearing a small pin on the lapel of one of his trademark checkered blazers. When I looked closer at it, I recognized it as the emblem of the Canadian Security Intelligence Service (CSIS), Canada's civilian domestic intelligence agency, which had been created to take over that role from the law-enforcing RCMP several years earlier. I had seen the obscure insignia before as an undergrad studying politics, and as a keen reader of books about the intelligence world. The internet had not yet come into being, and so the logo was not known among the general public.

"I couldn't help but notice your pin," I said, unable to conceal a smirk.

Kamal was caught off guard, but pretended not to be.

"Ah, yes," he said, looking down at his lapel—perhaps realizing that he should have removed the pin for the visit.

"New employer?" I asked, proud to have sniffed him out.

Kamal raised his chin and eyebrows simultaneously, in exclamation: a very Arab gesture indicating the word "no".

"Different organization. *Same* bosses," he answered with almost slight distaste, referencing the old RCMP leadership.

Kamal Bey's easy-going admission, a cryptic confidence, and a complaint about the stultified and police-minded men now running the new civilian spy agency, was a reflection of our relationship: we trusted each other and had grown more like-minded and closer. The two of us were also a similar mélange of East and West in our interests and attitudes; each the mirror image of the other. He recognized my desire to straddle and reconcile both worlds in the same way he did, and decided to encourage me. Henceforth he became a mentor figure who would impart his manifold stories, anecdotes and perspectives.

IN THE YEARS TO come we met regularly, though infrequently, at his triplex in the leafy and spacious Junction neighbourhood at the edge of downtown Toronto. The living room where we convened was filled with Middle Eastern bric-a-brac: from hand-etched brass antiques to Damascene mosaic inlaid boxes, as well as shelves-upon-shelves of books that seemingly contained every political memoir and Middle East work ever published. Kamal Bey's intelligence link was, of course, thrilling for me at that unripened age when I had not yet come to learn about the banal administrative and bureaucratic aspects of that line of work—as well as some of its ethical conundrums. Yet the quality that magnetized me the most, and drew me to Kamal more over time, was his uncommon perspectives born of an exceptional mental agility. Kamal was a man who recoiled from any form of extremism and was himself almost entirely without dogma. Unlike my wider family, who, like most people, harboured layers of prejudice, bias and emotion, Kamal had a built-in mental 'devil's advocate' on every issue that also made him calmer and more objective. He was the first person to articulate to me a flexible, global and multifaceted approach to seeing the world.

"Rather than looking at anything from one narrow angle, you should look on it, like an eagle soaring above it and around it, seeing it from as many of the different perspectives as possible," he said with his hand held aloft, mimicking a bird. "This is real objectivity." *

At that moment, Lilly, Kamal Bey's wife, appeared holding a platter with lemon cake and green tea. "I can tell you *all sorts* of stories about Kamal's objectivity," she said, rolling her eyes in comedic jest. Lilly was both a sharp and ironic commentator on Kamal Bey's monologues, adding details and correcting information, and also a foil to her husband's sometimes intense seriousness.

Kamal's study of Koranic law and the holy book as a student in Egypt, parts of which he knew by heart, predisposed him to the spirit of Islam, which he insisted most westerners had no real knowledge of and which they criticized in ignorance.† Islam, he reminded me often, was not an exclusive new religion at the time

---

* Kamal Bey always told me: "Think for yourself, look for both corroborating and opposing evidence, and don't take opinions at face value."

† "Most people don't know that alcohol consumption, in and of itself, is not forbidden in Islam," Kamal Bey said, trying to clear up misconceptions he learned during his legal studies at Cairo University. "Only drunkenness is frowned upon. Also misunderstood and taken out of context is the provision allowing for the marrying of four wives: it was for a time of war when men were in extremely short supply. And as a man, you could only do so *if you treated each wife equally, in every respect.* Tell me, how many men, having multiple wives wouldn't show favourites?"

of its birth, but was simply the last in a chain of major world faiths that built upon Christian and Judaic tenets known widely at the time. This was why Kamal Bey not only had no problem studying Islamic law in school, but also considered himself, at a certain philosophical level, something of a *de facto* Muslim.

Though he never spoke explicitly about his job, I came to see that it was impossible not to get a sense of what Kamal Bey knew, as his work suffused his ideas and very being. As far back as the late 1980s he was already talking about the coming ascendancy of China. Beijing, he said back then, planning many decades ahead, was making quiet inroads into certain parts of Africa and Latin America. He predicted the rise of Al-Qaeda and the resurgence of the Muslim Brotherhood in Egypt and knew every major religious militant in the Middle East down to the length and colour of his beard. Because he was allergic to extremism of all kinds, and believed that most people were like "sheep being led to the slaughter" by their authority figures, he took a particular dislike to religious demagogues, which I assumed were a focus of his work.

"These people are the furthest thing from Muslims," he told me, speaking about Osama Bin Laden and Al-Qaeda after the 9/11 attacks.

"So, how would you describe them, then?" I asked.

"They are a religious aberration, a sect, based on a warped literal understanding of their faith. Those pulled in are people looking for a purpose. People who are afraid of the ambiguities of life, and who need strict rules, structure, and certainty. And to be part of a clique in which they are virtuous and saved—while everyone else is wrong and damned. It is the sanctuary of literal minds. A spiritual no-man's-land. That's why they hate humorists, and can't laugh at themselves."

"As in disliking jokes?"

"Yes. Have you ever seen, or can you see, a religious firebrand, an Ayatollah Khomeini or an Osama Bin Laden, laugh heartily or take kindly to jests and wisecracks? Laughter and humour are keys to the soul."

Anyone who's ever had a mentor, or a role model, must one day meet the flawed and vulnerable persona beneath the idealized veneer. Fortunately, in the case of Kamal Bey, there was no earth-shattering skeleton in the closet, no dualistic Jungian shadow to his benevolent psyche that came flashing out menacingly in unexpected moments. Had that been the case it perhaps might have been more interesting; a grandiose character seems deserving of remarkable and grandiose defects. Yet I was confronted by the opposite at times: a deflated version of Kamal Bey, marked by silence, frustration, and even slight depression—a complete antithesis to the force-of-nature I knew. It was as if, at times, he had been rendered simply ordinary.

I had gone to visit him one day and knew something was amiss when I found myself speaking more than he did. He sat on the couch beside me drably, passively, while trying to show interest and nodding between moments when his eyes glossed over—indicating he was somewhere else. There weren't any of the usual interjections that segued into impossibly long yarns; no guileful, semi-cryptic insights about the nature of the world born of his life experience, or some epic tale that defied belief.

"What's bothering you?" I finally asked him.

He held my gaze for a while without revealing any expression, before turning to face the window. "You know, there are days I wish I had never come here."

"Where? To Canada?"

"Yes. To the West."

With frustration, he added that he was ill-suited to aspects of Canada: the cold weather, the wide empty spaces, the bureaucracy and small-mindedness of government work, the overly-polite, cool, and docile nature of the people he often met and had to deal with. I was reminded of certain criticisms he made of Canada in passing when I was younger. I realized that he was caught more between East and West than I knew; and in a way I didn't think possible. Without saying so I could see that he yearned in that moment for the more palatable aspects of Arab life and culture (which also constituted the firmament of his being), but which he had repudiated, and ultimately fled, because of the region's problems. I later realized that his storytelling impulse was partly a nostalgic incantation or benediction, an effort to keep alive some interesting and exciting version of the East that could drive away his periodic demons that came with the feeling of being exiled in the West. The stories helped him escape being caught at the loggerheads of both worlds.

When later I started living in the Middle East, lured by its cavalcade of colours and sound and the desire to reclaim a flagging sense of Eastern self, I too became paradoxically caught, much like Kamal. In cycles that seemed never-ending, I repeatedly found myself wanting, or being drawn again to, the once-staid, boring and cerebral West that I had previously fled. It beckoned me back at times, offering its poultice of calm to soothe the fatigue inflicted by an overwhelming and excessively emotional East that in small ways seemed to reject my assimilation efforts.

But in that moment in which he revealed his ennui, I had another more selfish thought. Having just complained about his work culture and colleagues, I saw a chance to ask him about his intelligence work to find out what he did exactly. Perhaps, in his mood of discontent he would open up and uncaringly tell me all, sating my curiosity?

When I asked him as nonchalantly as possible, and in the most clever segue I could devise, he was taken aback and assumed an uncomfortable posture on the couch. He looked away, clearly at a loss for words in the moment, while at the same time overcome with an emotion that resembled sadness—or perhaps even disappointment. I wasn't sure if his reaction was related to his mood that day, but I instantly regretted asking him. He took a deep breath.

"I don't need to tell you: I regard you as family. You are like my own son. I know that anything I reveal in confidence you would keep secret. But I cannot discuss this with anyone—not because of any blind loyalty to organization, rules, or even to country. It's because I promised I wouldn't. And where we come from, in our culture, *promises are kept—no matter how small or casual.*"

I nodded, embarrassed for being caught out. And although I felt ashamed, Kamal Bey, in classic fashion, mitigated that feeling by turning the moment into a seemingly unrelated, but crucially important object-lesson.

"Upright men," he said with deep emphasis and gravitas, "honour their obligations."

I ONLY SAW Kamal Bey more discombobulated on one other occasion, and for different reasons. It was about a year before his death from deteriorating health. I had just arrived at his home for a visit and found him gazing incredulously at the television watching CNN. He was 89 years of age and frail, but still clear-minded and full of vigour. The broadcast was about yet another acrimonious and violent collision between radicalized partisans of the left and right in the United States during Donald Trump's first term.

Kamal Bey threw both his palms atop his head in an Arabic gesture signalling calamity raining down from the heavens.

"*Yikhrib beitkom!*" he shouted in Arabic. *May God destroy your homes!* It was also a non-literal saying meant to convey extreme astonishment.

I was habituated to the growing turmoil in US politics, and I asked him what the problem was.

He extended his hand towards the television. "*This* is the problem! It has come *here!*"

"What has?" I asked.

"This tribalism… this fucking extremism," he said with his old expletive gusto. "Bickering between ignorant zealots—even between Republicans and Democrats. Every day these people look more and more like the fanatics of the Middle East."

In the moment I thought the comparison farfetched. I remained silent, not feeling like contesting him.

"It *is* the same," he said, as if reading my thoughts. "It is a puritanical moral superiority. Everything to them is black-and-white. I know these people well. We came here to escape them. And now this mindset is growing here too."

I instantly thought back to what Kamal Bey had said about the rigid, extremist mind of Al-Qaeda members, decades ago, and which I never forgot:

Those pulled in are people looking for a purpose. People who are afraid of the ambiguities of life, and who need strict rules, structure, and certainty. And to be part of a clique in which they are virtuous and saved—while everyone else is wrong and damned. It is the sanctuary of literal minds. A spiritual no-man's-land.

Kamal raised the remote control and turned off the TV.

"I hope I am wrong: but this will likely play out in the same way these things do back home," he added ominously, while holding my gaze. "People will turn on one another."

It was one of the last predictions he made in my presence, and the one I continue to remember the most to this day.

Addis Ababa, Ethiopia, 1964

Kamal Bey would never have seen the inside of Haile Selassie's palace, or been ordered to meet the Ethiopian emperor's pet lion, if he had not been declared persona non grata *in Sudan a day earlier.*

His expulsion upon arrival at Khartoum airport, while on a solo multi-nation business trip for the Egyptian Chamber of Tobacco, was decided on a whim and for little reason. The rude and foul-mouthed Sudanese customs agent, whom Kamal Bey had the temerity to talk back to, responded by simply deporting him. Egypt and Sudan were then on very bad terms.

Kamal was placed on the next flight out of Khartoum, which happened to be to Addis Ababa, in Ethiopia.

When Kamal Bey arrived there, he sought the assistance of the commercial counsellor at the Egyptian embassy, whom he knew. The men met for lunch, where the diplomat offered help rescheduling Kamal's trip. Afterwards, the man suggested they go to Emperor Haile Selassie's palace to sign his guestbook—a common practice, the diplomat said, with visiting Egyptian dignitaries and officials.

While at the palace, an English-speaking staffer accompanied by a pair of thick-chested henchmen approached Kamal Bey and the diplomat and took them aside.

"Which of you two men would like the honour of meeting the emperor's pet lion?" the man said, brandishing a forced smile.

Kamal and the diplomat stared incomprehensibly at the palace hand before seeing that the man was serious. "Thanks, but we're not interested," the Egyptians said in near unison.

"I'm sorry, but one of you must do so," the man replied. "It is by order of the emperor."

"How is this so?" the diplomat asked.

"You have been selected at random. The emperor's lion needs to be acquainted with non-Ethiopians. Visiting world leaders will be

meeting the cat and the emperor wants to know how the lion will react in the presence of foreigners. It will only take a few minutes."

The diplomat, who knew that Haile Selassie was given to bizarre and idiosyncratic behaviour, and that lions, like most cats were highly temperamental, panicked. He protested, saying that any harm that befell him, a diplomat, would cause an international incident. The palace hand let him go, and the diplomat scampered off, telling Kamal he'd meet him outside.

The Ethiopian, backed by his enforcers, then turned to Kamal. "Come with me, sir."

"Oh but, I cannot," Kamal Bey declared steadfastly.

"Why?"

"Because I am allergic to cats!"

The men chuckled. "That's okay. This is not a house cat. This is an African lion."

"A cat is a cat! And an allergy is an allergy! Do you not know how allergies work?"

The three Ethiopians stared blankly at him.

"I am Egypt's top doctor. You had better listen to me, or this will end badly for you!"

"Speak then," the palace staffer said.

"The effect of an allergy is not just one thing reacting badly to another. It is actually about the incompatibility of two things. Do you understand what that means?"

The man shook his head.

"It means that if I am allergic to that lion, then the opposite will be true. Harm will also come to the lion... who will also be allergic to me!"

"I've never heard that before," said the emperor's minion.

"Of course you haven't! How could you? If a man is allergic to carrots, can the carrots tell you that it is also allergic to the man? Can vegetables speak?!"

The palace hand looked blank-faced.

"Well, can they?" Kamal pressed him. "Answer me."

"No."

"No, is correct. Vegetables can't talk. And neither can cats. If the lion gets sick, or dies, because of its allergy to me, how will His Excellency the Emperor feel? What will he do when my embassy friend informs your leader that you let a man with a cat allergy come into contact with his precious lion?"

The staffer turned to confer with his retinue in Amharic, before turning back to Kamal Bey.

"We have discussed the matter and you are quite right. No harm must come to the emperor's lion. You are free to go, sir."

"There is No Mossad"

Your eyebrow and your eye play separately.
 – Turkish Proverb

It was the limp arm. That was the giveaway.

Up until that moment there was little to suggest that Yair Ravid, the man whose cozy and idyllic Mediterranean home I'd just entered, was the sort of intelligence agent who had fought hand-to-hand on the frontlines of real-life shadow wars. His countenance and manner were heavy—there was no denying it. A deep baritone voice filled with cold realism and a smile that exuded little joy rounded off a persona made all the more weighty by some palpable yet indescribable psychic baggage that announced itself in his every cumbersome step. But none of these things, I had heard, were rare among Israelis working in the wider security field. In fact, many such professionals the world over become hardened beings after a lifetime of swimming in malign undercurrents. But it was Ravid's paralyzed arm, which slumped comatose at his left side, cradling into his lap as he sat down for our video interview, that convinced me he was of an elite caste of combatants. My imagination, filling in the blanks, conjured images of him in a knife fight in the Port of Marseilles. Though given what he'd discuss in the interview, and what I'd learn about him subsequently, it would more likely have been the Port of Beirut.

Yair Ravid was a former *katsa*, the Hebrew word for "case officer" or "field agent" of the Mossad—Israel's foreign intelligence service. He spent much of his career working in Lebanon, eventually becoming the organization's head of station there.

"So, you are coming from Dubai," Ravid remarked a moment earlier, with more than a flicker of interest, as he led us into his living room where my assistant began to set up the camera. I got a similar starry-eyed reaction from most people who'd heard I lived in the United Arab Emirates (UAE). Many Israelis, who, in addition to being dazzled by Dubai's glamorous façades, also saw it as a place of sympathetic secularism and modernity. It was a part of the region they could understand.

"My home base these days," I answered.

"Aha," Ravid said, noting my response. "Lots of interesting things happening there, I hear."

I was in Israel in 2004, now in my 30s working as a journalist, producing a documentary for Al Arabiya, an Arabic-language cable news station based in the UAE. The program was about a rogue faction of Lebanese army soldiers called the South Lebanon Army.* That militia, also known by its acronym SLA, became a proxy force of the Israeli military during its 16-year occupation of south Lebanon. The SLA disbanded when the Israelis withdrew from Lebanon in 2000. Not strong enough to face their enemies on their own, and out of fear for their lives, most of its members simultaneously fled to Israel where they continued to live in exile.

---

* A Christian-majority militia, the SLA formed during Lebanon's civil war and fought against the Palestine Liberation Organization (PLO) and Shia guerrillas. The SLA later fought alongside the Israelis against Hezbollah, when Israel occupied a buffer zone along its border with Lebanon.

In retirement, Ravid became a critic of Israeli policy in Lebanon and a spokesperson for the plight of exiled Lebanese SLA members—some of whom he knew during his time in the Mossad. He agreed to provide an interview for the documentary, one of the first he had given to an Arab television station; and definitely the first for that network by a former Mossad agent.

Before we started rolling, I asked Ravid how he wanted to be identified. I knew from my fixer he was a former Mossad agent, as did many people in Israel. He had appeared before on Israeli television. But I needed confirmation, including his desired title for the banner graphic showing his name. I asked if he was in the Mossad.

"There is no Mossad," Ravid said deadpan without missing a beat, which he followed up with a grin so subtle and ironic as to be nearly imperceptible.

He is joking, I thought. *He has to be.*

After letting his quip sit for just long enough, he let me off the hook. "Just *intelligence*," he continued. "It's enough to say I was in the Israeli intelligence. Your audience will understand what that means."

WHEN WE ENTERED Ravid's home—located in a comfortable Israeli coastal community north of Tel Aviv—we did so with a mix of trepidation and slight awe. Even my veteran field producer and media fixer Nidal, a Hebrew-speaking Palestinian from East Jerusalem who was a legend for her bulldoggish soliloquies against the Israeli occupation, behaved respectfully, even deferentially, around Ravid. The Mossad, like all things of an elite nature, insinuates high status and an aura of mystification—even to their enemies. We all secretly scanned the inside of his home looking for evidence of the ruthlessness which, by reputation, attaches to his kind. I, for one, saw it in his limp arm. But that was the extent of my initial impression. Looking back, I perhaps should have been more intimidated by the presence of Ravid directly before me. After all, if a member of the Mossad, the legendary samurai-style caste of dark knighted deceivers, was not the epitome of injurious Zionism for an Arab, then what was? But I was also different from many Middle Easterners: I had grown up geographically, and also psychologically, at arm's length from the conflicts there.

People of Jewish descent have always been part of the diverse ethnic mosaic of the Middle East—long before the region became the attention-grabbing problem child of centripetal blood feuds. But since the creation of Israel in 1948, which came at the high cost of Palestinian exile and subjugation, numerous regional wars, and a gradual moral debasement of the Jewish state and its collective soul, Arabs the world over have been implacable in their opposition to Israel and its polices. Israelis, and unfortunately Jews anywhere by association, became taboo for many Arabs. To most, they remain deeply hubristic foes that populate a beachhead of Western meddling in the East. Like kids anywhere, children growing up in Arab families often imbibe their parents' tribalism and politics with regards to Israel—ranging from suspicion and misgivings of the other, to burning hatred. The inverse, of course, is also true.

My upbringing and early experiences were of another quality and order, which made me an outlier in this sense. Because my parents were not fanatical on these issues, I was not subjected to the same level of indoctrination and dogma around Israel and Jews as many other Arab kids growing up. Like nearly all Middle Easterners, they were, of course, contemptuous of Israeli foreign policy, often hurling curses and insults in Arabic at the TV when Israeli officials appeared on news broadcasts to recite the party line in times of crisis and war. But at the more core religious, ethnic and cultural levels, they didn't display the same degree of tribal antagonism toward Jews. As transplanted Levantine Christians living in Egypt with a hybrid East-West culture, my parents were subconsciously simpatico with Jews who also had that diaspora sense of rootlessness and alienation amid other peoples. Before moving to Canada, they had lived among the ever-dwindling Egyptian Jews of Cairo who had survived the waves of anti-Jewish retribution following the start of the Arab-Israeli conflict in 1948. My maternal grandfather was employed by Jews, and my father had even dated some Egyptian-Jewish women before meeting my mom. By the family's account, Egypt's erstwhile Jews were modern and educated, and therefore exemplars of the Western secularism that was vanishing in the region, a development they have lamented ever since.

It was therefore both the height of irony, and somehow apropos, that when my parents moved to Canada, they settled, unbeknownst to them at the time, in what would become the most Jewish neighbourhood in the country. Thornhill, a northern suburb of Toronto settled by Germans in the late 1700s, was not only demographically the most Jewish community by numbers in Canada, but, by some apocryphal account, was home to the largest concentrations of Jews per capita outside of Israel and New York.

It was odd growing up there. My parents, who were comfortable with the memory of the Arabic-speaking Sephardic Egyptian Jews they considered co-nationals, didn't warm up at first to the mostly Ashkenazis in our neighbourhood, who they equated more with the Israel they disliked. They were sensitized to and hyper-aware of that Jewish presence and would often speak of them as an entity apart. As a kid, it was hard not to be influenced and affected by those reactions and sentiments, which rubbed off on my sister and me.

But living there was also an unusual blessing. Because I came into contact with Jewish people all of the time, it helped inoculate me against the sort of knee-jerk anger and dehumanizing prejudice that had gripped other Arab friends and acquaintances. The 'neutral ground' that was multi-ethnic Canada, at arms length from the world's hot zones, also kept tensions in check.

The fact that many Jews in my neighbourhood were either

genuinely, or wilfully ignorant of the Middle East, or were somewhat prejudiced themselves against Arabs, although awkward to endure, had less impact on my future attitude towards them and the conflict than the more benign daily interactions which demystified them as an enemy. Over time I learned to see them as other humans with their own, albeit perhaps sometimes more acute, version of the cultural conditioning, biases, and in-group thinking that affect many nationalistic ethnicities—heightened by the collective trauma of centuries of persecution that has defined and galvanized them. It wasn't that I was indifferent to the occupation of Palestinians in the territories. Quite the opposite: by the time I became old enough to better understand the conflict, and to travel and work in the region, I saw that the political onus was on Israel, holding most of the cards and power, to take the bolder steps to try to ameliorate their disastrous relationships with their neighbours, which their heavy-handedness had created or made worse.* It had been 2,500 years since Jews had a political entity in the region—far too long in the past to justify their forceful transplantation into the area on their own terms entirely. Something more had to give on their end to make it work.

The bizarre corollary to my growing up in a predominantly Jewish neighbourhood—perhaps an inexplicable cosmic consequence of this cross-ethnic entanglement—was that for much of my life I have been mistaken for being Jewish. This not only happened in Canada, where I had an inadvertent knack for attracting Jewish women, but also in the Middle East. When this misidentification occurs often enough, and even Arabs think you are Jewish, it has the rare effect of making you wonder if it may in fact be true. On my travels to Israel and Palestine as a journalist, I often found myself addressed in Hebrew—including in the West Bank among some Palestinians. The Israeli customs and security

---

* I learned to see the conflicts of the Middle East as being driven by the nationalists, religious fanatics and warmongers on all sides who held the rest of their populations—the less vocal majorities more amenable to peace—hostage.

people at the airport and land borders I crossed, especially the females, always spoke to me in Hebrew, and often with a rapid battering of eyelashes and beguilingly flirtatious smiles. When I informed them that I didn't speak Hebrew and that I also wanted them to stamp a separate piece of paper rather than my passport (to avoid being turned away from Arab countries that forbade visits to Israel), they frowned, sighed, and assumed their cold and aloof customs agent manners. In Egypt, and especially Sinai where Israeli tourists thronged, hustlers and souvenir salesmen chased after me yelling, "*Shalom! Shalom!*" My denials in the local Arabic dialect were unable to deter them. The more malicious of these characters would not at all be persuaded.

One night, while living in Egypt as a student and visiting Luxor with my roommate Daoud, we went for an exploratory walk through the backstreets after having tea and *sheesha* at a Nubian coffee shop. Suddenly a motorcycle with two men riding on it appeared at a crossroads ahead of us, stopping there. Both men glared at us with pained expressions of rage. It felt almost as if they'd deliberately headed us off, and I wondered for a second if we would be the victims of a militant shooting—as there was an armed insurgency in Egypt in the 1990s. The man who was piggy-backing pointed his finger at me accusingly.

"You are Jew!" he scowled in English.

Alarmed by his tone and glare, I shook my head and vehemently denied it in my most colloquial Arabic meant to leave no doubt in his mind that he wasn't dealing with a foreigner. But it had no effect. He was furious and impervious to my entreaties.

"You are Jew! *You are Jew!* You are not my friend!"

With that, the motorcycle revved in an angry roar and tore off into the Luxor night in a large plume of street dust and diesel exhaust.

A COUPLE of years before that incident, while as an undergraduate, I decided to work on a fourth-year honours dissertation, a one-on-one thesis paper, with a supervising professor. I chose to write about the jihadist insurgency against the Egyptian regime at the time. The only academic available and willing to work with me was a visiting Jewish professor from an affiliated university in Israel who was teaching courses about the Middle East at my school. The man, a serious minded and reticent character, was unlike many of the academics working at my university. Professors there were largely easy-going left-wing eccentrics that were more collegial with their dissertation students, often going for beers with them at the pub. Instead my supervisor was conservative, curt, awkwardly formal, and looked, spoke and moved like a bureaucrat with a security clearance. He often tore in and out of the department at lightning speed in a grey trench coat and briefcase as if he were moving between government crisis meetings. He had, in fact, worked in a national security role in the past, advising a former hawkish Israeli prime minister. None of those things alone, or together, of course, were necessarily implicating in terms of political dubiousness, or even being a spy—but it made me wonder, and fuelled my assumptions about what came next.

When I completed the dissertation, much to his satisfaction, he invited me to his office to discuss "the future."

"My colleagues back home are very impressed with your work, which I shared with them," he began. "Are you interested in pursuing graduate studies?"

"I am considering it," I told him.

"Well, if so, I could help get you a scholarship at my school in Israel. There is an interest in these sorts of topics, as you can well imagine. You could pursue an interesting balance of class work with research and travel in the region. Your familiarity with the language and your passport would make this very conducive—something not afforded to Israeli students."

With that he got on the phone and started calling people back home in my presence, laying the initial groundwork for the funding he was promising. He told me to "think about it" and to let him know.

There was a lot of flattery built into that conversation and I was excited about the prospects of an academic chapter in the Middle East. I had been itching to travel to and immerse myself in the region—and to explore my family roots there. But once my parents found out, a shadow of deep concern fell upon their faces. *Going to Israel? A full scholarship for an international student of Arab descent? Travel research in the region?* To them, the whole thing smelled. It was both too good to be true, and somehow too easy. It was also entry into potentially dangerous political waters. I dismissed their worries as the usual overprotection impulse of parents combined with Arab paranoia about the Israelis, and vowed to make up my own mind. They responded with an intervention, inviting over a close relative who told us the story of his brother who had been arrested and executed as a spy in Egypt in the mid-1960s—part of an alleged ring of traitors. The relative sharing the painful memory told us that he blamed the Israelis, although he had no evidence that they had been responsible for recruiting his brother.

Dragging such a skeleton out of the closet for use as a cautionary tale in order to save my hide was an impressive and dramatic maneuver. But how relevant was all of this to my situation? And how could anyone know for certain that the bad guys in that story were Israeli? It could have been the Americans, the Brits, or another Arab country—anyone. Even those poor souls who made the Faustian bargain, and were later busted, may not have been aware of who they were working for. This entire question was devolving into quasi-hysterical musings born of the conflicts to which we were all so tragically tied.

But the seed planted in my mind by my family sprouted, and the question began to weigh heavily as I imagined the possible scenarios. I needed to consult a more knowledgeable source. I decided to defer to Kamal Bey, who, I was certain, would know what to do.

Days later, I took my usual place beside him on his couch. He was fidgeting with a small set of yellow worry beads in silence as the cogs in his mind turned and turned. His brows buckled under the heavy weight of his deliberations. I'd never seen him take so long to answer a question.

"I can't say for sure," he began cautiously, "but this offer sounds much like the classic first steps to recruiting a source."

I related even more details to him, including new things that had struck me as suspect, or bizarre, after the fact: namely my professor's penchant for testing me to see how quickly I could think on my feet by asking me surprise questions I wasn't anticipating or prepared for. Kamal observed me gravely, like a doctor listening to a patient describe their symptoms, while nodding and repeatedly saying, "Aha... Aha." I was relieved to be speaking to someone familiar with this unusual subject. Yet I also felt silly, and more than a bit paranoid myself. I didn't have any hard proof beyond an uncomfortable and niggling feeling that there was more going on than was visible at the surface.

Kamal Bey scratched the back of his head and made a very dissatisfied expression.

"The truth is, it doesn't matter whether or not this man is what you think he is," he said. "Even if he isn't—and let's be fair, maybe he's not—you're still vulnerable by going over there to study. When *their people* find out about you, *and make no mistake, they will*, they will likely decide to approach, or even entrap you. Someone will ask you for a favour. Maybe to deliver something, or to get them some information which will seem innocent enough. They'll pay you a little something for it. And then..."

"And then what?"

"Then you're stuck."

This other scenario had not occurred to me.

Kamal Bey raised his hand into the air and made a pinching motion with his thumb and index finger. "These people, who you may be dealing with, live their lives hanging from a thread. You

"There is No Mossad"

don't want to be connected to them." I stared at the imaginary filament and saw, as he intended, how close it looked to snapping.

"I don't recommend you go there," he went on. "There's no need. You can study elsewhere in the region, if that's what you want. And besides, why be associated with the country and what it's been doing to the Palestinians?"

Just then the irony hit me square in the face: I was being warned off one group of intelligence people battling Arabs by another presumed intelligence person whose knowledge was likely put to similar ends.

"But you're also working..." I said impulsively, before cutting myself off.

"No," he said calmly, intuiting what I was about to say. "It's not the same. For us—for me—it is about preventing violence against innocent people here in Canada. I do not approve of the subjugation of another people. And it does nothing good for Israel. This conflict *will* metastasize. Many more people will needlessly die before this war finds resolution."

He was about to say more but then prudently stopped.

The look on his face conveyed the rest: *What I say may seem like a contradiction to you, but two opposing views* can *complement each other—even if they appear at odds.*

My interview with ex-Mossad man, Yair Ravid, and the documentary about the South Lebanon Army émigrés in Israel, whose Arabic title was *The Bitterest Exile*, is said to have shocked viewers in the Arab World. Not only had the film followed a group of Lebanese trying to cobble together new lives in an Israel that had largely abandoned them (Lebanese people living *in* Israel was a sight unseen to most Arabs), it was also one of the first Arabic language programmes to feature an interviewee who was a former Mossad case officer. Here was one of the faces of the notorious shadow organization, in all of his sly candour, delivering his sound bites in a flawless Lebanese dialect—showcasing an aspect of his former cover whose pseudonym, he revealed in another documentary years later, was 'Abu Daoud.'* *The Bitterest Exile* convinced my own family living in Beirut and who were incredulous of the film and my access, that I myself was some kind of political operator.

After we finished the interview and turned off the camera, I asked Ravid, off the record, if he personally knew a man by the name of Victor Ostrovsky. He was the former Mossad case officer who wrote a famous international bestselling book called *By Way of Deception*, which recounted his experiences inside the Mossad and blew the whistle on what he alleged was corruption within the spy agency. I had read the book when I was a teenager, after my dad bought a copy. When Ostrovsky's name was mentioned, Ravid's face darkened as if thunderclouds had gathered above him.

"That man was a piece of shit," he blurted. "He was a nothing," he added, making a little inch-long symbol with his thumb and forefinger. "He even mentioned me in that book."

While we spoke, my camera and sound technician, a Palestinian from Haifa, began to watch and listen to the footage we had just recorded. She had her earphones on and was watching the playback on the camera's viewfinder. Suddenly Ravid's annoyance at my question turned into rage and panic when he saw her operating the camera as he spoke. He thought he was being recorded in that moment, while speaking off-camera. His razor-sharp life-and-death survivalist reflexes kicked in.

---

* In 2018, Ravid appeared in the documentary *Inside the Mossad*, a 4-part *Netflix* series about the history of the spy agency and some of its operations seen through the eyes of its former staff. I later discovered in a book that Ravid himself wrote, called *Window to the Backyard*, that his paralyzed arm was the result of an army training wound in his youth—and *not* a Hollywood-style knife fight in the Port of Marseilles.

"Hey, what are you doing?!" he blurted to her in Hebrew. "I said, *HEY!!*"

The sound recordist looked up, startled and confused. She pulled off her headphones.

Ravid stood up, bristling. "Turn that machine off or I'll come break it into a thousand bits!"

All colour drained from her face. "I'm just reviewing the footage."

"What?!" he asked, not understanding, and then looking to us for clarification.

Nidal, our fixer, chimed in. "The camera isn't filming. She's just watching what we recorded earlier. To make sure the footage and sound are okay."

The emotion drained out of Ravid's face and body. "Oh," he said, deflated.

The frightened sound recordist nervously walked over to remove his lapel microphone from his shirt as he stood staring into space, still flummoxed by the appearance of a demon from his old life that remained in him.

Ajloun, Jordan, 2001

Hadya lost control of her car while taking a turn down the steep mountain road below the castle. Reckless Middle Eastern driving, wits dulled by wine, and a steep grade was more than the vehicle could handle. Luckily, the compact car slid into the mountainside instead of the unfenced zone of empty air beyond the edge of the road.

We had just finished a romantic lunch beside a 12th century medieval fortress with a panoramic view of hilly scrubland and olive groves. All was well in our world. But now that Hadya had crashed her car, a crisis had been heaved upon her—and us.

She drove the vehicle to a standstill on the side of the road at the bottom of the mountain. We were only shaken, but the front right side of the car was smashed. She lit up a smoke, exited the vehicle and made a phone call to get herself out of the jam she was in. If her father, a big-shot international businessman and arms dealer—her financial wellspring—found out she'd crashed the car, there would be big trouble. Or so she believed.

"What are you going to do?" I asked when she got off the phone, posing the question with the appropriate gravity she would demand of me on such an occasion.

Hadya had tossed away her Davidoff Slims menthol cigarette and lit a more potent hashish reefer the size of a stage magician's wand and took deep pulls on it.

"Maher's coming," she said, as she began to relax. "He'll take care of it."

Maher was a former security official poached by Hadya's father to be the family fixer and major-domo.* Hadya had a special relationship with him: he did her bidding on the side, including aiding and abetting her various jet-set adventures and commercial pursuits, helping to keep them hidden from her parents.

Two hours later, Maher arrived from Amman. His car came to a dramatic halt beside us after a sly and impressive U-turn. The vehicle he drove, a rental, was identical in make, model and colour to Hadya's. The man got out of the car and went straight to examine the accident damage. He then stood up from a crouch and turned to look at Hadya, who was now on her second cannabis reefer. He glanced about worried that others were watching, and stormed towards her, snatching the joint from her hands.

"Maher!" Hadya cried, indignantly.

He dropped the joint on the ground and stomped it to a pulp.

"Where do you think you are, the Champs-Élysées?!"

---

* Maher, appropriately, means 'skilled' in Arabic.

Hadya threw her hands on her hips—a bohemian in designer jeans, a floral hippie shirt, and a crocheted skullcap—attempting to project anger.

Maher ignored her theatrics. "Quickly," he said. "Take these car keys and give me yours. We're switching vehicles. I'll bring yours back fixed in a week."

In just as fast and fluid a motion as he came in, Maher left the scene, acknowledging me with a neutral nod as he did.

As we sat in the rescue vehicle, I asked Hadya why she didn't just tell her parents the truth and avoid all of this senseless sneaking around. She stared at me through her sunglasses, seemingly affronted, and held her gaze for effect before she responded.

"This is not Canada. You naive Westerners are all the same."

The Hezbollah Encounter

The smallest hair casts its shadow.
– Goethe, *Maxims and Reflections*

Husain, the lithe 14-year-old tea-boy and multi-purpose tech prodigy interning at a small video production company in Beirut, was unable to hide his fascination with me from the moment we met. He fixated on my person with what looked like glowing adulation while an employee of the company toured me around their facilities. I'd seen that look before in parts of the world that had little or no exposure to foreigners. Husain lived in Dahieh, a predominantly *Shia* Muslim suburb of Beirut, which, because it was also the headquarters of the Lebanese political party and militia group Hezbollah, was somewhat shielded from Western culture and influence. Few if any foreigners ventured there—myself included. But given Husain also worked in a downtown production office and most of Beirut was hardly cut off from foreigners, his interest in my presence couldn't have been all novelty.

The Hezbollah Encounter

At that moment I chalked it up to a quiet admiration he had for the West.

"Where are you from?" Husain asked, in surprisingly good English. He had just brought me an Arabic coffee, as I waited to meet the office owner who was on a long call.

"Canada. But now I live in Dubai."

"Have you been to New York?"

"Yes, a few times."

"Is it as beautiful as Los Angeles?"

"They're different. I prefer New York—and New Yorkers."

"Did you see the Twin Towers before they were destroyed?"

"Yes, but not from close up," I said, thinking it was a strange follow-up question.

It was 2005 and I was in Beirut to shoot and edit a pair of political documentaries about Lebanon and Syria during my Dubai-based stint as a TV journalist. The docs were for the Arabic TV news station Al Arabiya. A Lebanese friend and colleague named Wissam was providing me with all of the production services and facilities for my work. But when I asked if he could also help me cut a new producer's showreel, a kind of CV containing my best video clips, he told me his studios were booked. Instead he referred me to another production house, the one where the young Husain worked, owned by Wissam's *Shia* co-confessionals and friends.

"They mostly do work for Al-Manar," Wissam said, referring to the official television station of Hezbollah, known for its explicit and vehement anti-Israel and pro-Iran bent. "Their studio is just down the road from here."

Wissam was one of the most secular and West-leaning Lebanese *Shia* Muslims I'd known, so I was a bit surprised about his referral, and jokingly told him so.

"Not to worry," he said smiling, swatting my concern away. "They're good people. We refer clients back and forth all of the time."

I met the production house boss once he got off his call. He told me Husain would upload the showreel footage I brought with me—and that I could come back the following week, once the editor was done with the job, to pick up the completed reel and source tapes. The boy beamed with delight and led me into a small edit suite where he took my paper-edit and started to digitize the footage. Between inserting tapes into the player, he showed me some of his pet-project videos and animation shorts on his laptop. Husain was an incredibly talented computer whiz, who was being groomed for a position with the company.

As I got up to leave, he became ever so slightly nervous.

"Can we exchange emails?" he asked, nervously in English. Husain, I noticed, preferred not to engage me in Arabic. "I want to practice English. Maybe we can do chat on Facebook Messenger?"

Husain seemed like a decent kid and I was more than happy to banter with him, if, and when, we found each other online.

"Sure," I said.

I wrote down my email address in my notebook. As I tore the page out, handing it to him, his face revealed relief, before settling again into a look that seemed almost heavy, calculating and encumbered.

I HAD ALREADY FORGOTTEN Husain and the showreel edit job, when I arrived in Damascus the next day. I was there on production for two documentaries: one about the history of the Golan Heights territorial dispute between Israel and Syria and the other about Syrian-Lebanese relations. Both were sensitive topics and required shooting not just inside of Syria, but also along its borders, which, given that I was a foreigner, was an extraordinarily iffy proposition. The Bashar al-Assad regime was, and remained up until its demise, antagonistic towards the West—and vice versa. It was also a secret police state, interpenetrated to the core by various intelligence services and citizen informers. Few Western journalists, prior to the regime's overthrow, were given access. Only independent travellers, skeptical about, or indifferent to, the Western media's blanket demonization of the country, ventured there. They reaped the rewards, the many aspects of Syrian culture that Western officialdom, in its myopic obsession with the country's mafia-style political system, filtered out. Syrians struck me as a warm-hearted, down-to-earth and generous people ennobled by a rich history and a bountiful cultural heritage, largely unsullied by time and gentrification.

I too had travelled there previously, fascinated by the preserved-in-amber nature of the place. I was drawn to Aleppo on those past trips, from where two of my grandparents, one from each of my parents' families, had originally hailed. I'd also explored Syria's wild and far-flung eastern rural border areas with Turkey and Iraq, near to where another branch of my dad's family came from.

My parents in Canada, and relatives in Beirut could barely contain their astonishment when they learned that I was about to go to Syria again, this time for work. All of them cited the oppressive nature of the regime, and told me to reconsider; even though I had already been there a few times and had really enjoyed myself. Their view of the country was coloured by negative media portrayals, and especially in the case of my Lebanese family, by political differences with the Syrian regime. But my sense, deeper down, was that Syria also represented an affront to their more Westernized Arabness. It was the gateway to the rough-and-tumble Middle Eastern and Islamic hinterland that segued into the baking plains of Mesopotamia and the unimaginable East-beyond-East that was Iran, Pakistan and Afghanistan. To be sure, one had to mind the delicateness of working in Syria as a Westerner, but it was manageable.

My Lebanese production partner Wissam had that angle figured out. He brought on board a Syrian *Alawi* news reporter, named Intisar, to be my fixer and field producer. Being a co-

confessional of the ruling Assads, who were also of the *Alawi* religious minority, she was trusted by the regime. She was so well regarded, in fact, that during our meeting with the officials who gave me and my Lebanese cameraman our Syrian press credentials—at an office plastered with old 1980s tourism posters of Palmyra and the Umayyad Mosque—they decided to forego assigning a government minder to us. They instead asked Intisar to do double duty in that regard. Mentioning my partial Syrian ancestry also seemed to help.*

"If you do good work, say nice things about Syria, you can come back anytime and we can have a long relationship," the press official said to me patronizingly in English with a wink, as we shook hands.

The not-so-veiled comment was not lost on me: and it wasn't all about my being a foreigner. The cable TV news station I was working for, Al Arabiya, was Saudi-owned. The Assads and the Saudis had considerable religious and political differences that periodically flared up. The Syrian press centre people had misgivings about Al Arabiya's editorial stance. But they were giving us the benefit of the doubt. And unfettered access.

We shot all over Damascus, largely unmolested, save for a few policemen who materialized out of thin air to check our papers. Our crew criss-crossed the Syrian side of the Golan Heights and filmed right up against the multiple barbed-wired and heavily mined no-man's land abutting the Israeli border; in one case coming within plain sight of Mount Avital—an Israeli signals intelligence station perched on a hill in a nature reserve on the occupied side of the Golan. On our last day we were granted an interview with the Syrian Foreign Minister at the time, Walid al-Muallem, and reached him through a rear door at the back of the

---

* I was Western enough to be granted the respect, privilege and partial protection of a guest, yet also Eastern enough that I was afforded sufficient warmth, trust and some degree of insider status, which it took Westerners years to earn.

foreign ministry building, which led by stairwell straight to his office.

The ease with which we carried out our work nonetheless belied the extent to which we were being watched. There are no surveillance 'get out of jail' cards under such regimes, even for the highest and most trusted politicians, all of whom are suspect. Even when there is no organized effort to tail you, there are so many informers among the public, pedlars of rumour and miscellaneous intelligence tips, that you are almost guaranteed to be watched in the hope you turn out to be a monetizable scoop.* During that trip, I more than once spotted the same pedestrians walking past us in different parts of the city. The same young men on motorbikes were also seen driving behind and alongside us. One had to assume they were part of a small legion that included others—perhaps even our own driver.

One such person who I'll never forget appeared to us, almost wraithlike, at the five-star Damascus Sheraton hotel, where my cameraman and I were staying. One day, after shooting, Intisar and I went to have drinks in the hotel's lobby with its shiny marbled floors, mahogany wood Arabesques and ornate chandeliers, a haunt for Syria's well-heeled. As we sipped gin and tonics and talked about the next day's production schedule, I noticed an elderly man in an oversized light grey suit standing beside the elevators. At first glance I assumed that he was just an elevator attendant. But I noticed that he never actually entered the elevators or did anything other than just stand there. He lingered, with his arms folded in front of him, watching people come in and out. What was more noteworthy and shocking to me were his eyes. They were completely and utterly lifeless: devoid of any twinkle,

---

* Some of these low-level hopefuls have the gall to approach you in public and ask who you are and what you are doing, as happened to me once during a previous trip to Syria, when I made the mistake of writing in my journal at a bus station.

emotion, or personality. His soul seemed forfeit, absent, gouged from his being.

When Intisar went to the restroom, I observed him longer from my distance, and I got the eerie but strong feeling that he was a former security official whose duty had probably involved regular torture or killing, perhaps in a prison environment, and who had been assigned this easier post in his retirement years. The man appeared like a zombie, his body, face and mind moulded into a permanent cast depicting pure fear in the blind service of someone else's absolute and ruthless control.

Hello Mr. John. You are having nice time?

Husain's appearances on email chat were more like sudden ambushes than tactful insinuations of himself. His opening salvos always appeared within 15 seconds of when I logged in, before I had time to check my email messages, creating the unavoidable impression that he was either desperate for human contact (which wasn't likely), or was lying in patient wait just for me.

His banter, a sort of banal question-and-answer sequence asking me how I was, what I was doing, how many siblings I had, and whether I was married, gave credence to his claim that he was looking to practice his language. In reality, and illuminated by the all-revealing rays of retrospect, it was a novice attempt to lull me into a sense of a normality with him, in order that his subsequent approaches would seem more nonchalant.

During our third chat, the conversation took on a whole new direction and tone. After I had asked him how he was, he wrote:

I go underground this weekend and made some filming.

"Where?" I responded, thinking he had probably gone with his production company to film tourists and stalactites at the popular Caves of Jeita in the Lebanese mountains.

Where resistance keeping the rockets.

I sat up in my chair. "The resistance" was another name and euphemism in Lebanon for the Hezbollah movement and the general struggle against Israel.

I simply wrote "Okay" in response, and waited. He took some time before he wrote back.

Some new big missiles to reach Tel Aviv. I have video tape.

"Sorry, I don't understand. Video of what?"

Rockets in underground. Do you know someone interesting in this? Journalist people who want copy of this video?

Husain, it seemed, was offering to sell weapons footage. Yet, I couldn't for a minute imagine that he, at 14 years of age, had happened to gain access to such a facility *and* shoot footage unseen, then get out with it, and work on his own to turn a fast buck. In my mind what was being proposed was a form of entrapment against me to see if I would bite—and uncover if I was a spy.

After considering the various ways I could word the same

response, I typed "No, thank you," and quickly wrapped up the conversation.

THE NEXT DAY I urgently asked to meet Wissam, who had recommended I take my showreel edit job to his Hezbollah-affiliated production house friends in the first place.

As we sat in his office with its huge window overlooking Riad Solh Square and the ornate buildings of Beirut's central district, I explained to him what had happened with Husain. Though I didn't consider myself in any imminent danger, I was feeling a creepy sense of betrayal and was upset about falling suspect. Also, my desire to be accepted in the culture to a point where such things would not happen so easily, faced a reality check. I wanted an in-the-know confidante to be aware of it all—just in case.

As I spoke Wissam's facial expression went from concern to shock to a jaw-throbbing rage punctuated by the most lurid and rancorous Lebanese expletives I'd ever heard him utter. "I can't believe this," he said disgustedly, shaking his head, and beating out his half-finished cigarette urgently in the ashtray.

Not only did Wissam have an aversion to the sort of religious dogma that Hezbollah espoused, but he was also part of that smaller subset of largely non-partisan Lebanese who despised the country's tribal politics and corruption that was fast corroding the country's foundations. He had worked as a cameraman on the frontlines during Lebanon's civil war and had seen what confessional politics did to a nation.

But there was also something more personal and more Eastern at play: in a way Wissam's honour had been besmirched. I was his friend, business associate, and guest, whom he felt a degree of responsibility for—and to whom he had referred his trusted production colleagues. In Arab culture, the young Husain's transgression against me—a form of disrespect—also made Wissam look bad in front of me. It was an implicit and unspoken violation against Wissam himself: I was in Lebanon working partly under his auspices. The production company owners who employed Husain, by association, had dishonoured Wissam, even if they weren't directly responsible for, or even knowledgeable about what Husain, their employee, did.

Wissam fumingly picked up the phone and called the head of the production house and sternly, but respectfully, protested Husain's behaviour.

"This is an upstanding human with no political bone in his body. He doesn't warrant such suspicious treatment," he said of me, nearly shouting, his face and body contorted into a tableau of deep emotive complaint.

I could tell that the man on the other line pleaded ignorance and spent the better part of his time apologizing and trying to smooth things over. The conversation, when it had cooled, went into a diplomatic phase of other work-related subjects that skirted the issue and was meant to re-establish normalcy and lower the emotional temperature.

Wissam hung up and lit another cigarette. He appeared relieved, and sufficiently mollified.

"Everything's fine," he said. "The owner sincerely apologized and said that the boy will be disciplined. Husain will also no longer be allowed to deal with you."

"Oh, good," I said, hugely relieved.

Wissam took a moment to think before continuing. "By the way, was any of your Israel footage included in the showreel?"

"Yeah, I'm using a clip from my documentary with the South Lebanon Army exiles in Northern Israel."

"Hmm. That's what did it."

I told Wissam I thought the footage might raise eyebrows, but didn't think it mattered. Most foreign journalists working in Lebanon, I said, had been to Israel before. It was almost always overlooked.

"Yes, yes, it's normal—there's no problem for journalists here.

But because the SLA fought with the Israelis against Hezbollah, and had close military relations with them, these people probably saw a more rare opportunity with you."

Wissam took a pull from his cigarette, and exhaled in a gesture of tired irony. "Welcome to Lebanon," he said.

Two days later, I went to pick up the finished showreel at Husain's production house. The company owner and staff were all sweet smiles and pretended nothing was amiss. It was so much business as usual that they didn't even offer to waive the cost of the work because of the scandal, as I thought might happen (but which would have also been an implicit admission of wrongdoing).

The young Husain was nowhere to be seen at first. After viewing the showreel and making the round of goodbyes, Husain drifted into my peripheral vision as I waited for the elevator. On cue, he reluctantly slipped into the elevator with me just before the doors closed.

Inside, Husain tilted his head down, and cast his eyes to the ground.

"I am sorry," he said in English. He remained silent, transfixed, awaiting absolution.

"For what?" I asked feigning ignorance, and putting him on the spot.

Husain opened his mouth as if to speak, but then ate his words. He wrung his hands nervously and pondered some more.

"I thought you were someone else."

When the elevator doors opened, he glanced at me with the same remorseful look he had had on his face upon entering the elevator. Then with the subtlest etchings of a smirk that indicated he had done his part for damage control, and for the resistance, he quickly dashed off.

Part IV: Borderlands and Liminal Zones

Escape from Lebanon

War is easy for the spectators.
— Ibn Asim al-Gharnati, *The Garden of Flowers*

He longs for war but dislikes the battle.
— John Lewis Burckhardt, *Arabic Proverbs*

The mad dash to Masnaa took place at dusk and under an unambiguous promise of bombardment. Our red souped-up Syrian hot rod, an old Buick Cutlass Supreme, sputtered and roared, achieving breakaway speeds on a Beirut-Damascus Highway nearly devoid of traffic. Majed, my burly Damascus taxi driver, originally from Homs, made it a point to ease his foot off the gas and stare for several seconds into the few other vehicles we passed. There is an implicit camaraderie between strangers plodding the same escape route under life-and-death circumstances: we were all hellbent on reaching the border before an airstrike rendered the shortest and most direct approach to Damascus unnavigable. Behind their frazzled and astonished looks, the other drivers seemed just as curious about us, as we were about them.

A few days earlier war had broken out between Israel and Hezbollah, the *Shia* militia group and political party that controlled Lebanon. A border skirmish, instigated by the latter, set off the conflagration which fast engulfed the entire country in the summer of 2006. That very day the Israeli military warned they would strike the Mudeirej Bridge—the highest bridge in the country, and which lay on our route just ahead.

"There is no fear," Majed declared boldly with a knowing smile meant to reassure. He saw that I was growing nervous as we raced towards the condemned concrete bridge somewhere up ahead.

I didn't respond. I was too distracted by the war in microcosm raging inside of me: torn, as I was, between the anxiety fuelling my escape, and the feelings of guilt, inadequacy and imposterdom for fleeing the country.

"No fear," he repeated. "No fear at all."

The road took on a ghostly countenance. Suddenly there were no other cars, and the highway lamps switched off. The moon skirted the mountaintops ahead of us like a beacon indicating our eastward destination.

"We can stop to rest when we reach Chtoura," he said. "There is tea. *Manouché*, too, if you're hungry."

I couldn't tell if he was joking. I merely looked at him and again said nothing.

"Even in war we have to eat, *habibi*."

At that moment I resolved to have him take me back to Beirut. Any outcome seemed better than the feeling of shame building with each kilometre. But when I tried to tell him to turn around, the words would not form. Some other part of me, an inner persona charged with self-preservation, grasped my throat with one hand, and held an index finger to its lips with the other.

'THE CALM BEFORE THE STORM' is a condition I've always understood and had an inexplicable talent for discerning. It comes as a feeling, the presence of a subtle and uncomfortable vacuum, like a marine tide receding before a tsunami. Or an equilibrium past its expiry date, such as a long stretch of great weather that is just too good to be true. That vague niggling precognition of an impending change in rhythm occurred just before the September 11 attacks. The same impalpable feeling had hung over me in Lebanon in this late spring and early summer of 2006.

I was working in Beirut. They were halcyon and unusually carefree days. The weather was idyllic and the nation was in an especially festive mood. Football's World Cup had started in June and was underway for the month. Every café, bar and restaurant had their TVs tuned to the games, attracting large, boisterous crowds. It felt like the entire city was out watching the daily matches—and nothing else mattered. Beirut, in classical Lebanese summer fashion, lived each day as if it were its last.

New experiences amplified that feeling of euphoria hanging in the air. My Lebanese friend and colleague, Wissam, who provided production services in Lebanon for my documentary projects, bought a small fibreglass motorboat, which he often invited me to travel on during the weekends. On our first few trips we hung off the edge of one of the runways at Beirut's international airport—adjacent to the local fishermen perched upon the giant concrete slabs that formed a jetty running parallel with the tarmac. We picnicked and swam the hours away as Middle East Airlines, Air France and Emirates jumbo jets landed in sporadic succession right beside us.

That feeling of attaining a new perspective on the city and country grew as we explored the coast around Beirut in Wissam's boat. Particularly surreal was watching the shoreline transform as we headed south from the city. After passing the Raouché district, with its slightly upscale apartment buildings, restaurants, and cliff-side cafés, the scene transformed revealing expansive underclass dwellings sprawled out along the coast. The water took on a hue of pea-soup green, while the sea suddenly teemed with garbage. Children played on the beach while their mothers watched nearby, covered head-to-toe in black *abayas*. It was as though we had entered an invisible portal that transported us to a parallel realm of more hard-edged realities and sensibilities.

Yet, also not surprisingly for Lebanon, this neighbourhood contained its own contradictions.

"Agha Zada, look in the distance," Wissam said, pointing his small bottle of Almaza beer towards the shore. "Hizbullah-stan, the enemy of the West, takes a month-long vacation from its hatred of all things Western."

As I looked out across the vast and crowded shanty-scape of corrugated rooftops, I noticed that each home hoisted a country flag of a team taking part in the World Cup. France, Italy and Germany were the most common standards, along with Hezbollah's own yellow banner, with its black Arabic insignia sprouting an arm clutching a Kalashnikov. A brisk sea breeze caused them all to flutter wildly in unison as white breakers danced upon the ocean, just offshore.

It was an unusually lighthearted display of blurred East-West boundaries in a neighbourhood where one wouldn't have imagined it. But the scene also stood in brutally stark contrast with a work trip I'd taken, days earlier, to the southern Lebanese border fence with Israel, the so-called "Blue Line"—a landscape in which the transition between juxtaposing realities could not have been more abrupt and unyielding.* There we found layers of barbed

---

* At one section of the border we found the centuries-old stone grave of a holy man, situated above ground, literally bisected by the border fence. The place, known locally as Sheikh Abbad Hill, was named after the saint in question. A close friend, John Bell, a Lebanese-Canadian diplomat, first told me about it. He describes the area in his excellent book, *How to Tame the Political Animal: The Missing Piece*.

wire, steel fencing, sensors, surveillance cameras, blimps, drones, military patrols, and a tension characteristic of two antagonists facing one another in a staring competition. At one location we encountered an Israeli bunker manned by two conscripts gazing into Lebanon through large slits in the concrete. They could not have been more than 40 feet from us. Across the metal fence, on the Lebanon side of the border, stood a large billboard that Hezbollah had printed and put up to face the Israeli border post, containing photos of injured, dead and imprisoned Israeli conscripts kidnapped or killed in a 2000 raid near that spot. At the bottom of the poster, written in both Arabic and Hebrew, were the words addressed to Ariel Sharon, the Israeli Prime Minister at the time: "Sharon, don't forget your soldiers who are still in Lebanon."

I didn't know it at the time, but that border fence, and the tension there, would be central to the conflagration that was then barrelling towards us.

Back on Wissam's boat, after gazing amused at the flags over the shanty, he and I continued further south at full throttle, leaping over waves with a feeling of rapturous freedom. In such a tiny, hemmed-in country, with limited privacy and space, the sea is the only frontier where one can throw off all restrictions and shackles. In that moment of relaxation and widened perspective I remember, at one moment, thinking to myself that things felt inordinately quiet and calm. Too much so.

DAYS LATER, not far from where we were on the Blue Line, Hezbollah guerrillas ambushed a border convoy of Israeli soldiers, killing three servicemen and kidnapping two others. Five other Israeli soldiers were killed in an attempted rescue of one of the abductees. The incident, one of hundreds of Hezbollah military incitements since Israel ended its occupation of southern

Lebanon in 2000, provoked an unusually heavy response. The Israeli strategy was to retaliate punitively and massively against the entire country, including Lebanese civilian infrastructure, and not just the areas that fell under Hezbollah's control. Israel was going to make all of Lebanon pay for the actions of one party, in order to try and create a rift between the Lebanese population and the *Shia* militia group. The fact that Lebanon was a fragmented and increasingly failing state, not just incapable of controlling, but controlled by Hezbollah, didn't seem to matter.

The morning the bombings commenced, the Israelis instituted an air and naval blockade of Lebanon and struck the runways at the international airport where, in suitable irony, I was slated to go that day to catch a flight to Cyprus. Within hours the entire country was in the anxious and fevered grip of war, with southern Beirut and the border area near Israel taking heavy aerial bombardment and artillery fire. Meanwhile, Hezbollah fighters unleashed their erratically aimed rockets with wild abandon at any and all Israeli towns south of the frontier.

I was staying with my uncle and his family at their summer apartment in the village of Beit Meri, in the mountains above the city. In the crisp air and relative stillness of the surrounding green hills, you could hear the distant gruesome rumblings and reverberations of the death machines; the thrusts and parrying of weaponry. The sonic booms of Israeli fighter jets, which up until that day was maybe a weekly occurrence in the psychological war of nerves, was now an hourly phenomenon.

I watched in a sort of fascinated horror as my family, who had survived the Lebanese Civil War between 1975-1990, with its post-war deprivations and aftershocks (including on-again, off-again sectarian flare-ups, a Syrian occupation, and altercations with Israel), assumed a kind of dissociated and skeptical mental posture bordering on denial.

"Normal," my cousin Eddy said unconvincingly, with a wave of his hand and a nervous smirk. "We'll stay here. The Israelis won't bomb the mountains. You stay here too. It'll be over in a few days."

"The Israelis just threatened to turn the clock back in Lebanon by decades," I said. "That doesn't sound like a few days of fighting across the border."

Eddy raised his chin and clicked his tongue dismissively. "Don't believe it. It's just talk."

Say what he might, I had my own read on the situation. When Israel announced its air and naval blockade of the country and stated that not a place in Lebanon would be safe from attack, I decided that enough pressure had built up, with red lines crossed by both sides, that this would be no run-of-the-mill skirmish. Given the severity of the Israeli response on the first day, the possibility of the conflict widening to include Syria, a close ally of Hezbollah, was also not remote. Hunkering down was the last option I was entertaining.

In just a few hours the country assumed an ominous air unlike any I'd ever felt before. Lebanon's culture of anxiety and its incessant attempts at mental diversion (the frenetic pursuit of social distraction, status, and hedonism), now had grafted upon it a deep neurosis triggered by war. A psychic hand-wringing took over. People paced around in the streets, on their phones, calling in favours and exchanging the latest gossip and rumour, while also scrambling to make Plans B and C in preparation for the worst. Millenia of apprehension, the cumulative angst of tribal life at the crossroads of empires, were again coming to the fore.

As much as I liked to consider myself also an Easterner, someone who could deftly navigate the cultural borderlands between civilizations, I found myself reverting to the default foreigner mode. I was unaccustomed to tribal wars and other unsavoury quotients of Eastern existence that I hadn't given enough thought to. I decided to leave, to return to my home base in Dubai, where nothing more than sandstorms, erratically-driven Lamborghinis, and vodka-Red Bulls posed a danger. Part of the appeal of straddling two worlds was the privilege of reverting to the other when convenience, or necessity, demanded. Although "fleeing" was perhaps the more operative word in this case.

"Go?! Go *where*?!" my uncle asked with deep angst, raising his voice in alarm, and both arms in protest.

"There's a war on. And I don't live here. I should probably leave, no?"

"But where are you going to go?! For God's sake, the Israelis are bombing the roads in and out of Syria! Just stay here. It's safer."

In moments of fear, of all heightened emotion, in fact, the perceptual field narrows. All I could see was the need to escape. And the border with Syria was only 90 minutes away by car. How difficult or problematic would it be to make a quick getaway, even that very day?

I resolved to pack my things and make a run for it—aiming to get to Amman in Jordan, via Damascus, where I could catch a flight back to the UAE.

That afternoon, after a round of rushed goodbyes amid the psychic pandemonium, Eddy drove me down the mountain to the Charles Helou bus and taxi depot in Beirut. The plan was to hire a cab on the spot and make my getaway to Damascus. But when we arrived, the station was completely abandoned. There was not a bus or taxi in sight. At that moment my uncle called to tell us he'd heard there was already an exodus of people fleeing to the Syrian border and that the few cab drivers willing to make the trip had already been hired out, and at many times their usual rate. Furthermore, he said the Israelis were occasionally bombing targets in The Bekaa Valley—another Hezbollah stronghold—through which the road to the main Syrian border crossing passes.

"*Wallah*, I think it's better that you stay," Eddy said, as we drove back uphill to his place, past long queues of frustrated drivers lining up to panic-buy petrol at the gas stations.

. . .

I DISMISSED my family's repeated supplications to ride out the war and, upon our return to Beit Meri, pressed harder to find a vehicle. I hit up every contact I knew, and even phoned other Lebanese friends outside the country, in the off-chance they knew someone who could take me to Syria. By the mid-afternoon I had somehow secured a local limo driver from the nearby mountain town of Brummana, who picked me up almost immediately.

We set off via backroads through the mountains towards Bekaa. But there was a problem: my driver was deeply anxious and spent all his time on his phone soliciting info from his friends in the field who spoke hysterically on speaker phone. Most of what I understood sounded like wild rumour, fantasy even; and all of it of poor veracity. The Israelis were everywhere, my driver was told, and were shooting at anything that moved: dogs, cats, birds. After one absurd conversation about Israeli paratroopers hiding in Lebanese cedar trees and sniping at shepherds, the driver got off his mobile and did a U-turn.

"Sorry," he said, visibly shaken.

"What are you doing?"

"I'm taking you back."

"*What?!*" I shouted. "*Why?!*"

"There are Jews everywhere. We can't go further."

"Nonsense. There hasn't been an invasion. It's just the odd fighter jet."

"They are circling over Zahlé, just ahead. They'll bomb my car if they see us now."

"Why would they bomb our car? They're fighting Hezbollah, mostly in Dahieh and at the Israeli border."

"Didn't you hear what my friends said? The Israelis know *everything*. They're probably listening to our phones. Look: I'm turning off my phone now."

"But we're already part-way there. I'll pay you more!"

"So I could drive through Bekaa again on the way back? Forget it. It's a suicide mission."

"Jesus Christ," I moaned.

"Don't go to Syria after this. Better that you stay with your uncle. You're a foreigner. Listen to what he tells you: he knows best."

By the time the snakes-and-ladders routine had sent me back to where I started, things had gotten worse. Hezbollah fired rockets at the city of Haifa in northern Israel—a bold and provocative move. More worrying for me in the short-term was that the Israelis announced that they would knock out the Mudeirej Bridge on the Beirut-Damascus Highway that evening, making escape to Syria afterwards much more difficult, and, I assumed, even more expensive.

At that moment a friend in Dubai, who I had contacted earlier, texted me the number of a Syrian driver who was in the city and was ready and willing to take me to Damascus that same evening—as he only liked to drive at night. But here was the rub: we would have to cross that condemned bridge en route to Damascus. Because the Israeli military didn't advertise at what time they would be flattening the bridge, or any other target, there existed the utterly remote, yet highly angst-inducing possibility that the Israelis would strike the viaduct at the exact moment we were crossing it. Nonetheless, I seized the opportunity.

My uncle, who paced around with an old battery-powered transistor radio held to his ear, looked at me with horrified eyes as if I was doing the unthinkable. His wife and my three cousins all felt the same: it was an unnecessary risk, they said. It was also one which came on their watch. I was certain that so long as I was still on Lebanese soil, even while en route to Syria, they still felt responsible for me. When I reflected on things further, I realized it was bad enough that I was running away and leaving them behind to an uncertain fate, but being so hellbent on escaping was probably also a snub to their hospitality and offer of safety.

I wasn't usually prone to feelings of guilt, yet in the hours after hiring the latest ride to Syria, I was overcome by a sense of inadequacy around leaving; and that I didn't have the mettle to face these matters properly like my family. It was admittedly petty, but I also wondered whether, by fleeing, my Lebanese family would no longer see me as the special Eastern-leaning cousin among the Western branch of the family. Oddly, my status and reputation, my sense of self, seemed to hang in the balance. In the intervening hours before meeting the driver, I thought seriously of cancelling the trip and staying put. But, I didn't.

The third round of goodbyes was the most tense. Worry and disappointment on their part, guilt and apprehension on mine, intermingled as I reminded them with great diplomatic flourish that my parents were worried sick about me and that I was risking life and limb for mom and dad—and had no choice in the matter.

This time my uncle, his wife, and my youngest cousin, drove me to the rendez-vous spot: a large roundabout in the Beirut suburb of Sin el-Fil, where the Syrian driver, Majed, and his souped-up Oldsmobile hot rod awaited in steely anticipation.

"This is my nephew," my uncle said to the driver, when we arrived. "Make sure you get him to Damascus right away. Do you hear?"

"*Inshallah*, learned one," Majed said amused. "As you can see from its appearance, my car is fast."

I immediately thought of Han Solo from *Star Wars* plugging his Millennium Falcon to Obi-Wan.

"I once drove a couple from Damascus to Tadmor to pick up their son from prison," Majed continued. "The three-hour drive took just under two. My car is the fastest in all of Syria. Maybe in all of the East."

"Don't get into an accident!" my uncle added, verbalising another of his worries.

"Accident? Do you see dents anywhere on this car, old man? There is no fear."

I found out years later from my youngest cousin that once I

sped off with the swashbuckling Majed, fleeing the war that would last 34 days and which, thankfully, my relatives survived, both my cousin and his mom looked at each other and, thinking the exact same thing, simultaneously uttered these words about me, as if on cue:

"He's not a spy."

Beirut, Lebanon, 2006

The Port View Hotel sits unobtrusively, almost invisibly, at the far end of the city's Gemayze district, directly across the dysfunctional Électricité du Liban headquarters—the only building in Lebanon that enjoys round-the-clock grid power. The low-rise budget pension lives, ever so slightly, up to its name, with a very partial and unimpressive view onto the sea and the ugly industrial port infrastructure beside it. Its clientele includes French budget tourists, foreign sex workers, Lebanese military personnel, and shady businessmen from Russia, Sierra Leone and Nigeria.

An aging Christian Lebanese couple with deep Francophone pretensions run the hotel. The husband, Tony, is a charming man with a weathered, tanned face and a full head of jet-black hair, gelled back like a Spanish matador. He is debonair in an old school way but has the volatility of a Maronite mountain warlord. He comes to my table during breakfast, day after day, to show me the same photograph of him in an old Lebanese society magazine standing next to a former French ambassador.

"Jean-Pierre is still a close friend," Tony boasts. "He invited us to his chalet in the Alps. We're still thinking of going if we can get his email or phone number to remind him."

Tony's unruly, meddling wife, Giselle, a kind of Estelle Costanza in furry flip-flops and sweat pants, offers me 'jambon' during breakfast, from a special stash of Black Forest ham she keeps for favoured guests in a Tupperware container she carries clandestinely under her arm.

When not attending to hotel duties, the couple spend most of their time watching television and chain-smoking cigarettes.

During a speech by a black-clad Hassan Nasrullah, the head of the Lebanese Shia *militia, Hezbollah, the couple shed all business decorum and airs of Francophone civility in favour of confessional fisticuffs, shouting at the TV:*

Tony: Ayreh Feek! *('My penis inside of you!')*
Giselle: Kess Ommak *('Your mother's vagina!')*

The Forever Kingdom

The prophet said:
"The best of holy wars is his who speaks a just word in the presence of tyranny."
   – Abu Sa'id al-Khudri, in the *Collections of Tirmidhi*

It was billed as one of those serendipitous, providential, once-in-a-lifetime opportunities. The initial email from the head of the documentary unit at Al Arabiya, with whom I worked, revealed a man who wanted to keep his cards close at the start. "Special Job" was inscribed curiously in the subject line. "An interesting assignment that is unusually suited to you has come up," he wrote in the body of the note. "Please come see me and we'll discuss it." The email was cunningly crafted not only to waft the aromas of mystery but to reel me in to his presence in-person. Had he told me more from the outset, I might have hopped on the first plane to the furthermost point on Earth to escape.

When I arrived the next morning, predictably intrigued, at his office in Dubai Media City, Mr. Fakhry was finishing his morning Arabic coffee and watching an Al Arabiya news report about the death of one of its journalists in a US helicopter attack on militants in Baghdad. It was late 2004 and the insurgency in Iraq against the American occupation was well underway.

"That's our third employee killed by American fire since the war began," he said, raising the TV remote control to turn down the volume. "Hard not to think they're deliberately being targeted."

I knew Mr. Fakhry as well as one could know a commissioning editor with whom one worked at arm's length. I was producing and directing a documentary series for him called *War Zones* about the evolution of warfare into the modern age, in conjunction with the production arm of a Dubai-based think tank whose owner worked in partnership with Mr. Fakhry. The documentary chief was an amicable, multi-lingual and worldly Lebanese manager with shrewd business acumen who, like me, straddled East and West. He was gentle and fatherly with his employees, but was also a tough bargainer able to push back if things got difficult for him.

"So," he said, cutting our niceties short with a soft slap of his hand on the desk, "how would you like to take a break from the current project for a few months and go work in Saudi Arabia?"

Hearing those words was a bit like getting hit with a frisbee in the back of the head. *Fuck*, I thought in pained silence: *Saudi. For a few months*. I was likely visibly wincing.

The Al Arabiya documentary unit often took on productions in remote places—and on offbeat topics. I had prepared myself for getting dangled an assignment somewhere exotic like Tajikistan. Or maybe even Zanzibar. I knew a lot of people at the station who had formerly lived in Saudi, and heard about the uninspiring walled compounds, the non-alcoholic potables posing as real drinks, and the mind-numbing boredom of the place. I also wondered what—and how—on earth one would film there given the kingdom's secrecy and restrictions. That is, until I recalled in the next moment that Al Arabiya was owned by a powerful Saudi prince named Walid bin Ibrahim.

"What's wrong?" Mr. Fakhry asked, pretending not to know.

"*Saudi?*" I asked in a calculated tone of mild disbelief and disapproval.

"A government contract," he said, unperturbed. "But it'll be just as interesting as anything you're doing now—and maybe more so."

The Saudi interior and information ministries, he said, had teamed up to produce a series of public service announcements to air on Saudi TV, and on Saudi-owned stations in the Middle East, to discourage their youth from joining terrorist organizations, chiefly Al-Qaeda. A spate of bombings had targeted the country recently. Political analysts everywhere were speculating that the kingdom was in deep trouble because of that growing movement. The Saudis, Mr. Fakhry went on to say, were hiring notable directors from around the region to each work on a differently themed short video.

"So, it's a government propaganda video," I said.

"In a sense," Fakhry admitted without hesitation. "But *good* propaganda. And for a good cause. Our sister company in Riyadh is running the production. They've been having trouble finding someone skilled and trustworthy enough to work on their most important video."

He paused, dangling the obvious question in the air.

"And what would that be?" I asked.

"The one highlighting the strength of their special forces in fighting terrorism."

God, not another military video, I thought. "No I don't think so, Mr. Fakhry."

"This is a once-in-a-lifetime opportunity."

"Is it?"

"You're lucky. Few foreigners ever get to shoot *inside* Saudi Arabia. What is it called in the West: 'The Forbidden Kingdom?' And even *fewer* foreigners, if any, ever get to film these Saudi Green Berets. To call it 'privileged access' would be an understatement."

I held quiet.

Mr. Fakhry went on: "The idea is to dissuade young people who are thinking of signing up with Bin Laden. Given your work experience, and that you're a known entity to us, I naturally put your name forward. The fact that you're a Westerner is also a big plus."

I broke a tepid smile, both ever so slightly flattered and annoyed.

"So? Interested?"

I shrugged an indifferent shoulder.

"If it makes any difference it's also well paid," he said, cutting into my silent deliberations and naming an astounding, eye-watering figure soaked in crude.

"Aha," I said.

"I knew that might tip the scales. Anyway, you'll be out within three months, or sooner, if you can finish earlier. The videos are shorts—only 10 minutes long."

As I left his office, wondering if I had made a mistake agreeing to the job, I was pulled aside by Ahmed, a clownish Egyptian producer known for his troublemaking at the station.

"I heard they were going to ask you to work on the Saudi shoot. Is that why you were talking to Mr. Fakhry now?"

"I took the job."

"You agreed? Oh no!"

"What?"

'You shouldn't have."

"Why not?"

"Because you'll *never leave.*"

"Where? Saudi?"

"Yes."

I rolled my eyes.

"No, really. They'll take your passport when you arrive and they won't let you go home until you finish the job *to their* satisfaction—which is basically never."

"Who told you this?"

"Three people from the station who were supposed to be there only six weeks are still there, now—eight months later!"

"It'll be fine," I said, beginning to walk away.

"Don't go, John. You won't come back. You'll be there *forever*."

I raised my hand in the air defiantly, as I strode off.

"You'll wish you'd never have gone," he hollered after me. It's called 'The Forever Kingdom' for a reason!"

I MADE many positive assumptions about the Saudi assignment. You might even call them rationalizations. One of them, that I would be ensconced in stratospheric Arabian luxury befitting a VIP television director from Dubai hired to save the Kingdom from its malcontents, was shattered upon arrival in Riyadh, when my mini-bus driver pulled up to a bland-looking hotel with an empty beige interior that in my estimation barely eked out 3 stars. The second expectation, that I would be eased into the job, making the rounds of introductions over days, and by way of at least a few ceremonial—and grandiose—dinners of appreciation, also hit the shoals.

"We're going to the office for an evening meeting now," my Indian driver told me, moments before pulling up to the Hotel Disappointment. "Drop your bags off in your room. And bring your passport."

A very official and stuffy gathering of about eight men seated at a round table in their crisp white *dishdasha* robes and varying styles of headscarf arrangements was underway when I arrived at the production house board room. I was shown to an empty chair as a few of the men acknowledged me with tepid nods and mumbled greetings spoken under their breath. Another Indian man in a safari suit, who stood in the corner of the room with a large stylized coffee pot, approached me. He dropped a tiny thimble-like cup onto the table and poured a resinous and bitter green coffee, before going to another man to re-fill his cup.

I barely understood the Saudi dialect of Arabic being spoken, which sounded as alien to my demotic Egyptian as Hebridean English would to someone from Texas Hill Country. But from the few words I could discern, I surmised that I was in the presence of both the Saudi Deputy Ministers of Information *and* Interior, as well as with the principals of the production company.

Once the meeting broke, I was approached and welcomed by Abdullah, the head of the company. He had a politician's charisma, wore his red-and-white *shemagh* headscarf in the elegant *bint al-bakkar* fashion, and reeked of Arabian Oud—an expensive brand of medieval Arabic perfume made of resinous heartwoods which he used (I was later told) to announce his presence and status.

Abdullah shook my hand, touched his heart, and mumbled something unintelligible before shuffling towards the door to walk the assistant ministers out.

His deputy, Nasser, the company manager, followed on his heels. His manner was stiff and serious.

"You are working on our most important video," he declared, after his barrage of phlegmatic welcomes in English and Arabic.

"Mr. Fakhry told me."

"It will be called *Qowwat al-Haq* or 'The Power of Right.' You will film the indestructability of our Special Security Forces. You will show the world, properly, their indestructability, yes?"

"Yes," I responded, confidently. There was no other answer.

"The video will explain that with God's support the terrorists will be destroyed—and that any new recruits would suffer the same destructability."

When I asked Nasser who would help me with Arabic translation, given that my command of the written language was weak, he said that I would be working with a Syrian writer named Yasin. The Syrian would script the film narration in advance and translate it to English for me.

"Did you bring your passport?" he asked.

"Yes."

"Can I have it, please?"

I paused uncomfortably before answering. "What do you need it for?"

"To apply for your security clearance."

I handed it to him, relieved.

"But we will also keep it until you have done your job."

I remembered Ahmed's warning delivered as I left Mr. Fakhry's office: about the possibility of being held as a work hostage in Saudi.

"But the passport is my property," I protested. "What need is there to detain it?"

"Mr. John, please understand: this is a very serious work for the national security. Some foreigners in the kingdom sometimes run away, or escape, because life here is not as they'd like it. We cannot afford for this to happen with you."

"But that won't happen. I'm a professional. I'm from the West." I was about to add that I also wasn't some Malaysian housemaid wanting to flee the ill-treatment of her employers—but thought better of it.

"It is not a question of East or West. This job has to be completed and done correctly. King Abdullah, may God extend his life, will see your finished video and approve it when it's done. You will be able to leave once you are finished the project."

"Mr. Fakhry told me I would be here three months maximum."

Nasser paused, blinking rapidly in thought, almost confused. He then composed himself and nodded quickly, almost confidently, adding: "Allah willing."

MANY OF THE things we dread are more pronounced in the imagination than when lived out. After a few days roaming the city, I got the sense that Saudi Arabia wasn't the diabolical house of horrors that its hyperbolic detractors portrayed. But neither was it a flourishing society. What I saw of Riyadh at that time was a bland and sprawling expanse of storefronts, mosques, low-rises and walled compounds largely bereft of entertainment options that made its distant cousin Dubai, my home, actually seem quite charming. Much of the city had an austere quality, too. It was basic, uniform and modest: lacking frills and flourish. There was little recourse for leisure. The locally strict interpretation of Islam categorically forbade bars, cinemas, and live music. That same perspective lent a humourlessness and heaviness, a kind of forced solemnity that seemed to penetrate everything.

The most notable quality, however, was the dearth of visible females. Women were conspicuously and painfully absent, verboten, and in some cases discouraged from moving about in public alone. At first it just seemed like another conservative, male-dominated corner of the Middle East—of which there are many, even in the non-theocratic countries. But in Saudi it was next-level, and you could feel it viscerally. Not seeing females after a time had a strange effect on the mind: it was as if you inhabited only half a place, a realm of incompleteness and deprivation—one sporting the Yin but missing the Yang. I became utterly sensitized to their absence. As a result, I was able to pick up the faintest evidence of a woman's presence, even at the furthest reaches of my senses. I would catch fleeting glimpses of them: almost always in *niqab*, and often in the backseats of cars driving by, flitting between buildings on a side street, or trailing their husbands along the sidewalk somewhere in the distance. I soon found myself doing my shopping in the higher-end malls in the more upscale parts of town, where women were allowed to rove without their male guardians—just to experience something of the normality of my old life. The expensive malls were also where some women, including Western females, wore their hair coverings more loosely.*

This left the rest of the society to the men, whose presence was amplified by the lack of countervailing female energy. In the district where I stayed it was largely South Asian migrant workers dressed in *dishdashas* or *shalwar khamees*. A few moved with the restless determination of the workday hustle, but the majority stood idly on street corners, outside shops, or drifted seemingly with less purpose. Minutes before prayer times all storefronts closed and emptied suddenly, as if the day were ending. At that moment members of 'The Committee for the Promotion of Virtue and the Prevention of Vice,' the religious police, also known as the *Mutaween*, came out of the woodwork. This fraternity of literalist religious rule-enforcers fanned out across the urban landscape to ensure that shops closed during prayer times. They also herded men with batons into the mosques to pray, as if they were wayward sheep. The grave looking, steely-faced moral guardians were easily spotted with their long beards, loosely dangling headscarves worn hood-like, long flowing capes, high knee socks, and dress shoes. More than once I found myself staring face-to-face with these blinkered myrmidons, who would size me up and just barely, grudgingly, pass me by, owing to my obvious appearance as a foreigner—an identity I was more than happy to embrace and flaunt there in that moment.

THE RIYADH PRODUCTION company had done little to

---

* Kamal Bey once told me: "Most people don't know the hijab has its origins among Christian women in the Middle East, which Islam borrowed. There is also nothing in the Koran that states women must cover their hair—but only 'not to reveal their adornments' and 'guard their private parts,' out of modesty. The Prophet was trying, in part, to bring greater civility to the pagan tribes at the time."

prepare for our arrival, causing us to languish, initially, for weeks in the office with little to do. The fact that our departures were inevitably delayed as a result, didn't help us cope with the feeling that we were living in a sort of purgatory. I began to regret coming and soon desperately wanted to leave. Had it not been for the friendships that I struck up with other film directors brought in for the project, I might have tried to renege on the job, or failing that, to escape.

While there I met two film directors, Anas and Elie. Like myself, both were amalgams of Orient and Occident. Anas, who was based in Beirut and born of Danish and Syrian parents, was hired to work on a video about the successes of the Saudi education system in thwarting extremism. Elie, a tough-looking French-educated Maronite from the mountains of Lebanon, was there to direct a short fictional drama about a Saudi kid drawn into a circle of militants, and who ends up rejecting them.

Like prisoners adapting to their circumstances by fostering rituals to pass time, the three of us implemented an evening socializing routine that centred around food and drink and jocular dialogue. Each night after 'pre-gaming' in our hotel restaurant drinking "Saudi champagne" (carbonated fruit juices served in champagne glasses) and eating shrimp cocktail served out of a can,* we visited one of a number of small hole-in-the-wall eateries with garish neon lights, mirrors, and white-tiled walls for dinners of *kabsa* and *mendi*—local meat and rice dishes. Like everyone else at those establishments, we ate sitting on the floor, with our shoes off, and without the use of cutlery. Over meals we gossiped about office politics, exchanged cultural observations about Saudi, and swapped stories about our lives back home and our production experiences on the road. The crucible of deprivation

---

* We once broke with routine and took our pre-game to a 5-star restaurant at the Dubai-like Kingdom Centre skyscraper. Their Saudi champagne and shrimp cocktail were not much better than what our modest hotel served. Incidentally, the 41-story tower was a dead ringer for the fortress of Barad-dúr from the film version of *Lord of the Rings*, atop of which the all-seeing flaming Eye of Sauron roved.

had turned us, almost instantly, into the best of friends. A kind of family even.

Anas and Elie were also forced to surrender their passports upon arrival. They heard, through their respective grapevines, that our videos might not be initially approved upon completion by the authorities, even if they were honed to perfection. As directors, we needed that approval to wrap up and go home.

"The committee of judges apparently don't get along," Anas said. "So, they take turns spoiling the unanimity needed for a video to be approved, just to piss each other off."

I dropped the ball of rice and chicken I was kneading in my hand onto my plate, and put the dish down in disbelief. "That's only a rumour," I said in nearly heart-stopping angst to Anas. "Tell me it's a rumour."

Anas took a sip of his Mecca Cola and went on: "No, I heard it from Talal, who used to be one of the production judges. Khaled and Abdul-Aziz are rivals. Anything one of them likes, or supports, the other opposes out of spite."

"Normal," Elie said cynically in Arabic as he gnawed on his leg of lamb. "You basically just described Lebanon."

None of us wanted to become victims of The Forever Kingdom, working endlessly to get the propaganda messaging on point. Neither did we want to be the last to leave; condemned to pathetic Saudi champagne toasts and greasy mutton feasts alone amid the dusty palms and wide boulevards of a city whose maniacal avoidance of sin also had the effect of keeping the greatest virtues out of reach. We each kept tabs on one another's progress in our own silent races to the finish line, which couldn't come soon enough.

A GROUP of black-clad soldiers in bulletproof vests and metal helmets, and clutching semi-automatic weapons, dart stealthily towards the walls of a dilapidated compound in the desert. The men keep low to the ground, out of sight, and along the walls on both sides of its open main gate. The soldiers appear determined, lethal in countenance.

More troops appear holding ladders, which they prop against the compound walls. They await the signal to climb them like sprinters crouched at the starting line in a race. Further swarms of gun-toting warriors arrive from every direction and amass along the walls. The targets on the inside—two young militants playing video games—are oblivious to the forces amassed against them.

The leader of the commandos, a lean and muscular paragon of courage, the spear tip of God's retribution, deftly flings two grenades in quick succession into the compound from the open gate. His cohort at the other wall opposite him lobs tear gas canisters in the same direction.

Explosions shake the compound.

The black-clad fighters, uttering war cries, pour through the gate and scale the walls onto the gas-enshrouded grounds, firing their weapons in every direction. Pandemonium, a rabble of excited confusion, erupts. Endless bullet rounds pour forth in American-style action film overkill.

Moments later, the commando leader marches out of the house, through sheets of wafting tear gas, holding the two dejected-looking young men by the scruff of the neck. The other soldiers stand with their weapons aimed at the criminals, who are dragged from the compound to an awaiting vehicle.

"Okay, CUT!"

When we stop filming, the lead commando comes out of character, as if from a hypnotic state. He seeks me out and saunters up to me.

"Mr. John, there is a problem."

"What is it?" I say, suddenly worried we'd need to shoot the scene again.

"If this were real, we wouldn't have been so lenient towards those criminals," he said.

"But this is how we've outlined the story."

"Fine, but if you really want to frighten the young people watching, make sure you tell them in the video that the terrorists were lucky. In real life not one of them would be spared—even on appeals to Allah's mercy, or in sympathy for their mothers."

I WAS GIVEN complete and unfettered access to film the Saudi Special Security Forces at a secretive desert facility beyond the outskirts of the capital. The drive to their clandestine sanctuary, hidden by huge rocky outcrops, a place informally referred to by my driver as "The Nest," was long and monotonous, taking us through endless suburban sprawl that abruptly gave way to empty wasteland. We travelled in zigzags along dirt roads flanked by sand, kicking up enough dust to be seen from space, until we reached the gates of the compound. The facility was ringed with gargantuan coils of barbed wire fencing and enough humourless armed guards to keep both Godzilla and King Kong at bay. Inside, soldiers divided according to section, task and uniform, manned the stations where they would demonstrate to us their special warfighting prowess.*

The Saudi Special Security Forces were a hybrid entity mixing riot, SWAT, and paramilitary functions. The force was created after the poor performance of the Saudi National Guard in trying to quell a revolt at the Grand Mosque at Mecca in 1979. Their specific remit among the constellation of eight military entities in the kingdom, was fighting domestic terrorism and providing riot control and bodyguard service for VIPs. The force was front and

---

* The Saudi authorities used the military display and production day to also host a group of British special forces officers from the celebrated SAS. They were inspecting the troops and facility in advance of sending their own counter-terrorism trainers to instruct the force as part of the coordinated 'war on terrorism.'

centre in the war against Al-Qaeda in Saudi Arabia, a conflict which climaxed that very year. The militant group's many attacks across the country killed several dozen people, including a handful of foreigners.

For days in succession, we filmed the soldiers in highly choreographed scenes: belaying from ropes down helicopters and cliff faces, doing group karate and kung fu, mimicking hostage rescues from hijacked busses, and engaging in high-speed chases with terrorist villains, who in some cases were gunned down and smeared with fake blood for the cameras.

"By God, Al-Qaeda will run like frightened children when they see this video," one of the base commanders, the first military officer I'd ever seen sporting a massive white beard, exclaimed with pride. A group of us sat on the ground around an eight-foot wide brass dish, eating from a gargantuan mound of chicken and rice.

"Even the unborn children of the terrorists will flee from their mother's wombs," he added, sucking the cooking juices from his fingers. The other white-bearded officers, all wearing berets, nodded and chuckled along in unison as they ate.

In spite of those 'lighter' moments, there were also difficulties on set: I didn't have much agency during the shoot. Although I was the proverbial 'director', I actually made few directorial decisions. An Egyptian production manager named Wael, who led the mostly Syrian and Egyptian crew, took nearly all the decisions. He only came to tell me what he had done, after the fact. When I tried to impose myself more and take the reins, he feigned obedience but still did what he wanted.

At first, I took Wael's behaviour as a kind of insubordination borne of jealousy—a snub against the foreigner and pure Westerner he took me to be. I knew that, in Middle Eastern culture, power and strength had to be exercised in order to earn respect, so I decided to establish my authority.

During one take of the bus hijacking scene, I huffed, got off my director's chair and walked straight to Wael and took him by the arm, pulling him aside.

"You're staging this wrong. The Minister of Information has put me in charge. Going forward you and the crew are going to do exactly as I tell you. Understand?!"

Wael stared at me in disbelief. "But *why* do you want to work? You are *the director*."

"Yes, that's exactly who I am. And you're going to do as I say."

"*But...* the director *doesn't* work."

"What are you talking about?"

"You are the Big Man. You are the boss. *We* do the work *for you*."

"*What?*"

"We do the direction. Your job is just to watch and yell at us for doing it wrong, and to tell us to do it again. *You are the boss.*"

Wael was trying to tell me that I was too high up the production chain-of-command to be involved in any of the directorial decisions. Directing was a small job and he was asserting his duty in deference.

"You're from Canada—a VIP," he reiterated. "Foreigners don't work."

"My parents are born in Egypt. I'm like you!"

Wael became horrified. He looked around him to take stock of who was listening, and pulled me further aside and began to whisper.

"Keep your voice down, *Sidi*. You don't want everyone knowing that about you."

"I don't care."

"You should. Only Indians, Pakistanis and Bangladeshis are worse off than Egyptians here—and not by much. Listen, you have a Canadian passport, right?"

"Yes."

"Then you're officially a Canadian director—praise Allah. Now go sit down and let us finish the shooting. We want to go home today!"

After several days of filming anything and everything to do with Saudi paramilitary and law enforcement, I finally met Yasin. He was the Syrian script writer on our project, a veteran government propagandist who formerly worked with the Syrian state broadcaster—but had fallen afoul of his masters because of his pro-reform ideas.

"I'm taking you to the best restaurant in Riyadh to celebrate our great collaboration and friendship," Yasin said during our first meeting, leading me to a modest hole-in-the-wall eatery across the street from our production building.

Yasin was originally from Tell Abyad, a small Syrian town on the Turkish border near my paternal grandfather's home town of Mardin. Tell Abyad straddled every ethnic fracture in the area and would later be fought over, several times, by all factions of the Syrian civil war. Though Yasin was all smiles, flattery and compliments, he also had a contentious and duplicitous side. No matter what you spoke to him about, he would constantly fish for information while his head turned with schemes. He embodied an old Syrian proverb: "Kiss any arm you cannot break, and pray to God to break it." He also loved eating lamb chops, and took me to his favourite kitchen where the staff knew his name.

Yasin waited for the delicious food to be served—and our dopamine to spike—before telling me that he didn't abide by my story outline to write his narration and script.

"I've changed the video," he said in passing, putting down a gnawed lamb chop onto the heap of bones he had accumulated.

"What do you mean?" I asked in horror.

"I've added more narration about the Koran, and written a longer condemnation of the unbelievers and their attacks. The king will be watching it. We have to make the leader happy."

What he told me was bad news. It meant I needed additional

footage that I didn't have to cover his new narration. What I had shot was no longer enough. I protested vehemently.

"*Inshallah*, it will work," he said, unconcerned. "You'll see."

He picked up another chop from the plate of mixed grill and bit into it with relish.

"Easy for you to say, Yasin. Even if the stock footage exists, it'll take weeks to gather—and more weeks to go through. You know how slow things move here. I have to go back to Dubai soon."

"So, what are you saying?"

"You have to change back the script to what we had agreed on!"

Yasin assumed a pained look. He pulled out a cigarette from his pack, lit it, and then rubbed his temples gravely with his free hand as he leaned forward on his elbow staring at his heap of bones. The deliberate display of melodrama lasted for half a minute.

"Brother John, as God is my witness," he began, looking at me again, and pointing to the ceiling, "as the Lord of Majesty and Bounty himself hears me now: I'll do all in my power to help you in this matter. I'll speak to the big boss for you. Not Abdullah, the head of the company, but someone even more powerful than him. We'll get your footage in two days. By Allah the Wise, this is what will happen."

"Yasin—"

"Brother John. Listen to me. *Please*. I am from Tell Abyad. Your grandfather is from Mardin. We are like cousins, family. Brothers, even. We're far from home in this horrible, horrible place. We have to help each other while we're here. We only have each other. I would never let you down."

"So, you'll change the script back?"

"I cannot, but by Allah, you have my word that I live each moment thinking how best to serve you and this great video that will save the kingdom, and the entire Arab World, from these unbelievers. *Inshallah*, all will be fine. You will see."

I received my English translation of Yasin's script the next day, but afterwards he was nowhere to be found. He didn't pick up his phone, or respond to my text messages. Neither, I found out later, had he spoken to any bigwigs about speeding up the process of getting the needed stock footage.

It took weeks to get a stack of a dozen or so tapes containing short and anaemic snippets of old news footage to cover his new narration—most of it of varying and poor quality. I barely had enough to work with.

Meanwhile, Anas had told me that two other directors hired to work on our project in the city of Jeddah on the Red Sea coast, had completed their videos—but had their works rejected by the committee. They were being forced to shoot additional material and recut their films. The Forever Kingdom had claimed its next victims.

I myself had already been away for three months and was feeling the strain—a monotony of existence that had no precedent. To make matters worse, my girlfriend back in Dubai was complaining to me about my absence. Other men, she added, acquaintances from our wider circle of "friends," had begun hitting on her thinking that my being in Saudi meant I was gone for good and would never return.

"Are you really going to come back?" she asked.

"What kind of ridiculous question is that?" I fired back over the phone.

"Everyone says that people who go to Saudi stay there forever. That the money is too good to leave."

I realized I had to take a more active and strategic approach to ensuring my timely escape. The only way to do this would be to dazzle the committee of judges with the final product, such that they wouldn't detain me indefinitely with endless changes. I would have to create a video that would fill the Saudi reviewers with immeasurable pride: a film so action-packed and emotionally compelling that the higher-ups would never think of rejecting it. I decided to maximize the bling factor. I would employ split-screens as well as the best electronic music with fast cuts in action sequences to create a sort of public service announcement-cum music video whose voice of God narration scripted by Yasin the arch-propagandist, would sow fear into every would-be Saudi militant from Dammam to Dhahran.

WEEKS LATER, as I was nearing completion of the video in the manner I had envisioned, I received a phone call in the edit suite.

"Mr. John, please, come to my office now," Nasser, the production house manager, said curtly before hanging up.

I looked at Mazen, my Syrian video editor, and told him that Nasser wanted to see me. He averted his eyes and said he would take a cigarette break.

When I got to Nasser's office and sat down, he closed the door behind me. He was grim-faced, and wringing his hands in worry. I too became anxious. I was only days away from finishing the job and, I hoped, leaving the country. I didn't need any more setbacks.

"We have a very serious problem," he said, sitting down. "It's with the footage you used of the king."

Yasin had written a new sequence into the film demonstrating the Saudi regime's previous attempts to be merciful and lenient towards Al-Qaeda members. In it, King Abdullah reads a past amnesty declaration encouraging all militants to turn themselves in voluntarily. In return for doing so, they were offered forgiveness and no jail time. As it happened, only one person surrendered himself after that declaration: a strait-laced and clean-shaven middle-aged man wearing a safari suit. The man looked very much like an actor pretending to be a terrorist, so that the regime would save face when no one actually turned themselves in. We had old news footage of that man surrendering, which I placed side-by-side in split-screen with footage of King Abdullah reading the amnesty declaration. Mazen, the editor, insisted that it was a bad creative idea to use the split-screens there. I didn't ask him why and simply overruled him. Mazen had obviously gone and told Nasser.

"What's the issue exactly?" I asked. "You approved that scene in the script. And you chose the footage."

Nasser took a few seconds to find the right words. "In our country," he began, "the king is a very special man."

I nodded in agreement.

"He is very powerful. Respected. He can do anything he likes, unlike the Queen of England or the King of Spain who are bound by rules. He has the power to make you a millionaire, or sentence you to death, with a snap. He holds all of our lives in his hands. Because of that the king cannot be shamed or criticized. Do you see what I mean?"

I tried hard to connect the dots. "No, I'm sorry, I don't."

Nasser became ever more uncomfortable and frustrated. He took a breath and sighed deeply before speaking: "Mr. John, we cannot make a video showing the king with a criminal. I feel filthy just saying it."

"Which criminal?"

"With this... man who surrendered himself in the amnesty!"

"But the news reported it. We're using footage that was already shown on TV. Everyone has seen it already."

"You don't understand. You put the two men *in the same shot*. You placed them physically next to each other. The king and this man would never be seen together in real life. It would be an insult. It would be *haram*."

"But, Nasser, they're not actually with each other *in the same place*. It's not literal. It's just an illustration showing cause-and-effect in the same moment."

Nasser shook his head vehemently and tsk'd rapidly in disapproval. "No. This logic and philosophy is incorrect," he said. "We don't think like that here. In our country what matters is *appearance*. That's all that counts. It's simple. The video shows them together—and so *they are* together. If the king sees this, if the committee sees it, it will be not just a big problem, but a *very big* problem for us. And just as much for you."

"Okay, but—"

"Please, Mr. John. This is very sensitive. You will need to change it right now and hope the royal palace doesn't hear about it. Mazen told us—and he also told Yasin. And Yasin stupidly told everyone. The whole office knows now. The sooner you fix this, the better for you."

IN SPITE OF THAT HICCUP, the Forever Kingdom, in the end, did not claim me. I completed *The Power of Right*, my first and only government propaganda video, set to deep baritone narration and electronic music that threatened death and destruction to Saudi Al-Qaeda members, in just four months—one month later than I was promised to be out. The committee who screened it enjoyed and approved it, though likely also because the videos they watched just before it were tepid and poorly produced—and were thus rejected.

I was finally free to go.

Since then, the Forever Kingdom has turned out to be less "forever" than expected. A bolder, more brash, and less conservative faction of Saudi leaders, led by the crown prince and de facto ruler of the country, seized power in Saudi Arabia some years later. The new clique modelled themselves along the more Westernized and forward-looking countries of the Gulf: places like Qatar and the United Arab Emirates. Saudi underwent a large transformation as a result. The government clipped the wings of the once all-powerful religious authorities whose influence over all aspects of society and life were greatly curtailed. The country enjoys more social freedoms, partly as a result. Women have been granted some rights: they mix more freely with men in public without persecution or shame. They are not required to cover themselves with an *abaya* and *hijab* and are now permitted to drive cars. Cinemas, too, have opened.

Yet at the same time, a mafia-style clan politics and domestic political repression have deepened. Those same people are trying to establish Saudi as a non-aligned middle power that more aggressively seeks to shape the Middle East in its image, while it cozies up to fellow autocrats in China and Russia, and has at times made strategic inroads with Israel.

It is said, by a few people who know, that the *ancien regime*—the previous power-wielding branch of the Saudi royal family that was overthrown—though it may have had its own excesses and vices, also maintained a kind of dignity, refinement, or etiquette in behaviour even, compared with its current stock of rulers.

This flip-flop, this new configuration of positives and negatives, was entirely unexpected. Sudden, sweeping change, when it comes, occurs on no one's terms but its own.

Somewhere in the Arabian Gulf, 2003

"So, whaddaya think, guys?" the American naval officer asks, wearing a wide smile. "She's a beaut, inshee?

The uniformed man keeps his voice low so as to not disturb his colleagues working diligently all around us.

"I've never seen anything like it," I say, truthfully.

"No one ever has. I mean... before they actually do."

My Lebanese cameraman Zouheir doesn't break concentration as he films the litany of glowing screens manned by sailors in military attire working with intense focus.

"Yup. Five acres of sovereign American territory we can take anywhere in the world. Wait till you see the night landings. You all say you're from Al-ERAB-eeya?"

We are in the Flight Deck Control area of the American aircraft carrier USS Nimitz during the Second Gulf War in 2003. It is nighttime. "The Tower," as it is also called, glows like an old video arcade parlour cast in clinical blue light. It has the mood and feel of a quiet hospital ward during a nightshift. A medley of F-18s, A-10 Warthogs, AWACS planes, and troop carrier aircraft, just back from their missions and bombing runs, are circling overhead, waiting to land.

Since arriving a few days earlier, we've filmed planes taking off and landing, and weapons depots in the hangar bay. We've interviewed pilots before and after their bombing missions, and as they signed their names on the outside of ordinance with personal messages to Saddam Hussein and the Iraqi Army.* All of them told us in no uncertain terms and in the indistinguishable drawls of

---

* More surreal yet was discovering Hispanic indentured labourers from Latin America working menial jobs at the bottom of the ship in exchange for a green card after five years of service.

Nebraska, Florida and Montana that they were proud to defeat the enemies of The Red, White and Blue and bring freedom to the people of the Middle East.

Zouheir and I set up the camera and tripod on an outdoor walkway that runs around the side of the tower and overlooks the flight deck. We film the planes landing in succession. I try to take photos with my stills-camera. Because it is nighttime the flash on my camera goes off automatically.

Moments later the door to the tower bursts open.

"Who in fucking hell's name..?!"

An officer we were introduced to earlier, known in aircraft carrier lingo as "The Miniboss," comes storming down the walkway towards us. He has the look of an irate Walter Sobchak, the character played by John Goodman in The Big Lebowski.

"WHAT. THE FUCK. ARE YOU DOING?!" he screams at the top of his lungs, hurling spittle. "THAT camera flash will get those pilots killed! Do you know how risky these night landings are?!"

"Sorry, I didn't—"

"SOR-RY?! This filming session is now over! Get off the tower!

"But—"

"What are you people doing here, anyway?!" he scoffed, oblivious to the irony of his question. "You don't belong here! Go back to where you came from!"

The Cyclone

I shuffled out of Dubai airport, through the terminal's perfume-scented and futuristic shopping mall bling, in a stupor of fatigue. My friends, a generous crew of Arab media colleagues, were waiting to pick me up in the parking lot. I followed their text message prompts leading me to a shiny black Range Rover where I was met with a flurry of enthusiastic back-slaps and Arabic cheek kisses set to repeat.

"*Hamdellah 'ala el salama!*" rang the ritual Arabic greeting. ('Praise be to God for your safe arrival').*

Moments later we screeched out of the lot and onto the knotted highway overpasses of Dubai, framed by the distant glitter of sci-fi skyscrapers winking in the night.

It was 2005. I had just returned home from a month-long trip to the parched Nubian Desert region of Sudan. Though I was back to familiar haunts, another universe by comparison, the slower, timeless Saharan rhythm still held sway. In that state of heightened sensitivity, I discerned something was amiss in the vehicle. A faintly palpable tension hung in the air amid all the

---

* An expression harkening back to a period in history when travels were far more lengthy, dangerous and uncertain.

questions about my trip, and all the banter and laughter. My friends were behaving strangely. They appeared preoccupied, even entranced. They were also giddier than normal, while being guarded and secretive.

"Where are we going?" I asked during the first real pause in the conversation.

No one responded, as if they hadn't heard me.

I waited and repeated the question.

Basil, the driver, and Wajdi in the passenger seat, looked at each other. Basil then looked over his shoulder and said to me, "We're taking you somewhere *special*."

Sam, who sat beside me, wore an indecipherable smirk. He took a drag of his cigarette and grabbed my arm, saying, "It's a surprise."

I would have had no objection to this playfulness if it wasn't for the fact that the collective mood suggested something devious at play that I wasn't going to like.

It was only when we came into the city's Oud Mehta district, an undeveloped area of industrial buildings at the edge of the desert, that it dawned on me what was likely happening. As we drove through a lonely roundabout, an isolated shoebox-shaped building with bright lights appeared off in the distance.

"Oh God," I said, with a feeling akin to horror.

All three broke into boisterous laughter.

"Yes, my friend," Sam said, indicating the joke was up.

I placed the palm of my hand over my face. "The Cyclone?!" I asked, in a pained voice.

"We figured you experienced a lot of deprivation in Sudan," Sam quipped.

More laughter.

"You've started going there?" I asked incredulously. "I go away for a month and look what happens."

"It's our therapy for living in Dubai," Sam said again.

"I'm just back from the desert. I'm not interested. Turn the car around."

"It's for your own good," Wajdi said.

"You'll change your mind once you're there," Basil added.

Sam, beside me, looked at me again, still wearing that deep smirk, which was now etched even wider.

"Welcome home," he said, grabbing and squeezing my arm with enthusiasm.

WHEN I ACCEPTED a job offer to work as a TV producer in Dubai, I had little idea what to expect from this burgeoning renaissance city in the desert. Much of the Arabian Gulf was still a mystery to me, beyond some vague impressions arrived at by deduction. It was a blank spot on my mental map, a place of cultural vacuousness and empty spaces marked by its penchant for Western suburban perks that I had travelled to the Middle East to avoid. In terms of its people, I imagined a hunter-gatherer culture that had unhealthily leapfrogged into modernity overnight, embracing some of our worst trappings along the way. It also seemed a place for unadventurous expats, who could wall themselves within the protective womb of a housing compound.

But as I rationalized moving for the job, Dubai—or rather, the idea of Dubai—began to strike a chord in that part of me seeking a certain synthesis that included more East but which came with more than a dose of West. In fact, on paper it was brilliant. Here was a city racing to become an international crossroads and entrepôt par excellence; a William Burroughs-style 'interzone' of overlapping regional spheres, bringing everyone near and far into a mélange of longitudinal shades of Orient and Occident. By the time I boarded the plane, I resolved Dubai would be the answer to my vagabond quest to find a suitable receptor for my unusual mix of East and West.

Yet the reality was somewhat otherwise. Instead of civilizational fusion and the harmonious intermingling of people promised by the Dubai PR spin doctors, what I found was an incongruous graft of awkward and colliding influences: a mostly imitation West transplanted into an austere version of East. At the surface, Dubai was somewhat absurd and built on the formula that bigger was better: cutting-edge skyscrapers that raked the stratosphere, idyllic retirement-style suburbs with manicured grass on reclaimed desert, palatial hotels, and boundless shopping malls built with grandiose historical motifs and themes. We've long heard of the city's archetypal dolmens, most of which were under construction when I arrived: the indoor ski hill, the Palm-shaped island-peninsulas seen from space, the highest building in the world, the 7-star hotel, and other such superlative monuments to superficiality. Dubai was a giant residential amusement park, a plastic bubble. It's what the late American author Daniel Boorstin, writing about the United States, referred to in his classic 1960s book, *The Image*, as a "pseudo-event": the product of a culture that manufactures and worships virtual experiences over the real.*

At the human level, the country was a segregated patchwork of ethnicities and classes strictly subdivided into hierarchies of salary and status—which, regardless of how the nation's rulers framed their cross-cultural experiment, was an undeniable reality. The pyramidal structure became plainly obvious after only a short time there. The host Emiratis, a numerically dwarfed minority, occupied the peak and top echelon. They were the people apart. You'd speak with them at government offices, see them walking arm-in-arm in the shopping mall, or watch them speed past you in a cloud of sports car dust on the highway before you even saw them coming in the rear-view mirror. But unless you directly did business with them, there was little contact. Westerners, merce-

---

* 'Wild Wadi', a waterpark that simulates a desert flash flood, 'Ski Dubai', the indoor snow-hill inside of the Mall of the Emirates shopping centre, and the waterways at Madinat Jumeirah, a hotel-shopping-dining complex which fuses Venetian-style canals with old medieval Arabian architecture, were all examples of this.

nary workers, many of whom were entrepreneurs or held plum positions at financial and multi-national corporations, came next down the ladder. They flocked to Dubai for the tax-free salaries and lives that revolved around beach parties, binge drinking, and weekends in Sri Lanka and Goa. A whole mid-section of peoples spanning Arabs, Iranians, and various Eurasians occupied the merchant and managerial sectors. Further down, Filipinos tended to work in retail and fast food. Malaysian and Indonesian women often worked as maids for wealthy residents. And South Asians, Indians and Pakistanis, ironically those with whom the Gulf region had some of the longest and deepest historical relationships, did much of the manual and tech-support work.[*] They, along with the Sri Lankans, Bangladeshis and Nepalis (those lowest on the UAE status rung) comprised the indentured labourers in the construction sector—the untouchables in blue or orange uniforms famously housed in decrepit camps in the desert and worked to the bone, sometimes in extreme heat, for minuscule pay. There were hundreds of thousands of them across the country. This underclass built everything in the UAE, including the countless skyscrapers and office towers, which grew like bamboo, seemingly overnight.[†] So deep did this caste system run that there was even a separate older terminal at Dubai's fancy international airport devoted solely to the war-zone and underclass destinations on the map: the Kabuls, the Quettas, the Baghdads, amid whose unglamorously bland walls and crammed gates thronged a bouillabaisse of extended families in flip-flops, *niqabs* and *shalwar kameez*.

Orbiting Dubai's foundational humanity like sub-atomic particles was another stratum of more weakly-tethered souls drifting upon currents of greed, desperation or ideology: these

---

[*] There were of course many exceptions within this class structure—and increasingly so in time as India became less impoverished in subsequent years.
[†] Nepalese Sherpas, because of their acclimatization to Himalayan altitudes and a lack of fear of heights, were sought after as workers for the super hi-rises. The word *Sherpa* means 'Easterner' in the Nepalese language.

were the underworld elements. An unsavoury pastiche of shysters, charlatans, grifters, spies, smugglers, terrorists, organized criminals, and sex workers existed in sufficient numbers that seeing them in plain sight, or even meeting them, was unavoidable for anyone living in Dubai. The Afghan and Pakistani Taliban and Al-Qaeda could sometimes be reliably spotted in some of the more traditional quarters, especially parts of Deira and Bur Dubai. The UAE was a neutral zone for them. Rumours circulated that the country's rulers had struck a deal with the militants to let them operate in the country, largely unfettered—in return for them not attacking it. Dubai was arguably the softest target for Westerners in the entire Middle East. And indeed, the inconceivable lack of such attacks, or even known attempts at them, suggested the rumours were likely true. Even Kamal Bey, who was usually tight-lipped about security matters, could not help but make ironic and oblique comments about how "every *bête noire* from the 'Who's Who of the World's Most Wanted'" was passing through and operating in Dubai.

The common denominator, however, that linked nearly all of us magnetized to Dubai at that time, was that we all had a weak or tenuous sense of place—or were outright running away from something. The city became a sort of way station occupied by the itinerants, the lost ones, the drifters and exiles—some of them looking to make a fast buck, others seeking something they couldn't quite articulate.* All of this humanity spun in a cyclonic vortex, like a revolving door, that sucked in new souls, and spat out the inevitably disillusioned.

---

* More positively, Dubai has served as a surrogate home for many people from surrounding countries in need of one. It is a safe haven for the persecuted and those fleeing conflicts. It is also a place for the unemployed to find work. Annual remittance flows from expat workers to their low and middle-income countries from the UAE alone are in the tens of billions of dollars.

WHEN WE PULLED into the parking lot of The Cyclone—where a pandemonium of bottlenecked vehicles and people were coming in and out—I knew my kidnappers were utterly serious. Up until we arrived, I expected to be let in on the joke (and let off the hook) at the last second.

"After you left to Sudan, we came here *once*. But only out of curiosity," Basil said, after finding a parking spot. "We've been back a few times since."

In retrospect, I could have tried to snatch my travel bags from the trunk, bid my abductors *adieu*, find a cab and make for the comfort and safety of my apartment from which I had been separated for so long. But a powerful peer pressure (in some ways as coercive as that experienced in youth), held me in check. Any attempt to escape would have involved considerable resistance and a scene. More importantly, it would have meant an unacceptable breaking of rank with my friends.

And then, as Basil had said, there was the curiosity.

For obvious reasons, a reputation of roguishness attached itself to The Cyclone. I'd long heard about the place and wondered what it would be like to enter its semi-forbidden confines. I was a journalist after all, a chronicler. It was my job to bear witness to humanity and bring to light its manifold challenges and conditions. Could I not infiltrate as a detached observer for the benefit of others, without catching bordello fever or becoming debauched in the process? But my inner devil's advocate told my false rationalizer (working overtime in that moment) that I *didn't really* have any intention of writing about The Cyclone. And besides, I'd never be able to report on the place journalistically in the press while living there without possibly getting scolded by officials, and/or deported from the country.

This dialogue in my head ended as the pressure gradient forces of The Cyclone drew us in. We coughed up a hefty cover charge to the gargantuan brutes guarding the door and crossed into an alternate reality cast surrealistically in curtains of dry ice smoke and set to the thump of deep trance music.

THERE WAS much unlikeable about Dubai, but which one had to live with. Yet there were two things that really unsettled me about the place, and which greased the wheels of my eventual exit from the city. One was the sight of veteran expat Westerners who had remained there far past their 'best before' dates. These people had become a kind of inner mush (the soul equivalent of a flabby muscle left unexercised), protected in their bubble from the push-and-pull forces of the outside world. They were conditioned to façades and superficiality, and poisoned by the Faustian bargain of living in a city-state that emanated a meaningless pretence. Among other things, it made them conviction-less believers in both everything and nothing.

The second was the ubiquity of prostitution.

As a gold-rush town, labour camp, and international entrepôt, Dubai magnetized sex workers, who, like everyone else, also went there seeking opportunity. They hailed from countries like Senegal and Morocco on the periphery of West Africa, through to Europe and the former Soviet Republics of Central Asia, all the way to the Far East and Russia's Siberian Pacific.

Though it is inevitable that some of these women were tied up with criminal syndicates and human trafficking, many others weren't professional prostitutes, or otherwise coerced into the work. Some came to try their hand, so to speak, at sex work for the first time—and to claim their slice of fortune, tantalized by legends of gold-lined thoroughfares commandeered by filthy-rich businessmen in Jaguars. Some sought wealthy husbands carrying passports to prime destinations in the West.

I came to be acquainted with these women, albeit at a

distance, because they were literally my neighbours. They lived in my district of Mankhool, a middle-class rent-affordable conglomerate of newly-built behemoth low-rise condo blocks in the Bur Dubai quarter. By day, the ladies walked these streets on foot, often in groups of three or four, as long queues of mostly Middle Eastern men cruised past them in their cars. This technically made my neighbourhood a red-light district. My future Bosnian-German girlfriend, who I later lived with in Dubai, would sometimes return home in tears from an excursion on foot to the grocery store, after being mistaken for a sex worker and luridly and aggressively propositioned by one or more of these lecherous drivers. Meanwhile, I often got the other end of the stick: I was sometimes accosted by these ladies, and at times, tenaciously. In fact, only days after first arriving in the city, I was ambushed late at night outside a 24-hour Kinkos Copy Center, and chased down the sidewalk by a desperate Chinese sex worker in a glittery black dress and thick florescent eyeshadow, begging for my patronage. She didn't speak English and probably hadn't worked for many nights.*

Given the Middle East's mercantile culture and its preponderance of *souqs*—markets—some of them specializing in the most specific commodities, it was no surprise that the preference in Dubai was to corral prostitution into venues that were self-contained physical marketplaces. Hotel bars and nightclubs across the city, especially most of the 3-star joints in and around the older Bur Dubai and Deira areas, took on that role and became especially known for them.

However, one venue in particular was the apotheosis, Mecca, and supreme clearing house of Dubai's sex *souq*s. It was located surreptitiously behind the American Hospital at the edge of the desert in Oud Mehta, and, unlike other bars, was *not* inside of a

---

* East Asian sex workers didn't fare well in the primarily Middle Eastern environment as Arab men were seldom interested in them. Racism and a perceived absence of cultural affinity informed that attitude.

The Cyclone

hotel (as strictly required bylaw). The Cyclone was a super nightclub, a quintessential marketplace and *maison de prostitution*, where vendors and clients came together in Dubai's garish attempt at a remake of Studio 54 at unimaginable scale. With a capacity of 5,000 souls, a "United Nations of prostitution" as it was called, The Cyclone was appropriately supersized to go with Dubai's other monuments to grandeur. The owners, who were reputedly Indians from London, must have had a moment of deep laughter coming up with the name, which was somehow oddly appropriate.

I had heard much about The Cyclone and about Dubai's sex workers, as some of my other Arab male colleagues at the TV news station became involved with them. It was culturally acceptable in the male-dominated society of the Middle East for men to barter for sex; and for them to brag about it openly. Though I wasn't puritanical or judgemental about the notion of sex work, it nonetheless struck me as problematic and sometimes tragic because of the tie-ins to human trafficking, poverty, health issues and exploitation.

Yet our psyches are made up of a collection of different sub-personalities. Thus, to a different part of me, where waking awareness meets the murkier unconscious, the very idea and possibility of accessible sex tantalized. It also appealed to a part of the mind that seemed to have its own appetites and will. The exotic overtones and sordid novelties of this very unfamiliar and far-away land of bartered pleasures appealed to my sensation-seeking and voyeuristic side. Which is why, taken altogether, even though I felt great aversion to visiting The Cyclone, I did nothing to extricate myself from the situation that landed me there.

When the dry ice smoke cleared and my eyes adjusted to the darkness, a fantastical scene revealed itself: women of all ages standing side by side in neatly-arranged human corridors—posing, glancing, smiling—as currents of men, some of them barely able to contain their enthusiasm, sauntered by, drinks in hand, surveying them. The women were as varied as one would expect from a place as international and multicultural as Dubai. I reflexively attached identities to all of them as I stood at a distance and watched: the bleach-blonde Uzbek from Samarkand in a halter-top and spandex, sharing a pack of Marlborough reds with her near identical twin from Bokhara; the Romanian brunette with a Marilyn Monroe beauty mark on her cheek wearing tight jeans, red high heels, and a blazer, straddling a bar stool while chewing gum and sipping a Piña colada; the busty Azeri from Baku in a glittering blue evening dress whose natural good looks were scuttled by the over-application of every sort of finery. Meanwhile, scores of others barely stood out, or looked the part: they could have been anyone—your neighbour, co-worker, or sister. The women appeared to defy all expectations and stereotypes of sex workers we hold in the West: bedraggled ladies of the streets whose ranks are filled with abused women from broken families, who have a hard drug addiction. The people before me seemed, and perhaps in many cases were, more volitional in their work. Although they were no doubt driven by a lack of opportunity or validation, there was still something of the party girl in their fragile yet brash demeanours. But then all of this, I realized, may have been applicable just to one sex worker demographic in Dubai: the nightclub set, the tip of a hidden iceberg that was likely more often criminal and exploitative. The men, ranging from handsome and sharp young professionals to rotund and sleepy-looking 50-and-60-somethings armed with Viagra in their back pockets, endlessly circled the floor, mustering up the courage to make their most suave approach.

    I came out of my daze and realized that my friends, who were just beside me moments ago, were now scattered to the cyclonic gales. I was gobsmacked by the strangeness of it all: how just hours before I was in the austere grip of the Sudanese desert, another universe by comparison.

I decided to move closer to the action and headed to the bar where I ordered a Heineken from one of the young bartenders. All around me, women, some alone, others in twos and threes laughing and enjoying themselves, turned to size me up, some more suggestively than others. I did nothing to encourage them, and resolved just to watch the dynamics unfold—close enough to sometimes read lips and body language, and in some cases to even hear words spoken.

I noticed that in the time it took for an interested man to ask a woman her name, she had already decided whether or not he was acceptable. With the clock ticking towards last call, no time was wasted on useless formalities. If she liked what she saw, she appeared to set her price and discussion ensued—often after a drink and some flirtation—until some kind of compromise was struck and the man left the nightclub beaming, with a lady on his arm. If she decided against him, as in the case of the tall curvaceous Muscovite and the nerdy IT guy from Bangalore, she would avert her eyes, perhaps triple or even quadruple her price and wait until he went away, while rocking her body unenthusiastically, impatiently, to the music.

By midnight The Cyclone reached its full fury. A dense sprawl of revellers haggled, drank and danced in unison, while waiters in white long-sleeved shirts emblazoned with patches showing black cyclonic swirls, attended to them. As the storm crested, and the establishment became incrementally less crowded, the seduction rituals went into higher gear. One dynamic replaced another: the seller's market became a buyer's market. Fear of leaving empty-handed—like the Chinese woman who chased me outside of Kinkos—goaded the women into ever more bold and flamboyant acts of salesmanship. Most came straight to the fore, literally lining themselves up on the main thoroughfare and axis with the nightclub's front doors, attempting in every way possible to lure a man to their side. Others went in search of guys they had previously turned down in order to restart negotiations. The men knew this and pressed their cards. New deals were struck just as the lights of the club blared on and waiters and bouncers asked people to leave. The remaining girls shrugged their shoulders, butted out their cigarettes, and strolled towards the doors in a pout. A large taxi queue of ladies whom luck, that night, had passed over, formed outside.

There I found my friends gathered amid the chaos of the exiting crowd. Each had a woman with them and they stood together as if they were a cohesive social group deciding on where to go next. As I headed towards them to get my travel bags—or hopefully a ride home—the woman in the tight jeans, blazer and red heels who I designated a Romanian and who was near to me most of the night at the bar, approached me head on.

"Hello," she said with a nervous but beaming smile charged with the last dregs of optimism. I greeted her back, smitten by her wholesome good looks, and the lack of anything untoward in her appearance. The feigned innocence of it all was almost touching. My heart fluttered.

"What are you doing now? You would like to go to some other place with me?"

From the corner of my eye, I saw that my friends had spotted me and were watching intently. That feeling of peer pressure came back and intermingled with my own longstanding desire to be accepted by the Arabs among me as one of their own. I looked at the woman and also felt captured by her. Countless scenarios raced through my mind. The illusory shift in my fortunes in that moment made me feel elated. Anything seemed possible.

But in that final second, another part of me, the clear-minded traveller who had just run the gauntlet of a different set of experiences in Sudan, and attuned to the utter strangeness of that moment, chose the other door. It was almost unthinking.

"I'm sorry," I said regretfully, wondering after how to have better worded my response.

I looked at the winking skyline of Dubai in the distance as I approached my friends. While doing so, I reflected to myself that nearly all of it was a mirage, and so much of it pretend: the city, The Cyclone, the scene.

Dubai, UAE, 2003

The Al Arabiya television newsroom is droning with activity and scurrying bodies. I am sitting at a side table alone logging a collection of Reuters video footage shot in Iraq. It is the time of the Second Gulf War. The tape I am watching shows a convoy of American military jeeps and APCs racing towards the city of Hillah, near the old archeological site of Babylon, south of Baghdad. The vehicles are blasting music by Rage Against the Machine, as they fan out to occupy the countryside in the days after the US invasion.

A Lebanese colleague walks over and drops another tape on the table where I am working.

"Saddam's home movies," she says, with a little smirk.

"Oooh, finally."

I have been eagerly anticipating the tape. It contains footage from old VHS cassettes found by an Al Arabiya TV news crew who were the first to get inside one of Saddam Hussein's abandoned presidential palaces. I asked to see Saddam's videos for possible use as archival footage in my documentary series. But I was also deeply curious.

I slide the tape into the player.

Footage runs of two men sitting aboard what looks like an empty commercial airliner. It is Saddam Hussein's infamous, tyrannical sons: Uday and Qusay. They are being entertained by a pair of terrified male flight attendants, whom the brothers are ordering to sing, dance and behave jester-like in their presence. The president's sons are clapping and laughing uncontrollably like little boys at a party, as the airline staff make fools of themselves by behaving as stupidly as possible. It is a life and death performance before an erratically ruthless audience. The brothers regularly maim and kill others at the smallest provocation or pretext, and sometimes for nothing, for simple pleasure.

The scene unexpectedly cuts to footage of Saddam and his sons, this time dressed in khakis and knee-high gumboots. They are holding shotguns and are out on a hunting expedition in what appears to be the marshes of southern Iraq. The men have just shot and killed a wild boar the size of a baby hippo. They are laughing and joking about the huge feast that is to follow, as the feral pig is carried off by the president's attendants.

Suddenly an Iraqi employee of the TV station, walking by me, recognizes Saddam and stops to watch the screen. His face reveals deep consternation. The man meets my eye and shoots me a look filled with daggers. Although most of the Arab employees of the station, especially the Iraqis, hate Saddam and are content with his ouster, they are just as enraged by the American invasion. Being a nearly indistinguishable Canadian, I sometimes find myself the target of their hostility—even though they know I am also of Middle Eastern ancestry.

"Kuffar," the Iraqi snarls in Arabic.

The word has many distinct meanings: 'Unbelievers.' 'Infidels.' 'Pagans.' 'Deniers.' 'Ungrateful Ones towards God.'

"Saddam and his sons?" I ask reflexively if somewhat obviously, wondering if the man is also reacting to Saddam's hunting of a pig —an unclean animal, whose consumption is forbidden in Islam.

The man's face contorts in further disgust.

"All of you," he grumbles, before striding off.

The Colonel's Caravan

> Ibn Khaldun based his system on the intuition that men decline, morally and physically, as they drift towards cities. The rigours of the desert, he suggested, had preceded the softness of cities. The desert was thus a reservoir of civilization, and desert peoples had the advantage over settlers because they were more abstemious, freer, braver, healthier, less bloated, less craven, less liable to submit to rotten laws, and altogether easier to cure.
> – Bruce Chatwin, *The Songlines*

Our entry into the greatest desert on Earth was not, as I expected, marked by the largest stone cairn ever assembled, and which we had passed earlier on the road: The Giza Pyramids. Instead, the real gateway, the last vestige of civilization, turns out to be a decrepit gas station located at the far edge of 6th of October City—a Cairo suburb named after the date of the surprise military attack against Israel in 1973. We pass its lone station attendant who sits limply on a chair, mimicking either sleep or death, beside its one and only functional gas pump.

Just ahead, the road stretches into a minimalist scene of open-ended infinity.

"We're in," I announce to the four others with me in the Toyota Land Cruiser.

Our driver, who is clad in an unusual mix of military camo, vintage sunglasses with leather eye shields, and a beige checkered *keffiyeh* wrapped around his head, looks across to me in the passenger seat with what appears to be a bemused look.

"In where?" he asks.

"The start of the desert."

The man gathers his thoughts before speaking. "We were always in," he says in a thick Arabic accent. "You just have to widen your perspective. All of Egypt is a desert. The Nile Valley is just a long oasis running through it."

We continue for hours, a caravan of four jeeps, running along a dark ribbon of asphalt through an endless sea of yellow sand that sometimes dribbles and spills onto the sides of the road. Long wisps of undulating cloud drift on a canvas of dark-blue sky above the shimmering earth-tone horizon.

A lone uniformed army soldier standing at an ugly concrete bus shelter in the distance, steps onto the highway ahead of us and waves his arms in the air. The convoy stops beside him. The soldier is called over by the jeep behind us. He throws his duffle bag onto the roof of the vehicle and climbs in.

Shortly after passing the tiny oasis village of Abu Munqar—a streak of palms beneath bright sandstone cliffs—my driver slows the vehicle to a crawl. With strained effort he scans the landscape to our right, while glancing at a computer screen sitting above his dashboard. At once he brings the vehicle to a stop, and parks.

"*Voila*," he says, and steps out.

The drivers of the other jeeps, and their passengers, pour onto the empty road. We all stretch our bodies below the vast, all-consuming sky. There is a deafening silence, like that which may have preceded the birth of the universe. A mood of solemnity, punctuated by whispers, hangs over what is to be a ritual marking our departure from the world of grids. The drivers crouch on the ground and release some air from each of the jeeps' tires in order to better drive upon the terrain we are headed into. The expedition crew then gathers together in a scrum, with their palms facing upwards, outstretched. The men quietly recite *Al Fatiha*, the opening verse of the *Quran*, before we all climb back into the vehicles.

Then, one by one, each jeep, slowly, meticulously, crawls off the asphalt in a near holy procession requiring the utmost mindfulness. All sense of direction vanishes as we begin, with increasing speed, to blaze a weaving path, avoiding rocks and small dunes, through a wilderness with yet no landmarks or beacons save for the waning disc of sun screened through thin veils of cloud. The sudden sense of freedom is both unsettling and euphoric.

My driver turns to face me in order to gain my attention, before looking back at the way ahead. He grins wryly to himself.

"*Now* we're in," he says.

THE PRAYER RECITAL by the side of the road was not the rote exercise that divine invocations can often be. By leaving the road, a sanctioned pathway and predictable trajectory, we had crossed into a realm far removed from the world and unfit for life beyond a certain scale. For all intents and purposes we had cast ourselves upon a vast and capricious sea.

The Egyptian-Libyan Sahara—also known as the Libyan Desert or Western Desert—is often described as one of the driest, emptiest and most forbidding places on Earth. Because deserts are generally anathema to life, all of them everywhere, large and small, tend to earn these same superlatives. But the Libyan Desert, because of its geography, physicality, and the historical dramas associated with it, somehow earns it more. Stretching over a thousand kilometres west of the Nile into Libya, and south for the same distance from the Mediterranean into Sudan, this vast wasteland of surreal moonscapes, towering dune fields, and plateaus of rock, is a veritable and ungovernable no-man's-land. Like much of the Sahara, it occupies an area that in prehistory was a verdant and even wet savannah, but was later transformed by climate change into a desiccated rendition of the surface of Mars. Beyond a few low-lying oases watered by aquifers, finding water in the Libyan Desert is nothing short of a pipe dream. Only desperation or daring—warfare, criminal enterprise, or exploration—has driven a few modern humans into its deepest recesses.

My driver has spent much of his life traversing this 1.3 million square kilometre desert—for all of the above reasons. Retired Colonel Ahmed al-Mestekawi is a former patrol agent and head of the Egyptian Border Intelligence Forces in the Western Desert. For 18 years he tracked Libyan military movements on Egypt's western frontier and hunted some of the most daring trans-Saharan smugglers and drug traffickers. After many intrigues, he rose to become commander of the entire Western Desert sector of Egypt's military intelligence. As an explorer in his retired life, he co-discovered a major prehistoric rock-art site, one of the largest in Africa, which is partly named after him.

Ahmed is also the co-owner of an outfitter that takes travellers by jeep to the furthest reaches of the Libyan Desert—where we are now headed. We couldn't have a better trained, and generally more suitable leader. Ahmed can predict the weather by looking at the glare of the morning sun, read tracks in the sand to tell you who or what made them, and drive through dune fields so menacing that they would overturn or swallow any other vehicle; all the while managing a crack team of driver-mechanic-cooks that preside over every aspect of the journey. Al-Mestekawi's commanding physical presence and primal instinct for survival are softened by his French-educated, gentlemanly manner reminiscent of characters from old Egyptian black-and-white cinema. His personality and charms put one at instant ease.

"This is my second home," Ahmed tells me as he navigates slowly through the low-lying dunes looking for a place to make camp on our first night out. "I can't be away from the desert for more than a few months at a time. I start to become, how do you say: a little bit crazy?"

MY FIRST MEETING with Ahmed was entirely serendipitous. While on a freelance writing assignment in Egypt in 2009, I met someone who told me about the ex-colonel and that he was about to make another bold expedition into the desert. The man suggested that I do everything I could to join, as it would be a once-in-a-lifetime trip.

From an adventure standpoint, no arm-twisting was needed. Plus, I was in another phase of my relationship with 'the East'— one conducive to pursuing such a trip. After years of not quite finding my place in the Middle Eastern society, I began to search for other conduits with which to connect more deeply to the region. At the time I looked to awe-inspiring landscape, with its sublime emanations and spirits of place, which identity can often be anchored to. I had based myself back in Canada at this point, but had also resolved to travel back to the region frequently and explore the Middle East's fringes, its remote parts, in search of the bewitching essence of place that helped make the East, *East*.

I contacted Ahmed and beat a trail to his expedition headquarters located in his residential suburban home just outside Alexandria. Sitting before me at a gargantuan desk befitting an army general and surrounded by military maps of Egypt on the walls, he told me that my luck and timing were impeccable: there was one space left on the journey. There was also, however, one big problem to my tagging along, he added.

"This is the first Saharan trip the military is allowing after bandits attacked and kidnapped another convoy of travellers last September," he began, gravely.

I must have had a blank, or astonished, look on my face because he immediately said: "You didn't hear about it?"

"No."

"They were African militias crossing from Sudan—criminals. The army killed them and rescued the kidnapped travellers. But there may be more of them still there. We don't know."

"So, how does that relate to me?"

"We need an extra special military permission for every foreigner on the team and it takes many weeks to get it. As you know, we're leaving in just a few days."

I was crestfallen. Then I had a thought.

"My parents have Egyptian citizenship. Doesn't that mean that I'm technically Egyptian too?"

Ahmed moved forward slowly in his swivel chair and clasped his hands together. "Both your parents? Your father, too? Born here?"

"Yes."

Ahmed reached for a blank piece of paper and pen, pushing them in my direction. "Write down their names and dates of birth for me here, please."

I did so and handed him the paper.

"So there's a chance, then?" I asked hopefully.

Ahmed looked at the paper and placed it down, before looking at me and pointing his index finger towards the ceiling, holding it there.

"With the will and permission of Allah," he said.

OUR DESERT CARAVAN is made up of 17 people. At its head is Ahmed who is accompanied by his early 20-something-year-old son, Ziad, a Bohemian Ahmed mini-me who is apprenticing in the ways of desert travel.

Co-leading the expedition is Mahmoud Marai, a younger but nonetheless accomplished Egyptian explorer with whom Ahmed has partnered to lead the group.

Five male crew members are in charge of driving, cooking and making and breaking our elaborate canvas-walled and roofed camps, fit for any caliph or emperor on campaign.

A uniformed escort from Egypt's military intelligence, named Maged, is also with us. He is there to keep tabs on us, to symbolically represent a government in-absentia from its own borderlands, and provide protection whose efficacy is questionable, given there are limitations to what one poorly armed soldier can do against a cabal of Kalashnikov-toting Saharan desperados.

Six introverted and exceedingly well-behaved German tourists who speak in whispers and silent glances, and one elderly Brit obsessed with the military history of the Libyan Desert, make up the rest.

Our mission, as Ahmed articulated to me days earlier, is vague and open-ended: beyond stopping at some historical points of interest, we are to explore and survey the desert along the entire route to the southwest corner of the country, and back—and see if we encounter any trouble.

"Obviously, given my past work with the borders, I have my own interests," Ahmed said, offhandedly on my first visit with him.

All of us are crammed into four jeeps that are stacked with provisions and equipped with GPS technology and a slew of shovels and metallic slates with which to dig out our vehicles when we get stuck in the soft sand. We carry all of our provisions with us: crates of bottled water, jerry cans of gasoline, propane tanks for cooking, bags of rice and pasta, cans of tuna, as well as vegetables, eggs, chicken and beef (as well as an entire small refrigerator-freezer, stove and oven) fill every last bit of space in, and atop, our vehicles. If we run out of anything there will be no place to replenish it because no settlements exist where we are headed.

On our second day, we enter a maze-like wilderness of eroded sandstone hills, shaped like pyramids that extend to the horizon. We stop at one of the large outcroppings, which is known as "Djedefre's Water Mountain." The site was discovered and named in 2000 by German explorer Carlo Bergmann while on a desert walking trip with two camels. Its rock face contains numerous prehistoric petroglyphs. One of them is an ancient hieroglyphic inscription in a cartouche which contains the name of "Djedefre," the son of the old Kingdom Pharaoh Cheops, beside the signs for "water" and "mountain." The etching is a crude-looking carving into the rock, made more with the impromptu informality of graffiti, than the exacting master craftwork of an ancient hieroglyphic scribe. But it is nonetheless old. Mahmoud Marai, one of our guides, tells us the inscription dates to 2610 BC.

"Few people know," Mahmoud says in flawless English, "that the Ancient Egyptians used to travel deep into the desert—far deeper than even here. But this spot is *officially* the furthest distance they travelled as recognized by Egyptologists."

"What evidence is there that they went further?" someone in the group asks.

"A gem found in King Tut's funerary jewellery is made of silica glass. That's the rarest crystal in the world created by a localized meteor strike and can only be found much further west of here. I've also found other ancient hieroglyphs hundreds of miles in the direction we're headed, at Jebel Uweinat," he added, referring to a huge basalt massif at the borders of Sudan, Egypt and Libya.*

---

* Mahmoud told me later that the hieroglyphs he'd discovered with fellow Maltese explorer Mark Borda at Uweinat were decoded. They mentioned the fabled 'Land of Yam': one of the most mysterious nations that the ancient Egyptians traded with in Old Kingdom times—and which has still not been located. Known from the biography of the Aswan noble Harkhuf, The Land of Yam is assumed to have been in Nubia, beyond the Third Cataract in northern [...]

As I listen to Mahmoud, a high school chemistry teacher, who is articulate and knowledgeable, I realize that he is a natural complement and foil to Ahmed—but also a potential rival. Though they both share a deep and almost mystical love for the desert and know its deeper recesses better than anyone, the two men are also opposites. Whereas Ahmed is older, wizened, quieter, more conservative, private, and carries himself with the cool, detached and planned air of his institutional army upbringing, Mahmoud is younger, self-taught, brash, spontaneous, and gushing emotion. He projects something, perhaps deliberately, of the eccentric poet-academic in his manner and personality, bolstered by his artsy neck scarves, brown corduroy professor's blazer and white headscarf worn Tuareg-style. Unlike everyone else, Mahmoud eschews a tent and sleeps outside, in the open air, on the sand and under a thick woollen blanket. And like Ahmed, he too co-discovered a prehistoric cave art site which is partly named after him. Both men lead the expedition like Roman consuls sharing power jointly, except that Ahmed, whose vehicles and staff we are using, has the final call on most things. I notice already that this is a source of tension and potential conflict between the two men.

Days earlier, before this adversarial friction revealed itself, I was privy to a rare conversation between Mahmoud and Ahmed; unusual not just for its sense of solidarity and bonding between the two men but also for its obscurity of topic. Both men, while riding in the same vehicle with me when we were still in Cairo, got into a long, detailed discussion about recent political goings on in the desert. I listened with utter fascination as Egypt's two foremost Saharan explorers talked shop and exchanged information and gossip—almost ritualistically to break the ice on their business enterprise—about things few people but themselves knew. The banter began with Bedouin tribal politics on the Mediter-

---

Sudan. Marai and Borda's find called that into question, suggesting instead that it lay much further to the West, in the direction we were heading.

ranean coast. The posturing and shenanigans of the various chieftains: Abu *this* and Ibn *that*. Stories of smugglers, blood feuds, and the contraband hashish routes from Morocco. The most recent Libyan border troubles. The conversation then moved to the deteriorated security situation where we were headed, which Ahmed referred to in passing earlier. This is what I was able to cobble together from their conversation:

There is a south-to-north African trading route that runs up western Sudan to Libya, and that also comes near the Egyptian border. Legitimate, but intrepid truck traffic in the desert follows this track. But so do smugglers, particularly human traffickers, who risk running into army patrols on the Libyan side of the border. The smugglers tend to ferry Somali and Eritrean refugees wanting to flee to Europe via the Libyan coast.

Armed rebels from the North Darfur region of Sudan had recently gone into that largely lawless Sudan-Libya border area and formed checkpoints to take a cut of the legitimate truck trade. But they also saw another lucrative opportunity: they set themselves up as middle men to facilitate smuggler traffic by way of an alternate route and detour into Libya—through an ad hoc corridor in southwest Egypt meant to bypass the Libyan patrols. That was the area of Egypt we were heading to.

These same Darfurian militias were the people who abducted the jeep convoy of travellers the previous September, and who, in the years before had also temporarily detained several other desert expeditions, perhaps as a dry-run for the September kidnapping, which had demanded a huge ransom. A multinational commando raid, led by Egypt, rescued those September hostages, who had been taken into Sudan. The rescuers also killed two of the kidnappers, including the leader.

"What do you know about this Darfurian named Akid Bekhit?" Ahmed asks, referring to the rebel leader killed in the army raid.

"He's not Sudanese," Mahmoud says. "He's Chadian."

"*What?*"

"Yes, all these people are."

"How do you know?"

"Because they abducted *me* last year. I was with them for 10 days!"

"You're kidding me. Where?"

"At Uweinat. The Sudanese side at Karkur Talh. They pretended they were the Sudan Liberation Army and arrested us for trespassing.

"Sons of bitches," Ahmed grumbled.

"They were barbarians. You should have seen them. They wore dirty rags and shoes with no laces and dangling soles. They cut down the acacia trees for firewood with their machine guns on their pickups. They left us in one spot, alone, for two whole days. We thought we were going to die. Then they came back for us, and mysteriously let us go."

At that point, Ahmed mumbled something under his breath that sounded like an Arabic saying, or curse, and for the first time in almost an hour of constant, animated banter, the two men went stone-cold silent.

OUR WORRIES ABOUT DANGERS, human and otherwise, fall into abeyance for a time, and are replaced by the drama and magic of our surroundings. For, although we had crossed into an empty and desolate void, we had also accessed a place that exuded celestial-like beauty—a liminal zone where time and space insinuated their malleable, relative natures. The deep Sahara seemed to bridge another reality for whose qualities the words 'infinite' and 'eternal' are the nearest approximations.

The desert has always been considered a place of otherworldly machinations. Its minimal and distilled nature, its purity and poise, the strange yet utterly simple artistry of its contours, calibrate the human mind. The desert quiets and calms us, thereby connecting us to other wavelengths. The fragmenting that results from the human tendency to mentally parse by way of parameters, borders, and division into parts, are absent here. As are most straight lines. While in the desert, we can discern a more palpable aspect of being—the kernel or core of our real selves that is often buried or muffled in the noise and activity of the outside world. Our perceptions, being free of such distractions, can widen here as a result. It is perhaps for this reason, partly, that the desert is associated with—and is often a backdrop to—magical fables, fairy tales and legends, and is a bountiful wellspring of mystics and religions. There is also an observed conjunction between the desert and the monotheistic faiths. The two together form a popular motif of the East in general, and I wonder if my impulse to more strongly identify with land and landscape here as a conduit to greater Easternness stems from that. Am I actually pursuing something else far bigger, cloaked in a more mundane concern?

As we push deeper into the Libyan Desert's abstruse recesses, the old familiar world becomes more distant and I begin to understand and appreciate Ahmed and Mahmoud's love for the place, in spite of the dangers. I see our journey not as a touristic excursion to points of interest meant to distract us from our urban ennui, but as a guided experiential journey into an unfamiliar realm *without*, that bears upon and sheds light on the *within*.

This realization becomes amplified, and illustrated, as we enter what could only be described as a world of Dali-like art. For days we coast as if across an immeasurably vast canvas containing the most unusual formations of sand, rock and cloud. One day melds into another, activities and events fall under a single unified endeavour of open-ended and leisurely exploration. Clock-time is reduced to the rising and setting of the sun, drawing out the span of our journey. The nights are crushingly silent affairs, in which we become an extension and node—one tiny but deeply connected point—in a boundless ocean of intergalactic light. The sheer mystery of the sky's transformation in the dark and the gravity of its dazzling oblivion is at once the utmost reflection of life while also somehow intimating death.

Meanwhile, the desert constantly shifts and changes as we move through it. The tones, hues and colours of the sand, the variety and shape of rocks, the types of windblown contours and symmetry of the dunes, all transform. It is one desert, yet it is made up of endless permutations, all slightly different from each other but sharing a common, underlying reality.

"People who accompany me into the desert, see the world through new eyes," Ahmed says to me the next day, as I stand beside him on the edge of a yellow dune watching the Germans, who are rolling around on its crest and slope, laughing and squealing giddily like children. "This is what satisfies me the most about this work."

We are at a location called Abu Ballas, also known as "Pottery Hill." A cache of large prehistoric Egyptian pottery shards is strewn across the sand. Later, while everyone is examining the archeology, I see one of Ahmed's porters remove several large bottles of water from its cardboard box and place them in a row on the ground for us, beside one of the vehicles: our liquid sustenance. At first, I notice nothing out of the ordinary. But as I keep looking at the sleek units of water, something happens: the labelling on the bottles, their commodified appearance, melt away leaving behind glowing blue cylindrical cells in their place. They look like vitamin gel capsules, alien, futuristic, glimmering in the way bars of gold might to those smitten by gold fever. Each radiate life and fertility like a miraculous Planet Earth set in the desolation of space. I then realize that the very absence of water here, the incessant and inherent subconscious yearning for it, causes me to regard it in this way: not as something I take for granted, but as the most rare and precious element—on which not just our lives, but all life everywhere depends.

THE NEXT DAY, as we're breaking camp and preparing to leave, Mahmoud appears deeply unhappy. He is pacing around and seems to be cursing to himself. When I approach him and ask what's wrong, he is at first reluctant to speak, but then confides in me.

"It's Ahmed," he grumbles, looking around to see that we're not being listened to. "We're moving too quickly and spending too much time in the jeeps. The guests want to explore the desert for artifacts and inscriptions. You can't find anything by car. It's totally useless. All real exploration must be on foot."

Mahmoud is not wrong. But I realize he is speaking as much about his own desires as that of the guests. It's also further proof of my earlier observation that fractures have formed in the group. Our surroundings are peaceful and calming, but they are not enough to offset ingrained human group dynamics. The colonel's caravan, as small as it is, is nonetheless revealing its tiny cliques and hierarchies with their subtle power dynamics and cross-currents of relationship.

Ahmed and his son Ziad together form one cohort. The driver-mechanic-cooks on their own—a group of underclass Egyptian labourers—form another. Mahmoud, Maged (our military escort), and the guests from Europe each comprise their own nodes. Everyone assumes both master *and* servant roles in the grand scheme of the journey, sometimes lording authority or obligations over others, at other times doing others' bidding. Alliances form, disintegrate, and then re-form over journey decisions based on concerns and preferences. As a random and more ambiguous member of the group—a Westerner who is also partly Egyptian and a journalist—I feel more like a free-floating unit who belongs to none of the cliques. Only our military minder Maged, an awkward and rigid man who knows no English, and whose presence and personality more closely resemble an arrogant policeman, has no friends. He is also unenthusiastic about being in the desert, likening it to a dangerous exile in some faraway land. It is reflective, perhaps, of the ancient Egyptian attitude towards the 'Land of the Dead': the desert realm of the sunset that lay west of the verdant Nile Valley. Both Ahmed and Mahmoud, being quintessential desert creatures, who value total freedom, view Maged as an annoying encumbrance and a reminder of the bureaucratic behemoth that all Egyptians must live under. What solidarity exists between the two expedition leaders is mostly generated by this fly-in-the-ointment agent of state.

But as we are about to leave camp, Ahmed and Mahmoud are not, as usual, quietly making plans away from Maged's prying eyes and ears—but are instead duelling passive-aggressively about the route over one of Ahmed's large Egyptian military maps. Mahmoud wants to riff and improvise, and look for rock art. Ahmed wants to keep to a plan, military-style. When the conversation becomes more heated, they take a walk so that there is no shameful display of discord—and neither's authority is undermined in our presence. There can be no loss of face.

Ahmed, as usual, prevails. Mahmoud for a while is stone-faced.

Later as we're driving, Ahmed, as if he had intuited all I had seen between him and Mahmoud, says, unprovoked, "If you watch closely, you will discover the real personalities of everybody you are travelling with in the desert. They often behave differently here. In the city you can escape and act like someone else. But here in the desert you cannot."

EARLIER I HAD ASKED Ahmed if I could accompany him in the passenger seat for the whole of the journey, to which he agreed. Mastership of every sort has always fascinated me. I wanted to understand the extent of his abilities and watch as he weighs situations and makes decisions.

That day we enter an ideal area for this display of skill. We're in the 'Great Sand Sea'— one of the largest sand dune fields in the world, one of several such regions in the Sahara. For the next two days, we catapult up and down the dunes, across their sand-packed plateaus, and through the hard ground corridors that run between them. Ahmed navigates all of it with the focus and intensity of an airline pilot landing a plane in a bad storm. If visual perspective is significantly reduced in the desert, it's completely lost in a huge dune field, where at times you can't differentiate at all between near or far. Without warning you may come to the edge of a 300-foot drop and not know it. Though, somehow, Ahmed does. And our only mishaps are getting stuck in occasional patches of soft sand, which all of us together in total solidarity, on our hands and knees, dig ourselves out of.

I notice that Ahmed follows paths of least resistance marked by the absence of undesirable signs and obstacles. In the sand sea he avoids visible patches of soft sand and the hard ground corridors that lead to cul-de-sacs between the dunes. On firm terrain he is especially wary, almost paranoid, of hidden or sharp rocks that can damage the bottom of the vehicles or puncture our tires. His focus is intense and unshakable.

"I'm always looking for multiple approaches at once," he tells me. "If the route I'm on turns bad, I'll quickly switch to another. I'm also driving *all* of the cars together—taking into consideration each vehicle and each driver, their strengths and weaknesses."

I ask him how he makes his decisions so quickly under such ambiguous conditions.

"You have to read the land. You have to feel it."

As I observe Ahmed, I think of the longer pedigree of passionate and half-mad Libyan Desert explorers who've come before him, and whom he and Mahmoud consider themselves heir to. The ancient Greek writer Herodotus reports that the Persian army of Cambyses II was swallowed by a sandstorm as it tried to cross the Great Sand Sea in an attempt to reach and conquer Siwa Oasis in the 6th century BC. Much later, in the 19th and early 20th centuries, Egyptian and European explorers breached that void in an attempt to map what had until then only been known to speculation. Epic and flamboyant journeys on camel-back and Model-T Fords gave way to the subsequent spy and combat missions of the Allied and Axis powers, who intrigued against each other in the Libyan Desert during World War Two.* We not only come across broken down military vehicles from that period, old rusted husks looted and stripped to their skeletons, but in some cases we even see older tire tracks cast in firm sand.

"Do you see how narrow those tire tracks are, compared to the others?" Ahmed says, pointing to a faded and dusted-over pair of thin parallel lines in the sand that run alongside us before swerving away into the distance. "They're from the car of Prince Kamal al-Din, from his 1926 trip," he adds, referring to the Egyptian nobleman who pioneered the use of the first motor vehicles for desert exploration.† Kamal al-Din turned down the throne of Egypt in favour of living his own independent life spent exploring the desert.

Astonished by Ahmed's abilities of perception, I ask him if his desert skills are entirely self-taught.

"No," he says, followed by a thoughtful smile. "There were three great mentors in my life. They're all dead now but each, a close friend, still lives inside of me. Suleiman Silmy, a Red Sea Bedouin soldier, taught me about camels, tracking and desert survival. Samir Lama, a Palestinian-Egyptian cinema actor turned explorer, taught me business and how to be a guide. Lama also showed me all of the secret routes to the hidden areas in Jebel Uweinat and the Gilf Kebir."

"And the third person?" I ask, after Ahmed goes silent at the wheel for a time.

---

* Those early 20th century episodes provided the real-life characters and setting for Michael Ondaatje's fictional novel, *The English Patient*.
† Ahmed constantly remarks on who made which tire tracks and how old they are. At one point he comes across his own vehicle tracks, and because of the specific tire treading, which he recognizes, he can confidently tell me they were from a specific trip he took 15 years earlier.

"The greatest influence was Ghenewa Abu Balooza. He was a Bedouin guide, tracker and camel driver from Sidi Abdel Rahman. Ghenewa didn't want his son to work in the desert because of all the dangers. Because of that, he didn't have an heir to impart his knowledge to. So, when I recruited him to be my personal guide and tracker to help the border forces catch smugglers, he saw an opportunity to pass along everything he knew to me. I became his disciple. When he died, I couldn't stop crying for days."

"You said he was the greatest influence. Why?"

"Because Ghenewa was a man of principle, strength and integrity. He was a man of truth, the wisest man I ever knew. His only condition for working with us was that he not be present, face-to-face, during any arrests our team made in the desert."

"Did he fear for his safety if people found out he was collaborating with the army?"

"No. Quite the opposite. He cared nothing for himself. He was considerate of everyone else to an unusual degree."

"So, what was his reason?"

"When I asked Ghenewa why he didn't want to face the men we arrested, he said to me: 'It is not for me—it is for *them*. Even though these people may be breaking the law and should face justice, it is a great humiliation for them to be captured. I do not want my eyes to add an extra ounce of weight to their embarrassment and dishonour—and which may fuel future criminality as a result. So, I will absent myself briefly while you detain them.'"

AFTER A WEEK'S TRAVELLING, we reach the southwest corner of Egypt near the Libyan and Sudanese borders—the furthest we will venture before circling back. The area feels immeasurably far-flung, a place of edges, indescribably out of bounds and subject to its own laws. The following days are spent weaving through the hidden interstices, the *wadis* and sandy corridors of the Gilf Kebir: a vast 1,000-metre-high plateau system the size of Switzerland. The area is sprinkled with prehistoric rock art, including Ahmed's namesake site, Mestekawi-Foggini Cave, which he co-discovered in 2002, and to which we are headed.

To get there we come off the plateau and descend a long *wadi* of red sand punctuated by the odd acacia tree. Our caravan skirts the Gilf's western face, a towering bluff, and the many high rocky outcrops below that together create mazes and passages at the plateau's base. To our left, to the west, lies Libya, with its long flat featureless horizon. Out of sight in that direction sits the country's most distant outpost, Kufra Oasis: the ancient seat of the Senussi sect, and an important way-station in the human trafficking routes going north from sub-Saharan Africa to the Libyan coast. It is through this area of Egypt that the African militias—and the smugglers they are helping—come through to access Libya and bypass its military patrols.

Mahmoud calls out to us over the radio and succeeds in getting us to stop to investigate possible rock art sites, but Ahmed cuts those pit stops short. Because of the bandit threat, he is wary of lingering in any place for too long. At first, we are unable to locate his cave, but we double back and Ahmed finds the spot with his typical, "*Voila*."

Mestekawi-Foggini Cave is more of a landing on an elevated rock wall with an overhang, and reachable by way of a natural ramp made of sand, than an actual cave. We exit the vehicles and excitedly ascend the incline in hurried steps just short of a run. Maged and the drivers, stay behind. I try to be the first to get there to cherish a few seconds of solitude and mimic the act of discovery. The wall is high and wide, a natural canvas containing a huge mosaic of mostly red ochre graffiti above a floor of perfectly wind-sculpted sand ripples. No one, it seems, has been here for a while.

There is a collection of hushed sighs as we come face-to-face with the amber kaleidoscope of handprints, human figures, and what appear to be animals—real and imagined—some of them disfigured. The huge armies of stick people in different poses and acts, some with muscular quads and wide backs and shoulders, resemble epic battle scenes. I recognize what appear to be elephants, ostriches, gazelles, and giraffes. In one corner of the wall, two lines of stick humans face each other, inverted, across a crack in the rocks, as if it were a reflection scene in water. Some of the images are cast in yellow, white and black dyes. Mysterious hybrid beings, monstrous, ghoulish creatures stand out in the crowded display.

It feels like we've accessed a time capsule, a message from our common ancestors that shouts, "We were here!" There is a stab of instant connection. Our quiet reverence, like that shown at a holy place, exists to silence the mind to hear their call. The handprints are what draw my attention the most. Each a distinct size, shows a different splaying of fingers. One hand displays four fingers with the thumb tucked in. Another is simply a fist, an image made by the rebel, a non-conformist, the avant-garde artist. Yet another shows a hand and forearm resting sideways, horizontally, amidst the bloom of upward thrusting palms. All are playful attempts to convey an individual soul, to leave their mark for posterity. These people might almost be alive, trying to make contact across a threshold.

I turn to Ahmed who is looking up at the wall and wearing a big smile resonant with deep satisfaction—as if seeing the place for the first time. We all find our own corners of the wall and sit on the sand and stare. As we take photos, Mahmoud tells us he thinks the art has faded ever since people started coming to the site.

"I know it sounds crazy, but I'm certain there is something about these cameras that steals the art's essence," he says in a tone of mild disapproval. "Each time people come here, they seem to absorb and take something of these pigments with them. I've seen it at other sites too."

Ahmed, who is eager to leave and make camp somewhere before dusk, tells everyone to head back down to the vehicles. I deliberately linger on and find myself alone in the enclosure. Before the group notices my absence, I approach the wall and find the largest and boldest palm print. I raise my right hand and place it directly over it, and hold it there. After a moment of solemn communion, I remember Mahmoud's comment about vanishing pigment, and I draw my hand back.

THAT SAME DAY we make a beeline south into the Uweinat Desert, a red sandy expanse punctuated by huge basalt outcroppings. We are tantalizingly close to the junction of Egypt, Libya and Sudan. Further south, the almost Mount Sinai-like massif of Jebel Uweinat stands in terrifying defiance, a natural marker or cairn, announcing the tri-border area and deeper hinterlands of Saharan Africa that lay beyond. Closer by, to the north, are the twin black volcanic protuberances known as Peter and Paul.

Since leaving the Gilf, Ahmed, Mahmoud and the military sentry have been on edge: we have entered the main thoroughfare of the bandits near to where both Mahmoud and the September tourist convoy were separately abducted. Ahmed doubles his effort in scanning tire tracks, and the horizon, using his binoculars at every stop. The worry is infectious and is made worse by one of Ahmed's surreal anecdotes. While on a pit stop to stretch our legs, he tells us that we're standing in almost the exact spot where he once found the dead bodies of three migrants who had either fallen off the truck they were on, or were deliberately left behind.

"They looked like mummies," he said. "Their flesh had become hard and dry like cured meat and just fell off their bones when you picked them up. I buried them just over there."

Mahmoud is most anxious. I notice him burying his satellite phone in a large Ziplock bag in the ground at night before going to sleep and after texting his position to his wife back home. He complains bitterly about having to do so—that he's lost his sense of distance from civilization by having to use the technology. The excessive fear, he tells me, spoils everything.

"These people from Sudan, or Chad, or wherever they're from, believe that this is also their country. Borders for them are an imaginary line. They roam freely here. And there are no real controls or anyone to tell them otherwise. For them, our being here would be both a violation and a surprise. Anything can happen."

Later that night in camp, Ahmed, Mahmoud, Maged and I are drinking tea and chatting by candlelight when suddenly we hear what sounds like an engine droning in the distance beyond the dunes we are hidden behind. Maged, who sees his chance to exert his authority, jumps to his feet, puts his hand on his gun holster and starts marching around in an ever-confused panic of zigzags, looking up and into the blackness, trying to determine what the sound is.

"Who's there?!" the soldier hollers. "Who are you?! Show yourself!"

The engine grows louder and we realize it's a plane, flying low and about to land.

Ahmed is unperturbed. He calmly takes a sip of his tea, and tells us it's possibly a military plane, but he doesn't know for sure.

"It doesn't matter," he adds, pensively. "Whoever it is won't know we're here. We couldn't be better hidden. Put it out of your minds for tonight."

Maged slips his revolver back in its holster. "I'll deal with them tomorrow," he says, trying to conceal his utter relief.

AT DAYBREAK the decision is made to approach the Sudanese border. It is the result of an unshakeable and almost feverish curiosity that has arisen with the appearance of daylight. Ahmed and Mahmoud frame their impulsiveness as an obligation of their trade: to venture forth in exploration, in spite of the risks. Ahmed,

I notice, can't help but slip back into his old border guard role. Maged, however, whines and protests.

Ahmed fixes a serious gaze at him. "We're Egyptians. This is our sovereign state. And you are its courageous protector—as I once was," Ahmed says. "We have a duty."

"True," Maged concedes, willing to accept the flattery, albeit uncomfortably.

"Good. We'll do a short border patrol and then head back."

We proceed south, but at a crawl. The jeeps circumvent a minefield which Ahmed tells us the Egyptian army laid many years ago after a skirmish with Libyan forces in the area. Uweinat looms commandingly in the distance, beneath a perfectly clear and deep blue sky. Ahmed suddenly stops the vehicle and begins searching the floor and jeep console.

"What is it?" Mahmoud, who rides with us, asks.

"I think I see people. But I can't find my binoculars," he says frustratedly. "It looks like there are several people grouped together in the open, off in the distance."

Maged radios us from his jeep, asking what the problem is. Ahmed responds to tell him.

"Don't move," the officer orders through the radio. The jeep Maged is in races past us and stops several hundred metres ahead—and which is still a far distance from the figures we've all now sighted. Maged gets out of the passenger seat with his handgun drawn and begins marching authoritatively towards the distant horizon.

"Who does he think he is? Tarzan?" Mahmoud asks incredulously. "What is he going to do alone?"

Just then I get an idea: I have a telephoto zoom lens on my camera and I decide to take a photo of the figures. I do so and enlarge the image in my viewfinder to find what looks like several abandoned oil drums with rocks piled on them. I show Ahmed, who had also just found his binoculars. He nods, as if he isn't surprised, but is also relieved. "Border markers. Close your door," he says.

We drive up to where Maged is marching and slow down beside him. The soldier is panting, covered in sweat, and wide-eyed with anxiety.

"They're not people," I tell him through the window and show him the viewfinder. At first Maged won't believe me and takes almost a whole minute to inspect the photos closely, as if he's never seen a digital camera before. Ahmed steps out of the vehicle and hands him his binoculars, which Maged looks through. He is then convinced.

The soldier sighs exasperatedly and begins to pace around, walking off his nervous energy. Maged then stops in his tracks and turns to approach Ahmed.

"By the authority granted in me by the President of the Republic, and by the Field Marshall of the Egyptian Army, I order you, retired Colonel Ahmed Al-Mestekawi, to turn around now and return us all to Cairo."

ONE WEEK and seven hundred kilometres later I am sitting on a bus that has just left Dakhla Oasis and is bound for Cairo. It is dusk, the sun has just set. Next to me is a young Egyptian man who looks no older than 18 years of age. He is wearing jeans and a hoody. His mood is flat and sullen, bordering on depressed.

I introduce myself. He then asks me, "Why did you come here? To see Dakhla?"

"I was on a jeep trip to the Libya and Sudan borders."

He jolts more alert. "Really? I was there too."

"Where?"

"Near a placed called Jebel Uweinat."

"When, just now?"

"Yes. I'm in the army. I've been stationed there for five months."

I recall the night a week earlier when we heard the engine of the plane landing somewhere nearby at night, and I realize that that was probably his base. And then I do the math: five months.

"So, you must have been sent there after those tourists were kidnapped in September."

The man stares at me, shocked, as if I had uttered a state secret. "That's right," he says, frozen.

"And how did you like being there?"

The boy's gloomy countenance immediately returns. "To be honest, it was the worst catastrophe that ever befell me."

"Why, what happened?" I ask, expecting a big story.

"Nothing happened—that was the problem. There's nothing to do there. Five months of nothing. No trees, no river, no birds, no people. *No girls*. Nothing."

"But you got to see another part of the country," I say, trying to find a silver lining.

He laughs at me. His brief mirth is tinged with bitterness. "That is not our country. To be Egypt it needs the Nile, it needs Egyptians."

"Were there no bandits and smugglers to chase?"

"No, brother, we were too busy battling the *djinn* to care about smuggling," he says, referring to the Islamic mythological spirit beings that are said to haunt certain places and dwellings. "Anyway, we weren't sent there to look for anyone. It's too dangerous."

"So, why were you there?"

"Only to have more of a presence."

Somehow, I am not shocked.

"We played dominos and cards. We slept. We begged Allah to take our lives and spare us this endless suffering in the Land of Eblis.* There's no worse place to be sent as a soldier."

"I found it beautiful there."

"You like it only because you are a foreigner and a tourist and don't have these things where you come from. Try spending five

---

* In Arabic *Eblis* is the supreme leader and head of all the *djinn*.

months there against your will, unable to see or speak with your family and friends."

"But what about the quiet, the calm, the clean air, the sense of space, and being out in nature? Was none of that a nice change?"

The man sourly flicks his head upwards in dismissal. He then sighs and looks out the window at the flat sand-sheet extending into infinity, and the last dregs of light from the vanished sun disappearing into the underworld.

Eastern Turkey, 2012

A dilapidated Kurdish tea house in the embattled town of Şirnak, near the Iraqi border, is occupied by a dozen brooding souls. Diffuse light casts their soft shadows over faded earth-tone walls that peel paint. The grizzled, greying Kurdish men in flat caps and woollen blazers, quietly sipping tea and smoking cigarettes, form a perfect tableau. Every man is transfixed on his own section of empty wall, or floor space. The air is oppressive. Nobody speaks.

From outside comes the incessant thumping of low-flying Turkish military choppers. Şirnak and its outskirts are occupied. It is a garrison town. High observation towers, sandbag hillocks, and armoured personnel carriers surround the community. Their opponents, Kurdish PKK rebels based in Iraq, and their local civilian supporters, flit around unseen, like ghosts. At night, firefights erupt, and Şirnak is transformed into a kind of Jenin or Kandahar—but entirely bereft of any news cycle notoriety. The town has already been pounded to dust once.

Inside the teahouse the mood is tense and awkward. I catch wandering, curious eyes, starved of novelty, taking me in. A few fixate on me, free of any self-consciousness.

You are drawing unwanted attention to us, *one pair of eyes says.*

You are going to get us into trouble, *says another.*

I have come to the area to take photos. But here in Şirnak I dare not touch my camera, or even lay a hand on its carrying case resting on the stool next to me.

The teahouse waiter, a boy of probably 15, wearing a peach-fuzz moustache and an oversize black blazer, shuffles over with his own tea and sits at a stool beside me. He half turns to look at me a few times—all aborted attempts to make contact. All eyes in the teahouse, in unanimity, now turn in our direction. The boy takes a few sips of his tea, and sits more upright. He pivots again to me, this time holding his gaze.

I turn to acknowledge him.

Meekly, but resolutely, and with a bafflement so poignantly genuine that it could not be feigned by someone else in a thousand attempts, he poses his question to me in English:

"*Why are you here?*"

Interview with a Partisan

Men can starve from a lack of self-realization as much as from a lack of bread.
— Richard Wright, *Native Son*

The less justified a man is in claiming excellence for his own self, the more ready he is to claim excellence for his nation, his religion, his race or his holy cause.
— Eric Hoffer, *The True Believer*

After our third round of tea, Firat Uzun, the chain-smoking 28-year-old women's clothing merchant I had met earlier that day in the *bazaar*, decided to trust me with his deepest secret. When I broached the subject of his life again, one in which he was unusually cryptic, I watched him ruminate heavily before making the decision to open up.

"I was 10 years in The Mountain," he said in English. The look on his face mixed nostalgia with remorse.

"Which mountain?" I asked, confused.

Firat raised his arm up, pointing towards the ceiling. "The Kurdish Mountain."

He shuffled to his desk in the far corner of the store, near to where the purses hung, and brought back his laptop. After clicking open a few folders he turned the screen to face me.

"This is me," he said, pointing to a photo of himself wearing a moustache and sunglasses and standing next to two young men in a landscape of forested and snow-capped mountains. They were all dressed in a khaki green military uniform made up of Kurdish baggy pants, long green vests, and traditional belt sashes. I could see the muzzles of AK-47s hanging at their sides.

Firat clicked on another photo showing a group of young men and women, similarly dressed, milling around what looked like a camp. He began pointing to people in the pictures.

"This person killed by missile. This one is killed in Iran. This killed by Village Guards. This one is dead from landmine. And this is me saying goodbye to my best friend before he went in an operation and killed by the Turkish commando. In the last year I lost 15 friends."

Firat looked at me to appraise my reaction.

"PKK," I said.

Firat nodded gravely.

When I ran into Firat earlier by chance amid the throng of bottlenecked shoppers moving through the Duhok *bazaar* in northern Iraq, there was no hint of the secret life and dark intrigues he would later share with me. If anything, I felt a sort of kinship and comfort in his presence. He both looked and sounded more like my Lebanese Arab friends than a Kurd. There was also something disarming about his lanky, easy-going stride, bookish Trotsky spectacles, and the slight German lilt to his broken English. All together, Firat exuded confidence. His probing and intelligent, if not slightly analytical questions and quips—in a way, very Western—put me at ease. Without articulating it as such, I must have detected he was something of a freethinker for the

Middle East. When he invited me to tea at his shop in the 'Dubai Bazaar,' a laneway of women's clothing stores built like a shopping mall above the old *souq*, I knew he had the makings of a real friend.

Only when I began to ask him questions about his life, en route to his store, did I discover there was something more complicated lying beneath his façade of nonchalance.

"I'm from Turkey—from Hakkari—but I can't go back," he replied coldly, almost with annoyance, when I asked if he was originally from Duhok. I waited for an explanation as to why, but none came.

Because I knew something about Kurdish issues, I figured his politicking had gotten him into trouble back home—it wasn't uncommon. And so I kept my mouth shut while we weaved through the shoppers.

Back at his store, as Firat nostalgically scrolled through the laptop photos of himself striking various rebel poses in the wild and bedraggled mountains that straddle the frontiers of Turkey, Iraq and Iran, the barest etchings of his story took shape for me.

He lit a cigarette and snapped his laptop shut. "I was a big man," he said. "You will not believe how big. Everyone respected me. Everyone loved me. Now I'm no one. I am less than no one. I don't even have a passport."

FIRAT WAS a former insurgent with the PKK, the *Partiya Karkerên Kurdistanê* or Kurdistan Workers' Party: an armed guerrilla movement fighting in the rural, mountainous region of Eastern Turkey and its adjacent borderlands. The rebel group has battled the Turkish state on and off since the early 1980s and espouses a mix of Marxist–Leninist dogmas and fervent Kurdish nationalism. They are considered a terrorist entity by more than a few countries. Initially the PKK sought Kurdish independence, a sovereign national homeland, but in more recent decades it has pragmatically scaled back its demands, calling instead for political and cultural autonomy within Turkey. It has even engaged, reluctantly, at times in peace talks—most recently declaring a truce with Turkey (going so far as "dissolving" in name) as a first step towards finally ending the conflict.

The Kurds are an ethnicity apart in the Middle East, a minority living among Turks, Arabs and Iranians. Numbering around 35 million in the region, they largely inhabit the rural landlocked border region where Turkey, Syria, Iraq and Iran all meet. That knot of frontiers grafted upon an area where the north Mesopotamian plain rises to meet an arc of mountains, is the homeland the Kurds refer to as "Kurdistan." In all those countries —currently with the exception of Iraq where the local Kurds have slowly forged their own *de facto* country in the north since 1992* —the Kurdish people are heavily oppressed. For its part, the Turkish government often denies that the Kurds are a separate ethnicity with their own culture and language, instead calling them "Mountain Turks". Ankara regards all their efforts at self-determination, including by peaceful means, to be 'terrorism' against the state. And though it is also true that many Kurds are contentedly assimilated in the countries that host them, many others harbour dreams of independent nationhood. Armed Kurdish nationalist movements have existed in all of their host countries since the early 20th century, resulting in an ongoing state of low-intensity warfare and upheaval in the areas they inhabit.†

---

* The Kurds in Iraq have historically endured some of worst atrocities among their regional brethren under Saddam Hussein and his 20th century political predecessors.
† By way of copy-paste journalism, the same casualty figures have been bandied around by the news media for decades (and thus no one knows for certain), but many tens of thousands of people have died in fighting between the Turks and Kurds in Turkey since the start of the PKK rebellion in the 1980s. Many thousands more Kurds have perished in various uprisings and battles in neighbouring countries including, most recently, during the civil war and its post-war upheavals in Syria, in which Turkey has been a regular participant.

Firat had been a PKK fighter and political operator up until six months before I met him in the shaded byways of the Duhok *bazaar* in 2012. He told me that thousands of other former fighters like him who'd left the organization, unable to return to civilian life in Turkey, were living in exile in the Kurdish Autonomous Region of northern Iraq—an area run by fellow Kurds of different political leanings. So there were caveats to being there.

"I live as a prisoner here," he said, lighting another cigarette, and exhaling smoke with a loud sigh. "I can't leave Duhok. I can't travel. I can't go back to Turkey. I can't even go to the capital, Erbil."

"Why?"

"The intelligence services don't like us."

"But the Iraqi Kurds also don't like the Turks. Shouldn't that be good for you?"

"It doesn't matter. We are communist. We are 3,000 people with military training. We can make bombs and know how to use C-4. We are a security threat and are very dangerous for them. So they keep us here and watch us."

I wondered why Firat left the PKK at all. This time, I asked him point blank.

He exhaled another plume of smoke and then waved my question away with his hand as if he had answered it a thousand times before and could barely stomach doing so again. "They kicked me out. Most of us here was kicked out—or escaped from the PKK hell. I can't go back."

As a journalist I was excited to have Firat, a former member of one of the most shadowy paramilitary organizations in the world, seemingly ready to share the details of his once clandestine life. That feeling was bolstered by a sense that our encounter was also felicitous. For weeks I had been travelling through southeastern Turkey and northern Iraq, talking to Kurds for freelances pieces I planned to write about the area. Even though I hadn't considered focusing on the PKK as other journalists had (some of them finding their way to the PKK's hidden alpine redoubts in Iraq's Qandil Mountains), its guerrillas were still at the forefront of my awareness given the close proximity of the conflict. As Maoist insurgents, guerrilla warriors, they were everywhere and nowhere: concealed by the mists of far-flung peaks and moving invisibly among the sympathetic townsfolk living in the hamlets and villages clinging to the mountainsides.

I had always been drawn to the Kurds since first learning about them and their struggles in the 1993 BBC television documentary series *Blood and Belonging*. Something about their daring and the extreme outdoor adventure quotient of their lives appealed to the explorer in me. But I also felt my intuitive fascination with Kurds had an even deeper source, which, for lack of any sufficient explanation, I chalked up, half-jokingly, to a past life. That is, until I was told about a family connection to precisely that part of the region: my paternal grandfather, who I'd never met, was born in a town called Mardin in the Kurdish area of southeastern Turkey, near the Syrian border—today a split city of Kurds and Arabs. That branch of the family were a fusion of Armenian and Assyrian Christians, communities who had lived alongside the Kurds for countless generations. I concluded that my interest in Kurds was likely due to some genetic memory of that deep past and place. The feeling of kinship, as a result, deepened. And though I was no political cheerleader for anyone in the region, let alone a communist guerrilla insurgency, I was taken by the mystique that surrounded these fighters: the irregular warfare, the Robin Hood-style bravado, and the enigmatic mountains in which they operated, jutting up like bear fangs where Mesopotamia, the Trans-Caucasus and Zagros Mountains of Iran come together in an otherwise obscure corner of the Middle East. It was to me the most exotic and little-known part of the region. Given that a branch of my family was tied to these same lands by way of Mardin—where I was planning to visit later in that trip—I wanted to make this region the new lodestar in the continued quest for my defining East.

Firat, I realized, could be a conduit in that process.

There was an unspoken covenant between us whereby I became his confessor: someone from the outside world to bear witness to his past and to whom he could confide without fear of judgement. He in return would take me on a rare and privileged journey into his life as a PKK insurgent, allowing me to live vicariously through his experiences and see the region through his eyes. He would put me in touch with the last of the Eastern locales to which I was tied, and which I would now try to make my own.

FIRAT, like most recruits, joined the PKK as a restless teenager. He and his family lived under an unrelenting Turkish military occupation in the restive town of Hakkari, a leafy high-elevation community of walnut trees, steep roads and old apartment blocks located in the far southeast corner of the country. That rugged nook, where the eastern Taurus Mountains of Turkey meet the northern edge of Zagros Range jutting in from Iraq and Iran, are about as Kurdish a place as anywhere in Turkey. Surrounded by wild jagged peaks similar to the Dolomites, and situated in a no-man's-land of ungovernable borders, Hakkari has always been a gateway for PKK rebels travelling in and out of the mountains— and to and from Turkey.* As a result, the town and region have been a flashpoint of tension and violence. When state paramilitaries shot and killed Firat's grandmother during a routine home

---

* The Çilo-Sat Mountains are an alpinist's dreamland of high granite peaks, deep river gorges, pristine tarns, wildflower-filled meadows, and sparkling glaciers. The area, a redoubt of ancient Assyrian Christians (and the final holdout of the straw-coloured Syrian brown bear), was ruled autonomously for centuries by local Kurdish chieftains, even under the Ottomans. It has also been off-limits to travellers for much of its recent history. Access to outsiders was barred by Ottoman officials in the early 1900s due to lawlessness and banditry, and later again because of the conflict with the PKK.

search one night, he made the decision to leave his old life and become a partisan. He had just turned 18.

"I felt no choice," Firat told me. "They wanted to erase our heritage. I needed to fight for my culture and people. And anyway, what else was I going to do in Hakkari?"

Our first real in-depth discussion took place at a restaurant in the open-air courtyard of a local Syriac Christian church, close to the *bazaar* where he worked. Firat enjoyed drinking *arak*, anise-infused liquor, and it was the nearest place that served alcohol with its *mezzes*, all of which were local twists on classic Arabic fare. In the days to follow, the conversation moved back to his store in the Dubai Bazaar, where we would speak over endless tea, sometimes in the audience of other store owners who wandered in to say hello and who often helped Firat find the right words in English, when his language skills hit the shoals. It dawned upon me that I was spending time in public with a known 'terrorist' who was also likely under surveillance, possibly by more than one entity. But by then it was too late. I would have to shoulder the risk of being associated with him.

Initially, Firat's reminiscences were nostalgic and romanticized accounts of his time travelling with, and later leading, his units through the mountains to attack remote Turkish military outposts. His targets were either the military, or their Kurdish pro-Turk allies, known as the 'Village Guards'—a faction of loyalist Kurds the Turks used to divide and weaken the Kurdish rebellion. Like everyone in the PKK, Firat had been trained in guerrilla tactics. He was adept at foraging and surviving in the outdoors, as he and his unit moved surreptitiously between locations, especially to and from cave systems, avoiding aerial reconnaissance. The Turkish military dispatched fighter planes or drones to bomb PKK rebels, or special forces to fight them, as soon as they were detected. Those field missions, which sometimes lasted weeks or even months, had something of the epic and desperate ring of Mao's Long March to them. Firat and his unit, sometimes in conjunction with others, ambushed Turkish garrisons, and disappeared back into the mountains, where they resupplied themselves, sometimes by way of local civilian sympathizers, to mount further attacks.

"Were the Turks good fighters?" I asked, curious to know how the physically diminutive but often stern-looking soldiers I'd encountered in my travels in Turkey had performed as a modern-equipped army, one of the largest in NATO.

"The soldiers in the mountain were scared of us, and not hard to defeat," Firat bragged. "Many were new soldiers, from poor families, sent to the worst places to fight. We were like ghosts for them. They were most afraid of being attacked by our women units, who were sometimes better fighters than us."[*]

After their tours of duty, Firat and his colleagues would return to their larger bases in the Qandil Mountains across the border in northern Iraq to be debriefed. While at base they would have their performances assessed, receive additional training or military indoctrination, and be paired up with new groups of soldiers for their next missions—sometimes to neighbouring countries to either help their Kurdish allies there, or to just re-enter Turkey from different nations.

"It was hard, but it was good," Firat said, starry-eyed, while shoppers browsed through his store. "The places we travelled to—you would never believe. You would never see these places in your life. Big mountain paradise where no humans can go. We were trained how to get to there. We learned how to survive. We learned respect: respect for the nature, respect for the trees, respect for the animals, respect for the mountain."

Firat used the singular word "mountain" to describe the many mountains in general. I dismissed this initially as just a grammatical mistake. But he may well have been speaking deliberately in

---

[*] The PKK is big on gender equality and liberating women as part of the general struggle for political freedom. The use of all-female units has since been emulated by the Syrian and Iraqi Kurds which, similarly, inspire fear of humiliation in the ranks of ISIS, with whom they fought, and still on occasion fight.

the singular, too. For all mountains were not just one in his mind, but also the progeny of one peak in particular: the PKK's holy summit of Mount Çilo, or *Çilo Dağı*. That third-highest mountain in Turkey is regarded with the same mystical reverence by the local Kurds that the ancient Greeks held for Mount Olympus, or the Japanese for Mount Fuji. Yet all of the lesser peaks were similarly respectable; part of a high council of mountain elders that made up the PKK pantheon of sentient alpine spirits. The PKK operations centred upon this sacred geography not just owing to the perceived protective power of those summits, but also because victory in warfare means fighting over and winning the high ground and holding it. If that ground is especially venerated, the fight for it will be all the fiercer. This worship of landscape, its deep ties to place, is one of the defining symbols core to PKK mythos.

Indeed Firat himself couldn't speak in detail, or at length, about his missions and travels without grabbing his laptop from his desk and opening Google Earth to show me his old mountain haunts, all of which had stories attached to them. He would point out a great ambush site here, a pristine secret swimming hole there, a mountain slope covered in boulders and in whose maze he fought hand-to-hand with the enemy. His knowledge of the geography and terrain of the southeast border areas was unequalled. It was as if that huge swath of mountains were like a wooded area behind his home that he had spent his life exploring.*

Days passed like this, listening to Firat's stories and anecdotes, which he pulled, one after another at random, from a seemingly bottomless cache of experiences.

Though I could have cut my stay in Duhok short and continued my travels across the rest of northern Iraq and Turkey sooner, listening to Firat was just too engrossing. I found myself day after day beating a path to the Dubai Bazaar entranced by my

---

* Firat's most interesting geographical quips concerned forgotten archeological ruins in remote valleys that have not been seen by visitors for many generations.

new friend's tales of life-and-death battles on the slopes of hallowed peaks, and of his secret missions to Iran and Europe in his later years as a political operative. Listening to his yarns threw me into a hypnotic state in which I could visualize and sensually experience everything—in effect, transporting me there. Not only that, but I began to understand better how anyone feeling disempowered and humiliated would be magnetized by such a life. To be in the PKK, it seemed, was to achieve the loftiest heights of Kurd-dom and its fulfilling and intoxicating fruits of kinship and belonging. Thus even just the act of joining such a community was to spite their enemy by way of the greatest disobedience possible: revelling in the culture that their oppressors aimed to negate. Those heightened feelings of shared blood ties and the nature-based camaraderie elevated out of all normal proportions, was what Firat missed the most, and what he dwelled upon first, when talking about his life as a mystic mountain partisan.

FIRAT'S STORY about joining the PKK, and what it meant for him in a positive sense, unexpectedly offered a rare mirror to my own circumstances—a sort of metaphor of my state. His motivations in joining the guerrilla movement revealed aspects of my own relationship to the Middle East that I hadn't before considered. The parallels were rough, but undeniable.

Firat and the many young recruits who were drawn to the PKK, beyond the impulse to fight for their culture or people, *also* sought a certain type of challenge, a level of excitement, the push and pull of life, that just wasn't there for them in their Eastern Turkish backwaters shorn of opportunity. Apart from attending school, there wasn't much for younger people to do in some of these communities. The metaphor isn't precise, but in a less extreme, though not dissimilar way, I sought my own immersion in a form of challenge living in, and travelling through, the

Middle East. My passive, docile and safe home environment in Canada had led me to seek that greater tension in existence.

In the 1990s, a scientific project called Biosphere 2 was initiated in Arizona in the United States, which created the largest enclosed ecological system on Earth. The experiment aimed to monitor several humans living in a giant indoor green space for a period of a few years to explore the viability of a closed ecological system supporting life in outer space. One very small but important finding stood out in the experiment. The project's scientists were confused by the fact that trees within the biosphere failed to grow to full height before they fell over. It was eventually figured out that the trees needed wind, which did not exist indoors. Under normal circumstances, both the core wood in the trunks and the root systems of trees are strengthened by wind, causing them to sway. Or, put another way, their growth is spurred by pressure and mild adversity. Since then much research and writing has shown that systems devoid of tension have a paradoxical negative impact on all living things, especially humans.

One of Kamal Bey's chief complaints about moving to Canada from the Middle East was that his new life was by comparison too easy, alienating and stultifying—bordering on inert. It may also be why Canada, in seeking to be and remain an idyllic place, a safe haven even, had the effect of driving me to an environment and situations of more robust challenge and greater difficulty. I also wondered whether this could have been the real underlying reason I travelled, rather than the pursuit of identity, which, though also there, was a trumped-up and confabulated motivation or rationale. Or maybe the weak social fabric and alienation of Canadian life caused me to seek a more vital human landscape and home abroad. Another form of belonging.

FIRAT and I visited the Duhok Reservoir, just north of the city, on his day off from work. We climbed to the top of the big earthen dam, which overlooks the lake formed by waters flowing down from distant mountains where Firat used to roam as an insurgent. To the northeast lay Mount Gara, a wall of semi-arid peaks. Saddam Hussein, an enemy of the Kurds, built one of his many pleasure palaces on Gara. My new friend became pensive and sombre as he stared out towards those hazy ridges and summits where he once clandestinely trod. Firat was not his usual talkative self.

"What's bothering you?"

His face hardened. "The PKK are there," he said pointing into the distance. "But I feel nothing. They were 10 years wasted. You cannot imagine how terrible these people are."

I said nothing and watched him pace about in an agitated fashion like a caged animal.

"The leaders of the revolution are the worst dictators. They are as bad as the enemy we fought."

Firat's ivory tower depiction of life in the PKK ranks had begun to erode. He started to grumble again as he had on the first day I met him. The mood, tone and details of his story changed in the manner of a Cinderella story caught at the stroke of midnight. Deep disillusion replaced dreamworld fantasy.

I had read that the PKK, below their much brandished freedom fighter image and façade, were really a dogmatic and authoritarian organization. Firat that day confirmed it by virtue of his own experiences. As we sat atop the dam, he told me the rebel leaders demanded absolute obedience to their ideology: that mélange of messianic Marxist, feminist, environmentalist, Kurdish nationalist and anti-imperialist beliefs that drove every decision, no matter how small, and which was weaponized against its own members when needed. Firat said that the PKK would regularly, sternly, discipline any of its members who even slightly stepped out of line—to the point of exile, imprisonment, or even death. A general mood of fear and paranoia permeated the organization.

Abdullah Öcalan, the founder of the PKK who was captured in 1999 and remains imprisoned alone on an Alcatraz-like rock in the Sea of Marmara off the Turkish mainland, is still worshipped as a veritable god by some within the ranks. His ideas and writings, studied by recruits, inform the PKK's agenda. Firat repeatedly harped on the fact that Öcalan encouraged his rebels to attack any Kurds who disagreed with, or spoke out, against the organization. The PKK leadership which came after Öcalan still held to those tactics.

"In war, killing is not difficult. To kill an enemy soldier, it is easy. You can do it—just like that," he said, snapping his fingers loudly. "In one second it is finished. But to kill your own people —this is wrong. To kill our civilians, our soldiers, who say things the leadership don't like, this is very wrong. And they wanted us to do it a lot. I did not like that."

In what would be the start of Firat opening up about why he was banished by the organization, he told me that group celibacy was a core PKK tenet and rule. Given there was an almost equal mix of male and female soldiers, recruits were strictly forbidden from engaging in any intimate relations. There was a three-strike policy where that rule was concerned, he said. The first strike resulted in a warning; the second imprisonment; the third warranted banishment or death. Execution was likely if the offending soldier didn't have any PKK political connections. Firat believed this was the height of hypocrisy since the top cadre, including the big man of the mountain, Öcalan himself, used to cavort with all kinds of women, including members of his all-female bodyguards, whom he used partly for that purpose. But you could say so only at risk of death.

"Well, now you don't have to live by those celibacy rules anymore," I said, as we descended the top of the dam.

Firat laughed, mockingly. "What do you expect me to do now?"

"Maybe find a wife? Get married?"

"How?"

"I've seen lots of young women come into your store."

"This is not what I mean. A woman would never understand my life. How could she understand all I've done: the mountain, missions in Germany, travel to Iran, Marx, *Kapital*...?"

"Does she have to understand?"

"You don't know the Kurdish women. She would be frightened."

"So, find a woman who left the PKK like you did. You said there are thousands of those soldiers here."

Firat stopped in his tracks and looked at me as though I was from another planet.

"You are crazy. It is impossible," he said.

"Why?"

"How can I believe?"

"Believe what?"

"Believe this woman?"

I paused to think. "Do you mean, trust? How can you trust?" I asked.

"Yes, how can I trust?"

"What do you need to trust?"

"She could now be an agent," Firat said, nearing the end of his patience. "Maybe a Turkish agent, maybe a Syrian agent. Maybe one day she'll leave me and go back to the mountain. Maybe one day she will kill me."

No sooner had I thought this was farfetched melodrama than I realized I had the luxury of assuming so with zero risk.

Firat crouched on the ground and stared at those same mountains into the distance.

"No," he said. "I can never trust. Believe me, if it was you, you would do the same."

OUR DISCUSSIONS, I think, acted as a sort of release valve for Firat. I watched him become increasingly unburdened. Though his stories had given me fascinating insights into a shadowy conflict seldom reported on in the West, a different sort of penny dropped around why, fundamentally, people join such groups and movements in the first place. Ideas I had read about previously, and which lay dormant like seeds waiting to sprout, were properly activated by Firat's life experiences. The resulting understandings would not only inform my views about the Middle East, its problems and conflicts—but also the way humans everywhere ticked behaviourally at the group level.

Prior to meeting Firat, I had developed an interest in group psychology and was reading a number of cornerstone works in that field. I'd learned that humans seldom had true agency where their thoughts and actions were concerned, and were instead deeply susceptible to a constellation of connected and overlapping pressures ranging from conditioning, indoctrination, brainwashing, groupthink, cult thinking, and the simple pressure to conform. Being group animals, we are all very easily influenced. Political ideas and beliefs have a tendency to 'go viral' as a result. How susceptible to these dynamics any of us are is to a large extent mitigated by how stabilized we are in our own lives.

One book, entitled *Human Givens*, which I found particularly helpful, makes this last point brutally clear. The work is based on, and named after, a relatively new bio-psycho-social model of therapy and well-being that also has roots in traditional Eastern psychology. The co-authors, Joe Griffin and Ivan Tyrrell, argue that humans have a set of innate emotional needs that are just as crucial as physical needs, and for which we are hardwired.

Those needs are:

- Security
- Giving and receiving attention
- Autonomy and control

- Feeling part of a wider community
- Intimacy
- Privacy
- Status within social groupings
- Competence and achievement
- Meaning and purpose

The authors argue that, when we get our emotional needs met in balance, we experience wellness and can thrive. But the inverse is also true: if some, or many, of our needs are not met, various degrees of anxiety, personal turmoil and even mental illness can ensue.

But here's the clincher: because these innate needs are so important, and because most of us are unaware of them, we tend to pursue them *unconsciously* when they are not met. Most human behaviour, and what we believe to be our true motivations, are driven by them. We may complain constantly to a server at a restaurant about the food, even sending the dishes back to the kitchen, thinking that was the real issue, but we may in fact be seeking attention and control. We may sign up for a night course thinking we are interested in the subject, but we may in fact be seeking community. These needs can also be met poorly in unhealthy or destructive ways, and/or be hijacked by others, leaving us vulnerable.

Firat's story about his time in the Kurdish guerrilla movement became an object lesson about innate needs being unconsciously pursued and met in a less-than-ideal setting. Most of the PKK's rank and file is made up of disillusioned youth like Firat, usually in their 20s, who leave behind lives bereft of meaning and opportunity to be part of something exciting and larger than themselves. More than half of recruits come from the impoverished Turkish provinces on the Iraq border. For these people, the appeal of being part of a large organization can be enormous. Joining the PKK immediately stretches them and offers instant attention, a sense of control, a tight-knit community, and a sense of status, competence and purpose—where none, or little, existed before.

In addition to being instructed in the tenets of a revolutionary political framework that has impacted human history, the partisans are trained to be entirely self-sufficient in the field, and are taught to live off nature for weeks, or even months, at a time. The PKK's policy of gender equality attracts scores of young Kurdish females, who feel stifled and oppressed by the traditional roles forced on them by their families and cultures. Overall, members find a new, exciting and honourable life of widened frontiers with an organization that is accorded great respect by many Kurds. Firat personified those understandings for me in our many talks. For him, being a PKK fighter gave him a sense of meaning and achievement, which was unattainable for him as an alienated youth living in Turkey.

As Firat himself had said to me days earlier about his decision to join the PKK: *And anyway, what else was I going to do in Hakkari?*

I saw that the hijacking of these innate needs in these militant settings—especially by providing a sense of meaning tied to a cosmic struggle which promised glory and honour—applied to numerous other groups in the Middle East, including: ISIS, Al-Qaeda, Hezbollah, Hamas and extreme Jewish settler groups. They could even apply more widely and moderately to many political parties, social movements, and religious organizations. Indeed, it is the deep and sometimes desperate desire to meet these innate emotional needs, which cults, and cult-like movements, take advantage of when drawing in new members. And judging by what Firat revealed to me, the PKK, whatever other definitional boxes it ticked, sounded very much like a cult—and Firat a cult survivor.

Dr. Arthur J. Deikman, late clinical professor of psychiatry at the University of California at San Francisco, explains in his book, *Us and Them: Cult Thinking and the Terrorist Threat*, that another fundamental factor, a need for self-respect, drives people like Firat to join such groups. Referring to Al-Qaeda, but equally applicable to other groups, including the PKK, Deikman writes, "... it is not deprivation or injustice that is the decisive motivation for terror, but the need to see oneself as good and heroic, esteemed by the community and blessed by God... It has been remarked that the basic human instinct is not self-preservation but preservation of the self-image."

The fundamental point Deikman drives home, and which Firat would undoubtedly have concurred with if asked, is that there is no free lunch when joining such groups. What the cult never tells you is that becoming a member is a *transaction* whereby they provide for your unmet needs, but at an unsustainably high price: absolute obedience and the inability to dissent from the group agenda.

IT WASN'T until my second last day in Duhok that Firat explained to me, more or less, why he was kicked out of the PKK. His mention of it came out of the blue during lunch at a busy kebab joint in the *bazaar*.

"I did not like their rules against sex," he said. "And I told them so. I didn't care anymore."

He had stood in support of two friends who were in love and were being persecuted within the ranks. I wondered whether he was actually speaking about himself, but I didn't ask. Firat told me that he resolved to defect from the organization when he began to experience pushback for supporting his friends. But the PKK found out about his plans to leave. They arrested Firat and threw him into jail for three months.

While we ate, Firat rolled up his sleeves and showed me the scars on his wrists which, he said, were caused by the tightly bound wire which clasped his hands together for the entirety of his imprisonment.

When I asked Firat how and why he was let go instead of being killed, he said that his contributions to the PKK over the years—including doing jail time abroad while on missions to the Netherlands and Germany—saved his life. Instead of being executed for his disobedience, the PKK leadership expelled him, citing the made-up charge that he was an agent for the Turks. Given that he was a wanted man in Turkey and couldn't go back there, Firat was ordered to walk down the mountains alone to the valleys of northern Iraq to begin a new life in exile. His father, whom he managed to contact beforehand, travelled from Turkey to Iraq to pick him up at a predetermined spot along a lonely mountain road. He drove him to the city of Duhok—just six months before we met.

Firat's story had come full circle.

WHEN I WENT to say goodbye to Firat at his store the next day, he was sitting with a few other shop owners around his laptop. He was downloading one of the several Harry Potter films.

"I was in the mountain so long, I don't know any of these movies," he said smiling. "It will take me years to catch up."

"I came to tell you that I'm travelling to Erbil today," I said.

"When are you coming back?" he asked, trying to disguise a look of disappointment.

"I'm not," I said. "I'm going to Shaklawa and Amedi afterwards. And then to Turkey."

He nodded, looking away, with a somewhat pained expression on his face. "You are welcome anytime," he added. "Remember Dubai Bazaar. You will find me here."

We embraced.

As we made that final small talk that all people everywhere use to draw out partings and render them less abrupt, I asked Firat how he'd feel about me writing about him and his story in the future.

He tilted his head from side to side, tentatively weighing the proposition.

"I can change your name," I said.

"Change my name?" he said mockingly, followed by laughter.

Firat then waved me towards the door, a distance from his friends. When we got there, he looked back to make sure he was out of earshot.

"Do you think I am really 'Firat Uzun'?" he said in a whisper. "Even my best friends here don't know my real name."

Firat held my gaze. His dead-serious look melted back into a smile. He then winked at me and took a few steps backwards before turning and heading back to his friends, and perhaps the first of a few Harry Potter films.

The Road to Mardin

Disorientation. The airy emptiness of the pitch black ether. A blustery mountain downdraft buffeting my ears. I return, disappointingly, to where I had been all along.

The replay in my mind of those Middle Eastern scenes, marking the trajectory of my journey leading to that moment at the Turkish military roadblock, couldn't have taken more than a few seconds; yet it was as if I had relived it all as it actually happened. The experience of time, I knew, was fluid and subjective—a matter of perception. But to recollect decades packaged into an instant was an experience of another order. Was this the end of my life? The proverbial flashback which precedes one's demise?

A soldier was suddenly before me, his illuminated hand holding my passport. He extended the document towards me. I took it disbelievingly. He said something in Turkish and with a tone and inflection that sounded like everything was more or less fine. When I didn't answer, he repeated himself, and I said "Okay" in a reflex to placate him.

Even though my eyes had grown accustomed to the dark

while standing down the road from the bus I had been yanked off, I still couldn't discern his facial features and body language to confirm whether I was being let go.

"No Mardin," the soldier said, just as as his colleagues had told me earlier, referring to one of my intended destinations. I was confused. The fear began to creep back.

When I was led by the arm again, this time back towards the bus, I repeatedly told myself that a condemned man, or a person to be jailed, would not be handed back their ID. The terror began to lift. I found myself back at my bag, in the place where I had previously been standing with the others who were pulled off the bus with me. The lineup of other men was now gone. The soldier waved his flashlight beam rapidly at my bag, saying something to me while pointing to the bus. I concluded I was to take my things and put them back into the vehicle hold. Two other soldiers stood by watching, holding flashlights. I closed my pack, which was still open, and took it to the baggage hold and tossed it in.

As I climbed back onto the bus and took my seat, I wondered if I had been walked down the road in order not to see what had happened to others pulled off the vehicle. The passengers who were awake and who, judging by their looks, were keenly aware of the situation, stared at me with what looked like worried interest.

The driver went out to close the door of the hold and climbed back aboard in laboured stomps. He started the engine and shut the door, which closed in a loud hiss. The bus made a long and tortuous three-point-turn that took forever to execute. As we headed back towards Erzincan in the other direction, I could dimly see the military vehicles at the earlier road block we had passed. There had to have been fighting, or an operation, along our original route, causing the army to close it. I assumed that the 'No Mardin' comment was the soldier trying to say that we couldn't travel any further.

So vivid were the memories of my flashbacks, combined with the intensity of the fear that had consumed me, that it took a while for me to register that the bearded Kurdish man who had previously sat beside me, and who had been yanked off the bus at the checkpoint with me—the man who loved the rebellious trio of Jesus, and Sayyid Qutb, and Sheikh Said—was no longer in his seat.

Part IV: Beyond East and West

Anatolian Dreams

Home is not where you are born; home is where all your attempts to escape cease.
— Naguib Mahfouz

Nuribrahim glanced at me guilefully as he poured the tea into small rounded Turkish tea glasses. "This is a special occasion," he said in Arabic. "You are the first foreigner who has visited our village in a very long time."

Three of us sat on plastic patio furniture outdoors behind his home amid the once-stately, but now crumbling and half-abandoned stone houses of the village of Dereiçi.

Thoma, Nuribrahim's cousin, another middle-aged man, whose mirth was amplified by his great handlebar moustache, lifted his hand in protest.

"What *foreigner*, Nuri?" he said, gesturing. "You heard him: the brother is from Mardin!"

Nuribrahim looked at me and nodded with a smile, as he continued pouring the tea. "True," he said, putting the teapot down. "Even though you weren't born here, brother John, you are still a son of Mardin."

I was on a day trip to the semi-arid foothills of the Tur Abdin region of southeastern Turkey—the historic cradleland of Mesopotamia's Assyrian community.* The village of Dereiçi, nestled circumspectly in a valley on my route, called out as we passed. I asked the hired driver to pull over. At first, I assumed it was the draw of the architecture—the handful of beautiful, restored, honey-coloured stone homes rising proudly from the rubble and ruins of the town's earlier incarnations. But there was also a palpably heavy mood, one of deep poignance, even a tragic feeling, emanating from it. The village, dating back over a thousand years, gave the impression of a place both alive and dead, awkwardly straddling dimensions in time. Even the town's few inhabitants moved about tentatively, skittishly, flitting about like ghosts, or squatters keeping a low profile, amid the stone and scrub brush. A troubled silence, occasionally shattered by a rooster crowing, or a donkey braying, amplified the strangeness.

After I met and befriended Nuribrahim, I was let in on the secret: Dereiçi was dealt a nearly mortal blow during World War One. In 1915, nearly a century earlier, Ottoman Turkish forces and its local allied militias, who were waging war against the invading Russians in the region, massacred most of the inhabitants of the town as part of the wider campaign to eliminate the Christians of Anatolia.† It was the same tragedy, involving the same players, that befell some of my father's ancestors who lived in nearby Mardin.

I shared with the two men what little I knew of my own family's story—to great fellow feeling and commiseration, which created an instant bond. But as the three of us sat sipping tea in

---

* Known by various other names—such as Chaldeans, Syriacs, Nestorians, Jacobites—the Assyrians are the descendants of the Assyrian, Babylonian, Chaldean and Aramaean peoples of ancient Mesopotamia.
† "Anatolia" is originally a Greek word meaning 'The East' and refers to the Asian area of modern Turkey.

that odd twilight zone where the emanations of past and present intermingled around us, the conversation took an unexpected turn. Nuribrahim reached into his pant pocket and removed his wallet. He opened it and showed me a faded old passport-sized hand-coloured photo of a stern-looking elderly man with a white beard and wearing a red fes hat.

"If it were not for this man," he said, "we would not be sitting with you now."

His name, Nuribrahim said, was Wehbe Effendi Seyin: an Ottoman Turkish army officer who had lived in a large house on a hilltop a few kilometres away. In 1915 Wehbe Effendi came to the aid of Dereiçi in the hours after the massacre and brought dozens of surviving villagers—wounded and orphaned children and youth—to his large estate, where they were later raised as his own. When they were old enough, the rescued kids moved back to the abandoned village to start new lives and begin the process of regenerating the otherwise dead settlement.

Wehbe Effendi's intervention was considered such a great act of kindness, and with such enormous repercussions for Dereiçi, that many of the villagers, like Nuribrahim, carried photos of the Turkish officer—as if he were a close family member or ancestor. The men told me that Wehbe Effendi's Turkish descendants still occupied the original home on the hilltop and maintained friendly relations with the village.

"That's a happy ending to a sad story," I said.

"We would be happier if there was an ending—but things still continue as they did before," Nuribrahim said.

"What do you mean?"

Nuribrahim shrugged his shoulders resignedly, as if to say he did not know where to begin.

Thoma leaned in. "We have trouble here still. With some of the Kurds. The PKK. We are caught between them and the state."

"Keep your voice down, Thoma," Nuribrahim cut in.

"And our relatives in Syria, the children of our ancestors who fled there in 1915, are now being finished off. One hundred years later."

Thoma was referring to the killing of Christians at the hands of Salafi jihadist militias in Syria's civil war, raging across the border just to the south of us.

"There aren't many of us left," he continued. "Soon we'll all be gone."

Nuribrahim, making an effort to lighten the mood after a lengthy pause in the conversation, smiled and moved a small plate of shortbread cookies closer to me.

"Have some more," he said reassuringly, before taking a cookie for himself. "Let's focus on the good news."

"What good news?" Thoma asked.

"Right here, before you. A son of Mardin, as you yourself just said, has returned home." Nuribrahim became pensive before speaking again: "It's very true what our old traditions say."

"What's that?" I asked.

"That in the end everything returns to its source."

THE SOFT LIGHT of Mesopotamia's rekindled dawn had ushered in my arrival in Mardin a few days earlier. Our shared mini bus, crammed with morning-tranquilized villagers swaying together to the rhythm of twists, turns and bumps on the road, raced towards the ancient citadel in the distance at a reckless sprint. Mardin's old town, perched on the slope of a rocky outcrop overlooking vast cultivated lowlands, bore the gentle incandescence of the rising sun in the east. The place resembled the Silk Road city of my imagination, hovering dreamily over a vast and hazy expanse of checkerboard farmland of the Syrian plain.

In some ways my arrival there was just another excursion to a place not yet visited; the unfurling of *terra incognita*, and the rendering of my mental maps of the yet-unseen Middle East into reality. But in another more important sense, it was a terminus. Mardin was the final stage of a long, meandering, and mostly ad hoc journey, backwards and upstream, in search of who I was and what I wanted to be. It was also a part of a larger reckoning with the Middle East and its disparate yet interwoven threads of East and West.

Given that my travels and sojourns in the region followed a trajectory leading back in ancestral time, and into the hinterlands of geography and memory, Mardin was the ultimate endpoint. It was the culmination of my feverish obsessions and complexes around belonging, if only for one reason: the town was the furthest and final locality tied to me that could yet satisfy my desire to connect more deeply with my Eastern roots. It was an obscure outpost whose seductive tendrils of historical exotica extended in all directions, and to seemingly everywhere remote.

Mardin was a northern outpost of historical Greater Syria, situated where the Arab World, Persia, Asia Minor, and Mesopotamia all converged in a dizzying melange of ethnicities and sects for whom the town, and its surrounding region, had long been a home: Arabs, Turks, Kurds, Jews, Yezidis, Armenians, Assyrians, Turcomen, Chechens, and Circassians.* It was situated not just at the crossroads of former empires, but along the East-West nexus of hemispheres and civilizations that was the Silk Road, which continued into Iran and eastward to Central Asian Tartary and the Far East. Mardin was a notable enough community that Marco Polo made a stop here. As too did the Mongols under Hulagu Khan, who captured the strategic perch.

Mardin's physical appearance embodied something of this long catalogue of associations and connections to the deep past.

---

* A typical *Mardelli* (the word denoting a person hailing from Mardin) spoke a brusque North Mesopotamian dialect of Arabic also called *Mardelli*, (or *Qeltu* or *Moslawi*), that is also spoken in northeastern Syria and in the Mosul region of Iraq.

Foundationally, there was something crude, almost Neolithic, in the town's craggy, rock-hewn countenance. The architectural refinements of a once-high and localized civilization both belied and complemented the almost neolithic spirit of place. The town's 12th century Islamic quarter, a beehive of terraced and beige-coloured limestone homes with arched windows and colonnades, built by the Central Asian Seljuks, glowed honey-gold in the morning light. Flocks of pigeons cartwheeled and careened joyfully over the town, skipping between the ornamented minarets and stone-carved madrassa domes redolent of the religious monuments of Bokhara and Samarkand.

After failing to find the sort of belonging I sought in Egypt, Lebanon or Syria, those more recent locales and way stations of my ancestry, all I had left was this lonely hilltop town. It was here that I hoped to settle on the profound connection to a place that once and for all would clarify and represent all things East in me. A place so unknown that not even Kamal Bey, in all of his Middle Eastern erudition, could speak about at any length, or with any authority.

I ALSO CAME to these parts with a more practical purpose: to write about the impact of the Syrian civil war on the nearby Turkish border area in and around the town of Nusaybin—an ancient satellite community of Mardin. Nusaybin had become an important border crossing on the eastern frontier between the two countries and was populated mostly by Kurds. But before heading there, I decided to explore and survey the landmarks of Mardin's old *medina*, where the dispossessed communities to which I was tied had once lived.

My connection to Mardin, now both faint and physically tenuous, was through my paternal grandfather. In 1915, he, along with his mother and siblings, fled Mardin as the ruling Ottomans massacred the local Armenian and Assyrian Christians, of which he was a hybrid mix. He was only four or five years old at the time. That episode was part of a larger historical chapter that Armenians call "The Armenian Genocide" and Assyrians refer to as 'The Sword.' When his own father was killed in that episode, my grandfather and his family, after years on the road, found their way to Egypt, where both my own parents were born and later met.

I spent the first few days in Mardin walking the byways of the old town, looking for evidence of those older vanquished communities, and speaking to people in an attempt to uncover any connections to the place. It quickly dawned on me that there was little left to work with. The fact that my family had long since left Mardin made connecting with it a more difficult undertaking. The nodes of community cohesion—the churches—were shuttered. Any kin, save a few descendants of the survivors, were long scattered to the winds. But there was a faint psychic echo, vibrational vestiges, of a once more diverse living culture. Some of the material artifacts of Mardin struck a vague but poignant chord inside of me: old Armenian mansions, the teardrop-shaped *Salbak* motifs carved in the ancient stone architecture, the local floral jewellery and linen embroideries, and a strange anthropomorphic image of a local demigod known as *Shahmaran*: an ancient two-headed mythological half-woman, half-snake deity of Indo-Iranian origin, depicted in art and seen everywhere in town. I wondered if as a child I had seen a few such objects, or motifs, at the home of family members. Or perhaps I was tapping into collective unconscious memories?

Ultimately, for all its old-world loveliness, Mardin felt somehow gutted of its patchwork multi-ethnic glory, a place taken over and converted into something of a museum piece. The best-preserved Armenian homes had been renovated and co-opted by the Turkish municipality. A national tourism campaign had recently branded Mardin the "City of Tolerance." That marketing initiative cited the town's manifold ethnic makeup which existed *before* it was deliberately erased in that notorious reflex of confessional bloodletting (which the tourist campaign didn't mention). The reality was that the remaining Kurds and Arabs, who each half populated the town, lived together in a mostly quiet yet tense coexistence. They, in turn, were watched suspiciously by the smattering of Turks from their high military perch atop the rocky crag, which, in addition to gazing into Syria, was also an operational base in its never-ending skirmishing with the PKK. What few Christian families remained, like Nuribrahim and Thoma who I met days later in Dereiçi, were too small in number and too powerless to matter.

Most people stumbling upon the place, knowing little about its history beforehand, would see Mardin for what it was in that moment: yet another politically-fraught community in Turkey's volatile southeast. After days spent there, not even I could avoid drawing a similar conclusion, causing me, naturally, to feel less connected to Mardin than I was to Egypt, or the Levant, where at least I knew some of the language, and could draw direct connections to family still living there.

I wasn't able to digest this realization before a kind of madness, partly the result of the disappointment with Mardin, overtook me. That episodic derangement began after I spent the day wandering around Nusaybin, the bustling Kurdish town near the Syrian border known for its smuggling, political intrigues and cat-and-mouse games between Turkish agents and the PKK. I had just finished photographing the anemic barbed-wire border fence and the no-man's-land separating Nusaybin from its estranged sister city of Qamishli in northern Syria. Manned Turkish military lookout towers ran at intervals along the fence. Tired of walking on eggshells that day with my photography, I decided to change tack, de-stress, and play the tourist for a while. I hired a car to go to the nearby Eastern Roman ruins of Dara: a 6th century Byzantine outpost that once straddled the old border with Sassanid Persia—a kind of East-West divide at the time. The unticketed site was located beside a poor village and contained large underground cisterns. Few, if any, of the trickle of travellers who came through the area, ever went there.

As I wandered the hauntingly still grounds to the clanging of nearby sheep bells and the occasional crowing of roosters, a young girl, from the adjacent village approached me. The urchin had auburn hair and was wearing track pants, plastic flip-flops and a pink t-shirt. As she came audaciously close, she held out her hand and spoke to me commandingly in Kurdish, calling me *Apo*—which I learned was the local word for 'paternal uncle.'* I assumed, at first, she was begging, but as she neared me I saw she was holding what looked like old coins, which she thrust into view. When I saw that, I turned and walked away. A kind of cottage industry in fake ancient coins exists at some archeological sites around the world. I'd seen them and their hawkers both at ancient Carthage near Tunis, and at Byblos in Lebanon.

Yet the girl doubled down in her resolve, screaming "Apo! Apo! Apo!" as she ran with surprising deftness and speed through the rock-strewn landscape in her flip-flops, keeping just a few feet behind me. When I realized the relentless pursuit would not end, I stopped and fished for some Turkish lira in my wallet. The girl also stopped in her tracks and fixated on my hands. I handed her a two lira coin and began to walk away.

"Apo!!" the girl yelled, louder than she had before.

I looked back. The child then transferred the coins into her other hand, picked one out and made a softball-style pitch, underhand, tossing it towards me before scampering off in the direction of the concrete huts. It was an honourable move on her part, I thought, given she didn't have to part with it.

---

* The word *Apo* is also the nickname, honorific, and *nom de guerre* of Abdullah Öcalan, the founder of the PKK.

I was about to continue to the cisterns, but my curiosity got the better of me. I headed to where the coin had landed on the ground, and started to fish for it. When I found it and picked it up, I saw that it wasn't a coin, but a circular pendant. On one side it had the profile of a man's head inside of a square. When I turned it over, the piece contained block Arabic writing, almost Kufic script, which was faded. I placed the pendant in my pocket, thinking it was a good forgery for some impoverished counterfeiter with limited means and virtually no clientele.

BACK AT MY hotel room in Mardin, I took a closer look at the pendant, which struck me as possibly genuine. I did an internet search on it and concluded, perhaps wrongly, that I was in possession of a real artefact based on others like it online. It resembled a copper dinar coin-turned-pendant from the Artuqid Dynasty—the Seljuk period in the Middle Ages to which the beautiful old stone architecture of Mardin belonged. I'm not sure how I became feverishly obsessed with this object to the point of losing my mind, but I remember the powerful feeling coming over me, euphoric in intensity, that I was in possession of an ancient and powerful tribal heirloom that was *meant* to fall into my hands.

From that moment on, I felt identified with Mardin—far more than my tenuous and distant connection to the town justified. I stared at the piece, seemingly forever, turning it over, feeling its markings and edges, imagining its bygone owners, and falling hypnotically under a spell cast by my mind about the identity it bestowed upon me—and validated. I imagined wearing the pendant as a marking of 'my people' and their deep historicity. It would be proof of my mysterious Eastern bona fides dating back to ancestors so obscure, exotic, and fabled—so unique and unheard of—as to make my Easternness infinitely more lofty and unassailable. None of the history tied to the piece was conventional, or cliché. It occupied a niche of its own. Instead of the conventional mélange of common ethnicities to which I was tied, and felt somewhat estranged from by my North American birth and upbringing, here was something new and exciting. Those uplifting feelings were expressed as a voice inside of me announcing the new mashup of trumped-up associations, as if from the rooftops:

> *Mardin! Silk Road station! The fairy tale lands of the octagonal-roofed buildings of the Seljuks and Armenians. Snow-capped mountains on the edges of the Steppes. Mesopotamia: cradle of civilizations! The Artuqids! The Assyrians! Ashurbanipal, King of the World, smashing lions with fists like sledgehammers and sinewy forearms thick as battering rams! All else who dare transgress: beware, for we are a hoary and ruthless nation!*

This was now *me*. I was "a son of Mardin," as Nuribrahim in Dereiçi had said. The pendant was bounty and reparation for my lost ancestors and my sense of place. I was embracing a new, more narrow, absolute. To hell with everything else that made up who I was. I had found the bold and attractive version of the East that I had long sought. All that I had endured, all of the travels and lives lived, all of the journeys criss-crossing the Middle East that flashed before me as a caravan of memories at the Turkish military roadblock, led to this moment. I had found my bearings, my true East! And the East, of course, as in all great and fateful homecomings, had also found me.

TODAY, when I look back, I see that pendent—owned and perhaps dropped accidentally by some faceless soul now long forgotten to the world, if not a forgery—held no magical power. There was no guiding Providence at play, no 'Fate' involved in my receiving it beyond my own repeating patterns of thinking and behaving which constitute a different sort of 'destiny'. I was desperately looking for something with which to attach, to identify with, and which was ultimately tied to something we might call ego. My desire to claim a more interesting heritage that was more boldly and fantastically Eastern, and that had slowly dampened with my failed attempts to assimilate into other parts of the Middle East, suddenly sprung back with a vengeance—as if it were fighting for its very life. A bad habit, repeating urge, or addiction is most tenacious when it is faced with its own extinction and mounts a return.

But in that moment, I was far from such clarity. Instead, I was faced with a more immediate and practical problem: if the pendant was real—and in that moment nothing could have been more so—by leaving the country with it I would technically be in possession of a contraband artefact. I was instantly torn between risking being caught trying to take it home with me, and leaving behind my rightful bequest and endowment—the ultimate symbol and evidence of my reawakened sense of self.

For the next few days I wandered around Mardin's quiet cobblestone backstreets and alleys in hand-wringing angst as the two roads forward, the two choices before me, battled to a draw. I schemed over solitary meals of lentil soup, *lahmacun* and *ayran*, in which the other restaurant goers, mostly older men, must have watched me as I mumbled to myself about how the pendant was mine—and that I would return with it; only to moments later make the decision, when slightly calmer, that I had best let the object go. During my endless deliberations and circuits of the old town, and the many pit stops for tea at cafes with panoramic views of the lowlands, I became almost paranoid that someone had seen me pick up the pendant at the ancient site. Or worse: that I was being watched, or followed even, by people who had somehow found out that I had. Two very ordinary-looking and middle-aged men in slacks and button-down shirts, who looked like local merchants but which my mind had tagged as plainclothes agents of the state, seemed to be tailing me that day. Soon I became suspicious that nearly *all* pedestrian traffic was part of an operation devoted to my surveillance. When one elderly jeweller-cum-pawn shop owner asked me in his store if I had anything to sell, I was certain he too was onto me and the pendant. I quickly and rudely slipped out of his shop and made a beeline to my hotel.

From then on, the indecision about whether to part with the pendant, the deep ruts of thought and obsession, became so acute and unresolvable that I entered a paralytic phase of my mania. I lay in bed, seemingly, for days. What coherency I had left was wracked by a kind of fever. I stared endlessly at the pendant in my hand, all the while withdrawn and caught in the terrible clash between two roads: the way of the ego, fixed identity and certainty, versus letting go and the acceptance of ambiguity. I had gone so far deep into the rabbit hole of irresolution that I had, for all intents and purposes, frozen myself stiff. Indecision, no decision, the avoidance of an uncertain outcome, is a far greater punishment than even a flawed or wrong course of action—but from which there is always a path forward. Deep indecision may stave off possible error, but the price is inertia. At that cul-de-sac one ceases to be present, or even exist.

I don't know how long this derangement would have lasted, or how things may have otherwise turned out had I not forced myself to break the impasse during a fleeting pause in the delirium. After another feverish night filled with the sounds of barking dogs fighting turf wars, and a few random gunshots across the plains, I awoke to some semblance of my old self, relatively calm and clear. I stared at the broken ceiling fan amid the horn-honking and hawkers shouting in the street below. In that moment, I realized that I had spent days, but a period that felt infinitely longer, in a kind of no-man's-land that I never again wanted to return to.

A *no-man's-land.*

Kamal Bey, years ago, had described the rigid mind, hellbent on certainty, as casting its owner into a spiritual Land of Nod: a kind of "no man's land."

I need to move quickly, I told myself, before the window of clarity slammed shut again.

I got dressed, left the room, and went down to Mardin's main square, where I boarded a *dolmus*, a shared minibus. I went back to Nusaybin on the Syrian border, where I had been days earlier researching and taking photos for my article. Once there I made my way to the scraggly barbed-wire border fence at the southern extremity of town, beyond which lay the fallow field and buffer zone separating Turkey from Syria. As I walked alongside it, I reached into my pocket where I was carrying the pendant. And with deep relief that has not since been equalled, I surreptitiously tossed it through the wide gap in the barbed wire—onto the several hundred-kilometre long thin ribbon of demilitarized land, filled with weeds, that remains unclaimed by any tribe.

A Turkish soldier in an adjacent observation tower, I noticed, looked on as I walked back towards the centre of Nusaybin in the light, buoyant steps of a person who has just shaken a monkey off his back.

THROUGHOUT MY OBSESSIVE monomania in Mardin, and in its lead up, I had missed an obvious message which stared me in the face. The town's main lesson, its most poignant legacy for the world, was that it was formerly a rare meld, an alloy, a patchwork, successfully combining many different cultures in a deeply tribal region. This erstwhile crossroads of the world in-miniature was trying to tell me that it is okay to eschew seeing oneself as strictly one thing versus another. Even the pretence of a strict East-West dichotomy and my mental conundrum tied to it is subsumed in this lesson. What is 'East' or 'West' other than degrees of movement, or positions, along a continuum of varying but ultimately complementary perspectives and experiences—and which have forever influenced each other? In one direction the sun rises, in the other it sets: two sides of the same coin. I was neither entirely one nor the other. I was both. And perhaps in a more metaphysical sense I was also none of these things and thus beyond it—it didn't matter. Canadian, North American, Arab, Western, Eastern, Syrian, Lebanese, Assyrian, Egyptian, Armenian, Torontonian—I am all of these things in different measure according to where I find myself in the moment. That pastiche is woven into one fabric that is now *my* patchwork cloak. This was how Kamal Bey, himself at times caught in the push and pull of belonging, handled the mélange of who he was. He embraced all his aspects, but none so much that it unhinged him, or came at the disparagement of others in the manner of jingoistic nationalism or the politics of identity. This is what drew me to him in the first place.

A few years ago, just prior to his death from old age, I related to Kamal Bey everything that unfolded on my trip to Mardin. He listened to me with an almost grave fascination, with his hand on his chin, as he affirmed my story with his repeating 'ahas.' Indeed it was Kamal Bey who once told me that it was the excessive preoccupation with identity and tribe that had laid havoc to the Middle East. That same obsession, a fixation in overreach, had metastasized, he said, like a cancer and begun to spread also to the West, revealing itself there in its "culture wars."

"As Middle Easterners, we've seen this story before and know what happens next," he said, putting his teacup down, as he fidgeted with his yellow worry beads in his other hand. "There is a Latin expression: *Homo homini lupus*. 'A man is wolf to another man.'"

"But this trend will probably reverse," I said.

"I'm not so sure—it may be the opposite. People playing this tribal game here have no idea of the fire they're toying with. It may one day erase them—and quite suddenly."

"What can be done about it?"

"What is there to do? Can you force another person to see before they have new eyes? Notice how it took years of travel for you to realize what you now understand: that no matter how hard you tried you could not force yourself into another mould. You could not find your place in Mardin, Cairo, or Timbuktu—those places together had to find themselves in you, and on their terms."

He leaned forward taking his tea cup and and sat back again.

"It could be that in five hundred or a thousand years, after much more drama, we'll come to our senses, reach a place of balance," he added. "Or perhaps we'll disappear like the dinosaurs, and a new species will rise to replace us. And everything begins all over again."

"Or maybe we'll sooner pull through," I suggested.

"There is no bigger 'maybe' as far as I'm concerned."

"So, how do you think it will play out?"

Kamal Bey glanced up briefly, then raised his index finger and worry beads to the ceiling and sky above it, keeping them there, before holding my gaze with a sly grin.

Afterword

"The only true constant in the universe is change," Kamal Bey would sometimes say, commenting, in part, on the ability of events to upend our surest expectations. The Middle East has undergone changes that were either unthinkable, or at least unanticipated at the time, as I was in the final stages of editing and publishing this book. Much of it has been an object lesson in causality and the law of unintended consequences.

The Hamas massacres in Israel on October 7th, 2023, set off a chain of events that will reverberate long after this book goes to press. Gaza has been obliterated, Hiroshima-like, by a thousand cuts. A great many innocents have met an undignified end in this most recent convulsion of an ongoing territorial tribal war of annihilation, kept alive at this moment by an extreme Zionist government at the helm in Israel. All this, partly facilitated by a novel military AI technology designed to destroy whole buildings, city blocks and large extended families, without thought or remorse, sometimes just to eliminate individual targets. This machine logic warfare tool, which received less media attention than it should have, will likely proliferate and reappear in future conflicts elsewhere.

The dramatically labelled 'Axis of Resistance' has collapsed.

Hamas and Hezbollah have been largely crippled. Syria's Assads have been overthrown and replaced by a Sunni government owing much fealty, for the moment, to the Turks, who themselves view Syria partly as a chess piece in their games of regional influence. Iran, for its part, has been effaced in the Levant, and has had its paper tiger dimensions exposed for all to see after a bombing campaign by the Americans and Israelis. Given the Israeli Prime Minister is exercising a near-perpetual military response largely designed to keep his political career alive, further instalments of that so called "12-day War" may yet be forthcoming—and with worse to show for it.

On the slightly more positive side of this ledger, the peoples of Syria and Lebanon, now freer from the constraints and difficulties forced upon them by their old overlords, are working, albeit under highly tenuous circumstances, towards possibly more promising futures. Convulsions of violence involving the *Sunni*, *Druze* and *Alawi* communities, and the Israelis, in Syria, has dampened some of that early optimism. The Turks and PKK, however, are talking again. One reason, beyond complex Turkish domestic political and electoral considerations, is that high-tech drone warfare has eroded the PKK's guerrilla tactical upper-handedness. But as we're also seeing with so much else, costly stalemates simply have their expiry dates.

All of these changes are in addition to the innumerable shifts in the physical and human landscape across the region not dramatic enough to warrant much notice: CCTV cameras in Cairo, the Russian military in the Libyan Desert, blingy shopping malls and Burger Kings in Baghdad, Formula 1 in Jedda, apocalypse in Sudan. As one Middle East-watcher friend who prides himself on being in the know said recently: "There's so much happening, I can't keep up anymore."

This concentrated pile-on of events can seem overwhelming for those of us witnessing it and/or feeling it more directly in the now. But looked at from the perspective of history—from a century ago in the aftermath of World War One in the region with the collapse of the Ottoman Empire, the formation of artificial nation-states and the redrawing of borders à la Sykes-Picot—things were just as fluid, ever-changing and momentous then.

I remember talking often with Kamal Bey, as I have with others close to me, about the Middle East and its possible futures —when things might once and for all ameliorate, settle, reach some kind of equilibrium. Kamal Bey envisaged a more Islamist Middle East emerging in which the political entity of Israel would be slowly, but more naturally, absorbed into the region, dissolving through a kind osmosis, as the medieval Crusader States once did. Another friend felt that the region might revert in the future to a kind of workable federation of interconnected cities, as it once existed under the Ottomans—but without the imperial yoke. And there were other musings. All of those visions, partly because we can't see past them, feel like cul-de-sacs, ends of history. But we are so habituated to thinking in terms of neat solutions, end states, and utopian finalities (i.e., the arrival to a place of human rights, justice, and the rule of law). They are the scenarios where things finally come to a rest in a manner that our brains, ever seeking to stabilize the world around us in an acceptable manner, would have happen—but which often don't. And in the ever complex and hidden reality in which things operate differently in a wider field of causality, each new human chapter in a story, anyway, is more of a way station than a destination itself.

We are now seeing that in the West: what was once felt and assumed to be a sort of permanence defined by unprecedented affluence and stability, and peak material power born of a Pax Americana with seemingly no end, is just another passing stage. We easily forget (or willfully deny) how peoples come and go, maps and place names change, oppressors and oppressed swap roles, great powers and civilizations shift: sometimes towards the East, other times to the West. One of the great untaught concepts in our Western culture and education system that underlies all of this (and more), is the reality and impact of a process known as entropy. In Eastern thought, the idea is partly captured in the notion of impermanence. We'd be less jilted and better prepared —if only philosophically—to deal with the political shifts we are now seeing, which the Chinese, in their past wisdom and subtle irony, referred to as "interesting times."

    I'm sure my ancestors in Mardin, for whom a workable coexistence with their many ethnic neighbours was always the norm, were just as caught off guard by the inhumane events of World War One that played out locally in Anatolia. They only survived, and subsequently thrived, due to tremendous luck, and by moving with the flow of change, both literally and figuratively, to another place. As did my parents after them. And as, even now, I sometimes ponder doing in light of changing realities.

Appendix: Some Historical Background on the Mardin Family Connection

In June of 1915, Girgis Manoushian, a respected Armenian merchant from the town of Mardin, was abducted from his home by members of an armed militia group. He, along with hundreds of other men, was taken to the ancient fortress built into the rocky hilltop overlooking the town and occupied by Ottoman Turkish troops. A local bishop had also been hauled there in chains and brought before Mardin's stern chief of police on charges that his church and its members were concealing and moving caches of illegal weapons on behalf of rebels fighting the Ottoman Empire. Over the next several days, Manoushian, the bishop, and the rest of the detained members of that community were beaten, tortured and forced to renounce their religion.

Three days later, for reasons that remain unknown, Manoushian was released—or somehow managed to escape captivity. By the time he returned home to his wife, Aziza, and his three young children, he was barely able to walk, as his captors had beaten his feet with cudgels. Armed men returned to his door a few days later and hauled him away from his family once more.

He was never seen again.

At the time, World War One was in full swing, and the Ottoman Empire, allied to Germany and the Central Powers, was in crisis. For decades the empire had been in rapid decline, losing territory and earning it the humiliating honorific, "The Sick Man of Europe." On the battlefield, the Ottoman Turks faced strong resistance from the Allied powers, including the advancing Russian army at the far-flung edges of eastern Anatolia. Some of the local Armenian Christian population living on, or near, Russia's borders, sided, and in some cases fought, with the Russians against their own Ottoman overlords. This didn't just happen on the battlefront, but also by way of fifth column organizations that had been agitating for Armenian autonomy, or independence for decades.

The Ottomans, in a panic, sensing the imminent disintegration of their empire and seeing the Russians pressing hard in the East, began to regard all Armenians as traitors, collaborators, and spies—and thus an existential threat. The decision was made by a coterie of ultra-nationalist Ottoman leaders to ethnically cleanse Anatolia of its Armenian and wider Christian population through murder and deportation. The tribal persecution and killing of minorities in those territories had been happening in staggered and de facto fashion since the late 1800s. The urgency and madness of war turned it into a pressing and organized effort, involving Anatolia's governors, the military and citizen militias.

The local point man for this project in the Vilayet of Diyarbakir (the Ottoman province where Mardin was located), was its newly appointed governor, Dr. Mehmed Reshid, also known as Reshid Bey—a fanatical pan-Turkic nationalist from the Caucasus who was close to the Ottoman Sultan's inner circle of hardline ministers executing the war effort. He was determined to prevent the Armenian collaboration with Russia at the Eastern front from spreading to his province—an arguably non-existent possibility for numerous reasons.* In his mind, that meant targeting other Christian denominations in his jurisdiction. That

---

* Mardin's Armenians were Arabized (they spoke mostly Arabic, the *lingua franca* of the town), unpolitical, and not connected to events near Russia.

included the mélange of Semitic Mesopotamians, primarily Assyrians, of which Manoushian's wife, Aziza Salmo, was one.

By June 1915, having disposed of all those in authority who opposed this plan, and with the killing having commenced in other parts of Anatolia, Reshid began the liquidation of citizens in his province. Those events would later earn him the nickname the "Butcher of Diyarbakir." For the few surviving victims, the events around 1915 would be remembered as the Armenian Genocide or as *Seyfo* in the Assyrian language, meaning 'The Sword.'

GIRGIS MANOUSHIAN and his widow Aziza Salmo were my paternal great-grandparents. We don't know too many details about what happened afterwards, as Aziza later spoke only in snippets about those events—if at all. But she did relate how her husband met his end, as told to her by witnesses. After Manoushian was picked up again by Reshid Bey's myrmidons, he was marched in one of the first long execution columns, with hundreds of other men, into the killing fields of the countryside towards Diyarbakir. Once there, Manoushian was taken with a smaller group of around 50 men, including a bishop, and killed. Because the economically strained Ottoman military sought to conserve its bullets for the war, most of the killings was undertaken with blades and scimitars. Victims had their throats cut and stomachs slashed, and when possible their bodies were thrown into deep wells to dispose of the evidence. Hence the Assyrian name for this historical episode.

The specifics of what came next remain obscure. What is certain is that Aziza, along with her three kids, which included my four-year-old grandfather, were either deported afterwards, or voluntarily fled—driven south into Syria with other displaced women and children. At the time, Ottoman officials were herding people from the Mardin area towards the remote killing fields of Deir al-Zor in northeastern Syria, where the displaced were barred from escaping, or going further, by the vast Syrian Desert. The big mystery is how Aziza and her family ended up in the Bedouin oasis town of Tafilah in the desert of what is today southern Jordan—a distant way station, where they would spend part of their desperate journey. Moreover, how did they do so without dying of hunger, thirst, exposure to the elements, or being killed or abducted by bandits or Ottoman soldiers—as so many other refugees had, en route?

Aziza most likely travelled out of Mardin in the direction of Western Syria, probably via Aleppo, where a combination of timely factors (including a more lax political environment, and presence of Westerners) would have helped them to survive and move much further afield: south by train. What also likely drove my great-grandmother forward, towards Tafilah, was that she, and her family, almost certainly had an ultimate destination in mind: Egypt.

Aziza was travelling with her sister and brother-in-law. The latter, Faraj Hanjozada, was an artisan who had enjoyed special privileges in Mardin as part of his job painting and decorating the interiors of mosques. He had survived the initial mass culling of men. Hanjozada had a wealthy businessman brother living in Cairo, and so Aziza and company were likely intent on getting as close to British-controlled Egypt, and the southern war front, as possible. British and Bedouin forces (led by the famous T.E. Lawrence) were fighting the Ottomans and were pushing north out of Sinai and Arabia towards Palestine and the Jordanian desert.

Aiming for Tafilah made sense. It was closer to Egypt and the southern front and the potentially liberating armies. It was also a better place to hold out than further north in Syria, where the allies may have never reached—and where the Ottomans might have still tried to deport my family back to the killing fields in the hinterland. In Tafilah, the Ottoman garrison and political officials were more preoccupied with the war to the south, than with the effort to eradicate Christians. The Turks in Tafilah sought to make use of the few Armenians and Assyrians who miraculously trickled into the town, as much needed war labourers.

Aziza and her family settled into a camp in Tafilah, where nearly all refugees either ended up working for the Arab locals or the Ottoman army. Many years later Aziza told family members that in order to feed herself and her kids she walked miles every day to fetch water for the Bedouins. She and her family remained in Tafilah for two years before moving on.

Those two years coincide timewise perfectly with events. Lawrence and the Arabs captured Tafilah from the Ottomans in January 1918, pushing the war front and British influence further north. With the way now clear, Aziza and the others continued on to Egypt, likely by the easiest route possible in that moment: by boat from liberated Jaffa in Palestine to Port Said.

Once in Cairo, she became acquainted with her sister's brother-in-law, the rich businessman Samuel Hanjozada—whom she married. Aziza and her new husband Samuel planned on having children in addition to the three she bore with her previous husband who was killed in Mardin. They decided to give the shortened surname Zada to her first batch of kids, which included my grandfather. Aziza and Samuel's future offspring would take their father's own surname: Hanjozada.

THEREAFTER, while in the lap of Cairo's western-style, *belle époque* luxuries and cosmopolitanism, the protagonists of this drama put their old lives forever behind them. Aziza, out of Eastern (and arguably universal) etiquette as a re-married woman, did not speak much about her former spouse who'd been killed. My grandfather and his siblings, as adults, had little recollection of Mardin or their murdered biological father. All they knew was that they had hailed from the town: a place that had since become vague, far-flung, and exotic even by Egyptian standards.

The next generation, which included my father, managed to pick up snippets of the Mardin story from his family. But by the time my dad and much of his direct and extended relatives travelled westwards out of Egypt to Canada, the USA and Australia, further distance and barriers to that faded and tattered memory had been created. Mardin at that point was completely out of reach, more of a fabled land, or even a lost legend, than an actual, real-life place.

I heard about Mardin when I was a young adult, and likely at one of the larger family gatherings in which the only tangible cultural artifacts from that phase of the family's history were the few culinary recipes native to the region. With time the city took on an almost apocryphal quality that sparkled with mystery and nostalgia as a place of origin, but which ultimately mattered little in a day-to-day sense. Mardin was just too far-flung and unknown. It was a lofty non-place, its name a faraway echo elucidating warm and familiar feelings, but occupying an ever-fading position in my family's changing constellations of belonging as immigrants to the West.

Acknowledgments

I'd like to express my thanks to both the Ontario Arts Council and the Canada Council for the Arts for their financial support for this project. I extend my appreciation to my two editors, Kisha Ferguson and Denise Winn, who separately and at different stages, helped shape the manuscript into something eminently more cogent and readable. Tragically, Kisha passed away earlier this year after a short battle with cancer. Kisha, a veteran journalist colleague from my time at CBC, was excited to see this work come to fruition, and so this book is also dedicated to her. And much gratitude to Michel Vrana, whose impressive cover design helped put the desired finishing touches on what has been a very personal project.

Thanks, too, to Lori Henry, Ramsay Wood, John Bell, Tarquin Hall, Andrew Boden, Holly Worton, Carolyn Forde and Christine Stephens for feedback and/or advice at various levels along the way. A few family members and friends, including long-time pals from the Mideast days David Rowntree and *oustaz* Anas, helped fill gaps and provide missing details when my journals, letters, old emails, photos—and my sometimes questionable memory—came up short. Bernadette Homsieh and Rose and Berdj Tanielian were instrumental in filling some blanks in the old Mardin family history.

And finally: special thanks to the family of Kamal Bey who, in the aftermath of his passing in 2020, shared additional anecdotes and information about him and his life that helped inform the book, as well as enrich our memories of him.

About the Author

John Zada is an author and journalist who writes about travel and the interplay between culture and politics. He's lived and worked extensively in the Middle East and has produced work for the *Globe and Mail*, *Toronto Star*, CBC, Al Jazeera, BBC, *explore*, *Literary Review of Canada*, *Los Angeles Review of Books* and others. He is a co-founder of The Conciliators Guild, a UK-based initiative highlighting the role of underlying human motivations in politics. John is also the author of two other nonfiction books: *Veils of Distortion: How the News Media Warps Our Minds* and *In the Valleys of the Noble Beyond: In Search of the Sasquatch*, which was a finalist for the Edna Staebler Award for Creative Non-Fiction in 2020, and was selected one of Amazon's 100 Best Books of the Year in 2019.

Request

If you enjoyed this book, please review it on Amazon and Goodreads.

Reviews are an author's best friend.

To stay in touch with John Zada, read his other writing, and to hear about his upcoming releases, you can connect with him at either, or both:

johnzada.com

johnzada.substack.com

And to follow him on social media, please go to any of the following links:

𝕏 x.com/senor_adaz
📷 instagram.com/johnzada
in linkedin.com/in/johnzada
g goodreads.com/john_zada
f facebook.com/johnzada
🦋 bsky.app/profile/johnzada

www.ingramcontent.com/pod-product-compliance
Lightning Source LLC
Chambersburg PA
CBHW071230070526
44583CB00017B/2118